Ports and Harbours
of Northumberland

Ports and Harbours of Northumberland

Stafford Linsley

TEMPUS

First published 2005

Tempus Publishing Limited
The Mill, Brimscombe Port,
Stroud, Gloucestershire, GL5 2QG
www.tempus-publishing.com

British Library Cataloguing in Publication Data.
A catalogue record for this book is available from the British Library.

ISBN 0 7524 2892 6

Typesetting and origination by Tempus Publishing Limited
Printed in Great Britain

Contents

Acknowledgements

I wish to place on record my thanks for the assistance given in preparing this book, to the following people, and to others not named who have nevertheless helped in one way or another: the staff of the Northumberland County Record Office, G.D. Younger, O.E. Craster, the Tweed Dock Harbour Master, Tony Rylance, Arthur English of Amble, Joe Clark, Mr McLaren of Belford. I am also extremely grateful for the support which my wife Tessa has always given me, and for the fact that through their attendance at my lectures over many years, and through participation in my research groups, my adult students at the University of Newcastle have always encouraged me to do better.

I

Introduction

The Northumberland coast is some 52.7 miles (84.8km) long, as the crow flies, from the river Tweed in the north to Hartley village in the south but its full coastline, together with that of its islands, measures some 84 miles (135.2km). That coastline is dotted with havens, harbours and ports, some active, others largely abandoned, and the purpose of this book is to explore the history of some of them. It is, perhaps, appropriate to define some terms at the outset. Firstly, a 'haven' is a natural and usually small, sheltered location for vessels – strictly speaking the term 'safe haven' is tautological. A 'harbour' may be a naturally sheltered location but significantly larger than a haven, or it may have been artificially constructed to provide such shelter. A 'port' is a harbour with terminal facilities and other services for shipping. Examples of all three are included here but this book concentrates mainly on locations where port or harbour facilities have been created at some time in the past. The port of Tyne is not included, for it lies without the area of the county's jurisdiction and, moreover, its control and fortunes lay with the town and county of Newcastle until it was placed under commissioners in the middle of the nineteenth century; the port of Tyne has also been well covered in recent publications such as Archer (2003). Cullercoats harbour is, however, included, for although it no longer lies within the county of Northumberland, it did so until the 1970s. A general introduction is followed by a study of each harbour, sequenced from north to south, wherein their sometimes turbulent histories are considered. These harbours range from simple fishing havens to the great industrial harbours built on coal export, Berwick in the north, once described as 'another Alexandria', to Cullercoats in the south. Each of these harbours has its own distinctive history and archaeology. Crates of eggs were once sent from Berwick to London; ships were once built on the Holy Island of Lindisfarne; the Beadnell and Craster harbours were created by quarrying away their foreshores; Alnmouth was shot at by the infamous Paul Jones; Blyth once shipped more coal than any other port in Europe; Seaton

Sluice may have been the inspiration for Sir Walter Scott's description of the small port of 'Ellangowan' in *Guy Mannering*; Cullercoats once boasted a son of Sir Richard Arkwright of Cromford and the Duke of Devonshire amongst its inhabitants, while one resident regularly put to sea in a coble to present bibles to French sailors in their ships in the offing. Many great engineers were involved in port and harbour development in Northumberland, men such as John Smeaton, John Rennie and Thomas Stevenson, father of Robert Louis, but some lesser and some unknown engineers were also involved. This story of Northumberland's ports and harbours weaves all these facets together and is set within the context of the growing industrialisation of the county.

PORTS AND HARBOURS AND TRANSPORT

Ports and harbours are components of transport systems, serving, as almost all transport systems do, both economic and social functions. Transport is about the carriage of goods between producer and consumer or the carriage of the consumer to the producer of goods, but transport can also serve as a consumer good in itself – most of us like to travel, sometimes just for the fun of it. So transport systems enable people and products to get around, more or less efficiently, and the nature of our economic life, and to a certain extent of our social life, is a reflection of our transport systems. Thus, the development of trade, the evolution of political systems and the growth of national trades unions, the nineteenth-century development of seaside resorts, the late twentieth-century expansion of overseas holidays and so on, are all bound up with transport; transport, trade, industry and travel, are all inextricably linked, and it has always been apparent that improved transport systems have been essential to expanding industrial economies. As features of transport systems then, our ports and harbours have been barometers of our local, regional, national and sometimes international, economic and social condition.

The nature and extent of any form of transport activity depends essentially on three factors: the value of the product which is being carried, the cost of the means of transport, and the risks involved in the journey, and it is important to note that transport has often been very costly and very risky. The cost of the product being moved is largely a feature of the market, while the cost of carrying it depends essentially on the transport system being used, but the risks involved in carriage, to humans, animals, the items carried or the mode of transport used, can be many and various. The risks in the north-east England coal trade in the days of sailing colliers, for example, were such that some sailors claimed that they would 'rather run the Hazard of an East India voyage than be obliged to sail all Winter between London and Newcastle'. And with good reason, for on one night in 1692 some 200 vessels, mainly colliers working to or from the north-east, and 1000 lives were said to have been lost off the coast of East Anglia.

All improvements in transport systems have evolved out of attempts to reduce the costs and risks involved in transport, and the preferred method of reducing transport costs was usually by speeding up the mode of transport, preferably without increasing the risk; as far as ports and harbours were concerned, providing protection for shipping during loading or unloading, while at the same time reducing ship turnround times, were guiding principles.

But the overall effects of an improved transport system can never be predicted with certainty, for the combined impacts of technological, market and social forces are not particularly amenable to scientific analysis; witness motorways today carrying traffic levels greater than originally anticipated. Technological, economic and social changes might lead to a more intensive use of a particular transport system, and possibly to further development of it, but the same forces might also lead to the diminished use of another transport system and even to its decay and abandonment. Thus the variable impact on Northumberland's harbours of the opening of the railway between Newcastle and Edinburgh in 1850, as will emerge in the pages which follow. Likewise the fact that Northumberland's ports and harbours have a much reduced commercial trading significance today but their waterfront locations have become desirable targets for art galleries, marinas and 'executive' dwellings.

THE NATURE OF PORTS AND HARBOURS

Although many of Northumberland's ports and harbours were active to a degree in the medieval period, the three main periods of port and harbour development in the county occurred in the centuries after the sixteenth. The first period of significant change, in the seventeenth and eighteenth centuries, was one of awakening interest in harbour improvement, mainly through the provision of sheltered waters by the building of breakwaters, piers and harbour walls, and also by quayside dredging; simple cargo handling facilities were also sometimes provided. The second period, around the middle of the nineteenth century, was marked by the building of wet docks at some harbours, and the third period, mainly occurring in the second half of that century, saw the provision of additional port facilities such as warehouses, repair yards, timber ponds, workshops, rail facilities etc. These periods were not, however, entirely discrete and such developments did not occur at every harbour, for the local factors which generated the impetus to improve a particular harbour might simultaneously result in arrested development elsewhere.

The basic reasons for the creation of a harbour concern the need for sheltered water for fishing fleets, for the export of the products of an immediate hinterland and for the need or desire to enable the safe import of commodities originating elsewhere. Today, provided that sufficient financial resources are available, a harbour can be built almost anywhere along a coast, but historically, a number of desirable prerequisites determined the optimum location for a harbour. Reasonably deep, sheltered water should be available, at least periodically, with the tide; the harbour should be fairly easy to enter and to leave; it should preferably lie adjacent to flat, hard-standing land. If these features were not to be found naturally, then an artificial harbour might have to be created. River mouths quite often met these criteria and it is no surprise that Britain's great ports, historically, were associated with its greatest rivers, usually at low bridging points where commercial centres existed. Thus, England's main ports in the Middle Ages, those such as London, Bristol and Exeter, were all located at sheltered upriver locations, dominating their regional economies but also acting as the main commercial centres of the country. Some inland ports like Selby, Nottingham, York and Yarm, located on navigable rivers, became quite prosperous as transhipment centres for varied imports and for the export of commodities generated by their agricultural hinterlands, even though they might be many miles from the sea; it is interesting to observe that, before 1950, all university towns except Durham had ready access to navigable water.

Most of Northumberland's harbours were 'river' harbours, but none were made the subject of the Navigation Acts common elsewhere in the country and consequently there were no cases where its rivers were improved for navigation, nor had their navigable lengths extended beyond their natural tidal limits. Their histories illustrate two inherent problems in the functionality of river harbours: firstly, that they are prone to flood and, secondly, that the water-borne silts and sands carried downriver are deposited to form both a bank on the seabed just beyond the river mouth (the 'bar'), and shifting sand banks within the tidal sections of the river. The bar can make entering and exiting the river problematic, for it always results in an unstable and shallow entrance channel and can sometimes prevent seagoing vessels from entering or leaving the harbour; in such situations ships may have to anchor beyond the bar and receive or discharge their cargoes via shallow-draft vessels such as keels; this happened on the river Wear in 1765, on the Tyne in 1860, and at Blyth in the late eighteenth century, for example. Much attention was given to overcoming the problems of bar formation in the nineteenth century; for example, by the construction of inwardly curving river-mouth piers to provide a narrow entrance, firstly, in the hope that sea currents, generally from north to south on the Northumberland coast, would sweep away the bar to the south of the river entrance and, secondly, in the belief that the channelling of the flowing river between the piers on an ebb tide would arrest bar formation; piers, of course, also played an important protective role for shipping. Sandbanks within the tidal section of a river always interfered with the free movement of river-using vessels and the only real solution to this problem was to dredge away the sands or, as at Seaton Sluice, low-tide ploughing to loosen the sands, followed by sluicing.

HARBOUR IMPROVEMENT AND THE PEOPLE WHO BROUGHT IT ABOUT

The essential function of a commercial trading harbour was to provide an interface between land or river carriage and sea carriage, and the main purposes behind harbour improvement were to ease and advance the carriage of seaborne goods, to provide protection and refuge to shipping and to accommodate a fishing industry where it existed. Basically, there were three forms of 'organisation' for harbour control and improvement. In some cases, as at Berwick upon Tweed before 1808, the local corporation took responsibility for the harbour; in other cases, elected or self-appointed commissioners/trustees were made responsible, as at Berwick after 1808; finally landowners or groups of interested individuals might bring about harbour improvements, as at Seaton Sluice and Craster. Railway companies also became very much involved in port and harbour development in the nineteenth century. Whatever the form of organisation, capital had to be raised to finance the required works in the hope, sometimes forlorn, that this money and more would be recouped through port and shipping dues or through reduced transport costs in the case of some private landowners.

Port and harbour design was generally regarded as a specialist task but, as it was, far from an exact science; harbour construction works often taxed and sometimes vexed the best civil engineers of their day. Reliable engineers were much sought after for harbour improvements, and civil engineering luminaries such as John Smeaton, John Rennie senior and the Stevenson family of Edinburgh all exercised their wits on harbour projects in Northumberland. Such men were essentially 'consulting engineers', and their role was to prepare and report on their proposals, plan and design the necessary works and estimate the cost of their intended works. It was not usually a simple task. If the brief was to recommend improvements to a river-mouth harbour by the provision of piers for example, decisions had to be made on the number of piers needed, their length, direction and cross section, their mode and materials of construction, the nature of their foundations and, in particular, how construction work should proceed in tidal and sometimes permanent waters. Moreover, some assessment would have to be made on the effect of such piers on tidal and river flows and on the bar.

The consulting engineer would produce a report on all such matters and he might also be required to attend a parliamentary committee to defend his plans against sometimes hostile cross-examination. It was for making such decisions, and writing persuasive reports, that the likes of Smeaton and Rennie gained their reputations and their incomes. Such men were ever on the move, for they were usually engaged on several widely-dispersed projects at any given time, and could never give their undivided attention to any particular project, hence the need for a reliable 'resident engineer' to be largely present throughout the project, providing continuity of approach and supervision. The resident engineer usually liaised between the client and the consultant, hired and fired the workers and dealt with problems as they occurred, but could always call on the consulting engineer should any significant doubts or problems arise. In a few cases, the positions of consulting and resident engineer were combined in the same person but he would usually be allowed the liberty to consult elsewhere even while harbour works were in progress. Sometimes, but not always, separate 'contracting engineers' were appointed, with the consulting or the resident engineer drawing up the contract specifications. Finally, most authorities with a port or harbour of more than modest size under their control, would employ a full-time salaried engineer for post-construction maintenance or repair, and to effect further minor improvements etc.; in due course most harbour authorities came to vest more and more powers in their own engineers, with outside consultants only being called in to express a second opinion on plans already drawn up and costed. As in all areas of professional life, there were frequent disagreements concerning the best approach to harbour improvement for the simple reason that port and harbour engineering remained an inexact science until well into the twentieth century.

HARBOUR ACTIVITIES

The harbours of Northumberland, as opposed to the natural havens, were created essentially to serve import and export trades, although maritime industries developed at most of them, ship and boat building and repair being the most obvious, for example at Berwick, Alnmouth, Seaton Sluice and Blyth. In the days of wooden sailing vessels these yards were sometimes supported by sailmakers, rope works, block makers, compass makers, chain and anchor smiths etc. Other harbour-based industrial activities were based on imported raw materials or on the yield of the sea itself – the fishing and salt making industries. Agricultural products dominated the export trades of Northumberland's northern ports and Seaton Sluice exported glass bottles for more than a century, while fishing, lime burning and salt making were common at many harbours and coal dominated those of the south of the county. It is appropriate to make some general comments about these activities, beginning with the fishing industry and the making of salt, two of the earliest known activities at Northumberland's harbours.

Little is known of the earliest days of commercial fishing from Northumberland's coast, but there were said to be 192 coast-based fishermen in Northumberland in 1547, 'whereof many be Scots'. It is difficult to assess the significance of this number of fishermen, for it may just relate to those who owned boats, but its general magnitude is confirmed by an enumeration of 1626, which recorded that the numbers of fishermen along the Northumberland coast varied between 40 at Spittal, 27 on Holy Island and 8 at Warkworth; in total, and including those at North Shields and Tynemouth, there were 284 resident fishermen along the whole of the coast between Tweed and Tyne. Fishing then, has been a significant coastal activity in Northumberland for centuries and although it was originally mainly inshore, for example in Goswick Bay and around Longstone, both of which were favoured fishing grounds, deep-sea fisheries were certainly being exploited by the sixteenth century, for six crayers (small trading vessels) were sent from North Shields to the Iceland grounds in 1528; likewise, the North Sea grounds, the seas around the Shetlands, and possibly also the Norwegian herring fields, were being fished at this time.

Other than that which was consumed locally, Newcastle was probably the earliest main market for Northumberland's fish catch, although much of it seems to have been then re-exported to London, but at some time part of the catch began to be exported direct from Northumberland to London, especially from Berwick. Fish such as salmon, turbot and lobster, were sometimes kept alive for the sea journey to London, being carried in specially designed smacks which contained water tanks. The market for most fresh fish was, of course, mainly local until the railway network was established centuries later and hence the drying, salting and curing of fish to be sold non-locally, for the London and foreign markets for example, was an absolute necessity. The preserving processes were quite simple, the fish to be salted being, in a sense, put back where they had formerly been, that is they were packed in brine in casks, usually (but not always) after gutting.

The eighteenth and nineteenth centuries saw a considerable increase in fishing activity from the Northumberland coast, both inshore and deep-sea, although the industry was, and still is, characterised by fluctuations in both the extent of its activity and the nature of its catches. Whitefish seem to have been plentiful in the eighteenth and nineteenth centuries, with good catches of cod, haddock, whiting and ling, while flat fish such as sole, plaice, halibut and turbot were also caught; Wallis had noted in 1769, that 'The haddock is taken in such abundance as to furnish all tables and to reward the toil of the hardy fisherman.' Salmon fishing also increased in importance, and by the 1790s some 300 men were involved in the Tweed salmon fisheries during a season, which lasted from 10 January to 10 October; eight Tweed boats specialised in whitefish and lobsters by the 1790s, although they switched to catching herring when in season.

Indeed, it was the herring – the famous 'Silver Darlings' – which were to become the mainstay of the fishing industry in the nineteenth century. The herring was quite a small fish, only reaching 1.5ft (0.45m) long at full growth, but it swam in shoals which could reach several square miles in extent. The herring did not move in a single shoal but in separate distinct shoals, each with a slightly different annual migration cycle. The shoals never remained more than a few days in any particular location; their former precise patterns of migration could alter without warning and this feature of their migration has, on occasion, left whole communities without a means of livelihood. For example, the herring forsook the Baltic in the fourteenth century, and they retreated from the Loch Fyne area of Scotland in the twentieth century. This very uncertainty, however, laid the seeds of bonanzas and although it varied in detail, the migratory cycle did follow broad trends over centuries, with herring shoals generally reaching different parts of the coast at particular times of the year; for example, off the north-west coast of Scotland in spring or early summer, Northumberland in mid-summer and the East Anglian coast by early autumn.

Salted herring was a major Scottish export in the later Middle Ages, but the Dutch had secured much of the industry by the fourteenth century, and they dominated the trade for some 300 years, developing the first drift nets, and also the necessary means of preserving the herring. The Dutch did not lose their pre-eminence, indeed, their near monopoly, until after the war of the Spanish succession, and England and Scotland began to make inroads into the lucrative herring fishery thereafter. In fact, the development of the herring fisheries in Scotland in the eighteenth and nineteenth centuries was seen by government as a way of providing a better standard of living in the Highlands and Islands, and was sometimes associated with the infamous 'Clearances'.

Much of this Scottish development rubbed off on Northumberland, as the nearest English county to Scotland on the eastern coast. In fact, the jurisdiction of the Scottish Fisheries Board extended along the Northumberland coast, and herring curing stations were established up and down the coast, as at Berwick, Holy Island, Seahouses, Beadnell, Hauxley etc. Thus, although it was noted in 1769 that there was insufficient herring taken off the Northumberland coast to allow for export, some 12,000 to 16,000 barrels per annum were being exported in 1906 from Seahouses alone to the Baltic ports. In addition, north-east fishermen began to seek more distant grounds, and although they often met with opposition, Berwick fishermen successfully increased the area of their operations up towards the Moray Firth in 1840-50. The herring industry grew unsteadily through the nineteenth century, being assisted by the railways after 1840. Indeed, the expansion of the herring industry off the east coast was partly railway-led by the middle of the nineteenth century but mainly at the larger fishing stations south of the Tyne.

Not all herring was cured, for some were sold locally, usually after gutting by women, but most were cured, either by simple salting, or to make bloaters (mainly at Great Yarmouth), red herring or kippers. Red herring were prepared by heavily salting un-split herring, and then strongly smoking them over a wood fire for about 14 days until they were cured to a reddish colour; this process was carried out at Tweedmouth from at least the eighteenth century to the early twentieth century. The 'kipper' was developed in the 1860s by William Woodger of Newcastle, surely to rank alongside the other great 'inventions' of north-east England. The herring was split, gutted and opened out flat, lightly rubbed in salt or sprinkled with brine, and then heavily smoked over oak shavings for 8 to 10 hours in a curing house. The curing house, also known as a smoke house, was usually a large oblong building up to about 45ft (13.7m) high with ridge or wall-top vents. There were no intermediate floors, but the house was divided vertically into bays, 3ft to 4ft (0.9 to 1.2m) wide, called 'loves', by partitions of horizontal rails beginning at about 7ft (0.1m) above ground level. The rails supported transverse 'spits' or 'speets', which were run through the gills and mouths of the fish for hanging in the smoke. Few curing houses are now at work in Northumberland but several curing houses, often converted for other purposes, still survive.

Another feature of the nineteenth-century industry was an increase in the size of fishing boats, and although this resulted in a reduction in the size of the fleets, from 64 to 9 native boats at Berwick and Spittal between 1855 and 1905, and from 52 to 8 at North Sunderland (Seahouses), the fishing ports were just as busy as before, with numerous 'stranger boats', from Cornwall to the Firth of Forth, coming to Northumberland waters every year between June and September; Berwick had 200 stranger herring boats in 1866, while North Sunderland regularly had 100 including, eventually, steam drifters and sailing boats from Yarmouth and Lowestoft for example. But the strangers did not immediately wipe out the natives. As an 1866 Fishery Commission noted:

> It is clear that at all these fishing villages [Cullercoats, Newbiggin, North Sunderland and Holy Island] there has within the last 20 years been a constant increase in the number of fishermen, the size of their boats, and the quantity of nets and other gear.

It was not to last, however, and the same report noted that 'Within the last 7 years [sailing] trawlers have made their appearance [off Northumberland]', and the depletion of inshore demersal stocks was apparent.

The development which had the greatest impact on Northumberland's fishing harbours was the introduction of the steam trawler. Up to the 1870s, demersal fishing had been carried out using beam trawls from sailing vessels which could only be absent from port for a few days, and of necessity the boats landed their fish at the nearest available harbour. Steam trawlers, like steam drifters, however, offered the opportunity of fishing which was independent of the wind and of longer periods at sea. Steam trawlers were apparently first used from North Shields in November 1877 when a steam tug hauled beam trawls having a 54ft (16.5m) beam; these greatly increased the catches of demersal fish. Steam-powered, screw-propelled trawlers made their appearance two years later and were in common use by 1906; these steam vessels could easily out-fish the sailing boats over a season. Few of the smaller fishing families along the Northumberland coast could afford steam drifters or trawlers and few local fishing havens could accommodate them; only harbours with deep water could take the steam-powered boats, and on the Northumberland coast only Berwick and North Sunderland were to have registered steam trawlers. Moreover, the effect of steam trawling 4 to 6 miles (6.4 to 9.7km) off the coast, further depleted the inshore catches by disturbing the inshore spawning grounds, making it necessary for the smaller fishing outfits to fish more distant grounds. The last sailing fishing boat on Holy Island was laid up in 1914; overturned, it was used as a store. The First World War was to play havoc with the entire fishing industry as the established European trade links were broken. Local industry was also to struggle in the aftermath of the war, even after the introduction of motor-driven fishing boats in the 1920s. The herring fisheries declined sharply in the 1930s; although catches revived after the Second World War it was only a temporary respite, and the local fishing industry had to fight to survive through the remainder of the twentieth century.

The making of salt was a natural corollary of the fishing industry, for the salt could be obtained by evaporating sea water in salt pans and then used in the salting of fish; sea water contains about 3 per cent salt. Water from the sea was either pumped into cisterns or they were flooded with it at high tide and the sea water was then transferred to a salt pan to be evaporated using brushwood or coal as fuel. Various ingredients might be added to clarify the sea water, by forming a coagulant which would entrap solid impurities and carry them to the surface for manual removal; at times ingredients such as calves feet, egg whites, bullock's blood, beer and the 'fat of dogs' have been so used. Salt crystals floated on the surface of the brine during evaporation and then sank to the floor of the pan, from where they could be removed with a wooden spade and placed into salt 'barrows' (conical wicker baskets). The latter were subsequently drained on a table or, sometimes, dried in flue-heated ovens.

Salt pans were made from lead sheet during the Roman period and throughout the medieval period, but riveted iron sheets began to be used in the later Middle Ages (probably in the fifteenth or sixteenth centuries), a development which was probably complete by the late seventeenth century. It has generally been argued that lead pans were not particularly suited to the use of coal as the evaporating fuel because of the intensity of heat generated by a coal fire and the corrosive attack by sulphur dioxide carried by the combustion gases; therefore, wood and turf were used rather than coal for the process of brine evaporation where lead pans were in use. On the other hand, a coal fire does not necessarily have to be maintained at a high heat, for it can be controlled by dampers or a covering of ashes and, moreover, if 'small coal', also known as 'pancoal', was being used, which was usually the case, it is unlikely that particularly high temperatures were generated; all the more so if sea coal (collected from amongst the shingle on the beaches) was used, for it is notoriously difficult to obtain a hot fire using sea coal. In any case, the manufacture of 'fishery salt' only required a brine temperature of about 105° F to obtain the very large-grained cubic crystals required for the salting of fish; higher temperatures were, however, usually employed for table salts. There is at least one piece of documentary evidence to support an early use of coal for salt making in north-east England, in a document believed to date from the fourteenth century which noted, of salt makers on the marshy areas on the north bank of the river Tees, that:

And as the Tyde comes in, yt bringeth a small wash sea-cole which is imployed to the makinge of salte, and the Fuell of the poore fisher Townes adjoininge: the oylie

sulphurousness beinge mixed with the Salt of the Sea as yt floweth, and consequently hard
to take ....

Far from having to deaden the effects of their coal fire, these salt makers
employed special efforts to keep it alight. It may well be true that sulphur dioxide
attack of the lead sheets reduced the otherwise effective life of lead pans when
coal fires were used, but that possibility cannot be used to justify the claim that
coal fuel was not used with lead-sheet pans. It is undoubtedly the case, however,
that wrought-iron riveted pans performed better and two such pans seem to
have been erected at South Shields in 1489, possibly in advance of their use
elsewhere, and there would seem to have been a subsequent swing from lead
sheet to wrought-iron plate for salt pan construction.

It is known that the religious houses of Newminster, Brinkburn and Alnwick,
all in Northumberland, had salt pans at coastal locations such as Blyth and
Amble from *c.*1150, and that the Prior of Tynemouth operated both salt pans and
coal mines in the thirteenth century. Thereafter, the evidence for salt making at
coastal locations becomes increasingly common, and although the main centres
of the salt industry came to be concentrated at the mouths of the rivers Tyne
and Wear, salt pans remained at work at several of Northumberland's ports. The
1740s probably saw the high-water mark for the local industry, followed by
decline thereafter, such that there were only about five operating salt pans in the
north-east of England by the 1820s, and these were mainly associated with soap
and glass manufacture rather than fish salting.

THE COAL PORTS

Certainly the salt industry came to be dependent upon locally mined coal and
historically there was probably no more important British industry than the
coal industry. Indeed, there was a popular belief of the early nineteenth century
that coal was the most essential commodity of the economy, and that Britain's
growing industrial and economic power was based on the twin pillars of coal and
iron. Much earlier than that, some would-be conquerors of Britain believed that
if they could only capture the sailing colliers operating between the north-east
of England and the Thames, then the economy of England would fail. Actually
this was most unlikely, for the major use for coal up to around 1700 was to keep
people warm and to assist them in their cooking: it was not until the eighteenth
century that coal became crucial to the nation's industrial economy as more
varied and widespread industrial uses for it were developed.

The origins of coal mining in north-east England are unclear. There is no
hard evidence for the use of coal in the prehistoric period, but there is abundant
archaeological evidence for the use of coal by the Romans. Consequently,
coal extraction in the North East has a near 2,000-year history. However, the

earliest documentary evidence for coal mining in Northumberland is from the thirteenth century, when 'sea coal' was being won from near Blyth before 1236, with at least the possibility that some such coal was being traded by sea; unfortunately 'sea coal' has meant, at different times and at the same time, either coal collected from beaches or coal destined to be exported by sea.

By the early sixteenth century, most coal mines in the North East were located on, or very close to, tide-water sites, the coal being extracted from above the water table where free drainage was possible. The possibilities for subsequent geographical and output expansion in the industry were primarily limited by the problems of overland coal transport and of mine drainage. From the sixteenth to the eighteenth century these two problems were potential and sometimes real restraints on output, even when demand was growing, albeit slowly; the London domestic market dominated demand, but there was a continued slow expansion of coal-using industries, particularly during the second half of the eighteenth century. The development of horse-drawn wooden waggonways proved to be the solution to the transport problem, first used in the North East in the Bedlington-Blyth area of Northumberland in 1605, the beginnings of a railway revolution which was to change much of the world. The solution to the drainage problem was to be solved by the invention of the Newcomen atmospheric pumping engine, which made its first appearance in Warwickshire in 1712 but was in use in north-east England by c.1715; later developments of this engine were to usher in the great age of steam power.

Thus, the use of waggonways and the railways which followed, plus the atmospheric pumping engine and the steam engines in its wake, wedded to controlled marketing by north-eastern entrepreneurs, enabled the Great Northern Coalfield to maintain its long-established position as the most important coalfield in Britain. These changes to the technical infrastructure of the coal industry required concomitant changes at the region's harbours, the most obvious being the introduction of coal drops suited to the carriage of coal by waggonway. Coal was clearly very important to north-east England and to the nation during the eighteenth century, but it was to become massively more so to both in the nineteenth century.

The pattern of coal outputs from the North East began to alter in the period 1810-30, and three factors seem to have been responsible for this change. Firstly there was a widespread adoption of steam-powered stationary engines in industry, and soon of steam locomotives on the railways; secondly there was a growing urban demand for coke and gas; thirdly, County Durham's 'concealed coalfield' was opened up, thereby quite suddenly increasing the supply of coal. Soon, indeed, north-eastern coal outputs exceeded demand, with the result that there was a depression in the industry in the period 1835-55 as both output and demand grew, but out of phase. However, a new, additional demand arose from the 1850s and 60s – that of steam shipping – and for a while demand exceeded supply. Many new pit sinkings were undertaken as a result; for example, in the

Ashington area of Northumberland from 1867 onward, their coals initially being shipped from the Tyne before belated improvements at Blyth harbour attracted their custom.

Outputs from the north-east coalfield continued to expand into the twentieth century, from about 15 million tons per annum by 1860, to a peak of 56 million tons in 1911. There were a few new sinkings in Northumberland in the twentieth century, mainly in coastal areas and ultimately aimed at undersea reserves, as at Ellington (1910-1913) and Lynemouth (1931), but as these pits were being sunk some of the older mines were already closing, particularly in neighbouring County Durham. Coal mine closures have, of course, continued, so that today, the North East has no deep mines, Ellington in Northumberland closing in 2005. All of these changes in the coal industry were reflected in harbour developments within the southern part of the county, their expansion and decay closely mirroring each other.

Before the launching on the Tyne of the steam-powered water-ballasted screw collier, the *John Bowes*, in 1851, every vessel that left Northumberland with coal was required to return with some form of solid ballast, in order to ensure stability at sea. Sometimes this ballast took the form of a useful raw material, for the glass industry at Seaton Sluice for instance, but much of it was of no use and was simply dumped on the shorelines and beaches. Again Seaton Sluice is a good example of this, as a walk along the flinty shingle beach to the south of the Cut (see later) will readily indicate. Solid ballast continued to be used after 1851 but was fairly rapidly phased out in favour of the new breed of *John Bowes*-inspired water-ballasted collier. Although coal exports came to dominate most of the county's southern ports and collier brigs or the later steam-powered colliers might crowd the harbour spaces, several other types of sailing vessel were once to be seen within the harbours, notably smacks, sloops, barques, snows, pinks, schooners and ketches. Some vessels, particularly the simply-rigged sloops in the London trade, were required to have striking masts, which could be lowered to enable them to pass under London Bridge.

SHIPPING AND HARBOUR DEVELOPMENT

Britain was not always a significant maritime nation, although its economy and culture have been heavily influenced by the seas around it and its links across them. The Middle Ages witnessed the growth of some important overseas trading links, with British exports of wool, herring, coal and so on and imports, which included cloth, wine, spices and timber; but while these links were important to the country, Spain and to a lesser extent the Low Countries remained the main seafaring nations, and they continued as such until the second half of the sixteenth century. By that time Britain had well-established trading links with northern Russia and the Mediterranean countries and, in addition, its developing coastal trade, assisted by the improvement of river navigations from about 1700, fostered much inter-regional water-borne trade especially with London, always the most demanding market for home and foreign products. The 1604 Anglo-Spanish Treaty, which had enabled Britain to settle the American colonies, was the final spur required by British seamen to advance their dominion further, and the English in particular now put to sea in considerable numbers, often at considerable discomfort and, indeed, mortal danger to themselves; it may be that the long-standing coastal trades eased this expansion into extensive overseas trade. The Baltic timber trade became especially important to Britain's east-coast ports, while the west-coast ports concentrated on the Irish trade and on rum, sugar, tobacco and slaves.

A very significant factor in Britain's eighteenth-century coastal trade, although it had begun centuries before then, was the increasingly important coal trade. Four out of the 10 leading provincial ports in England in 1701 were coal-exporting or collier-owning ports; some 1,400 ships were involved in the coal trade, equal to about one third of the total English shipping tonnage. The North East accounted for most of this trade, especially the port of Tyne, but with collateral advantages to harbours elsewhere; for example, the harbours at Scarborough and Bridlington were essentially created to serve as harbours of refuge for the north-east coal trade, their development being financed by a levy on that trade. The creation of canals assisted Britain's inter-regional trade from the middle of the eighteenth century but not in north-east England, for no canals were ever built there. Some of the earliest British canals linked existing river navigations – the Trent & Mersey, the Staffordshire & Worcester, the Forth & Clyde etc., and thus they enhanced the role of pre-existing, often inland ports. 'New' ports, such as Liverpool, responded to the new opportunities presented by the canals, with appropriate harbour developments, but the 'old' ports, such as Bristol, without the advantage of an early canal, suffered slow decline. But port developments in the immediate wake of the canals were often limited, for canals and their boats were themselves restricted in their carrying capacities. The sea presented no such limitations and with a rapidly expanding trade in the nineteenth century, especially after the Napoleonic Wars had ended, port and harbour developments were to reach a peak of activity in Britain. The absence of canals in the north-east of England made little difference to the progress of its ports and harbours, for they were essentially exporting ports, taking their main commodities from a narrow hinterland; the overland carriage of coal, the main north-eastern commodity, was served by horse-drawn waggonways rather than canals. However, with the gradually increasing size of ships during the nineteenth century and with the introduction of steam-powered shipping, port and harbour authorities were required to regularly revise their provision. The better harbour authorities planned for tomorrow, but some seem, in retrospect, to have planned for yesterday, as this study will show.

2

Berwick, Tweedmouth and Spittal

Without contradiction, there is not such a regular and ready communication between any
two places [Berwick and London] of equal distance in the whole kingdom, nor perhaps in
the whole world. (Fuller, 1799)

Although the coal trade came to dominate port and harbour developments
in north-east England, there were nonetheless developments outwith the
coalfield, spurred on by the opportunities to export agricultural produce,
general merchandise, lime, stone, fish etc. The creation of harbour facilities in
Northumberland at locations north of Amble was a response to some of these
trades. None of the more northerly harbours competed with the coal ports
in volume of trade but in serving their local communities, and in the case of
Berwick more distant communities, they brought a degree of prosperity to their
settlements which might not otherwise have been achieved.

The Tweed is simultaneously England's most northerly river and Scotland's
most southerly on its eastern seaboard, and the harbour facilities which were
developed at its mouth served both countries; Berwick lies almost equidistant
from the rivers Forth and Tyne. Berwick stands upon a steep slope on the northern
bank of the Tweed, where the wide estuary narrows, while Tweedmouth stands
opposite on the southern bank, with Spittal about 1 mile (1.6km) to the east on
low ground. Like many significant ports of the Middle Ages, Berwick owed its
early commercial development to its location near the mouth of a river which
formed a natural harbour at the lowest point of the river which was fordable at
low tide and, therefore, potentially bridgeable.

A timber bridge at Berwick is recorded as having been swept away in 1199 and
there are further references both to bridges and ferries during the succeeding
centuries before the present 'old' bridge was completed in 1624. Berwick may
have been settled in the ninth century but nothing positive is known of its
history until the late eleventh century at which time it was a Scottish town.

Even so there is little available information on the commerce of the town during the later medieval period, partly because it was the scene of the much debated and therefore frequently shifting border between Scotland and England. Under David the First of Scotland (c.1085-1153), the town was made a Royal Burgh and participated directly in the burghal parliament of the twelfth century, together with the Burghs of Stirling, Edinburgh and Roxburgh. When David founded Selkirk Abbey, he presented it with gifts which included a share in the fishing of the Tweed, a sure indication that salmon were already important.

By 1156, the Tweed at Berwick was said to have more commerce than any other Scottish port, Scotland's foreign trade being entirely in the hands of Berwick merchants. Although the town was taken by the English in 1174 it was regained by the Scots some 15 years later, a reversal which was to be often repeated in subsequent centuries; the town is said to have changed hands between England and Scotland some 13 times between 1147 and 1482. During the uneasy peace which was maintained up to the end of the thirteenth century Berwick's power, wealth and influence continued to grow, such that it could be described in 1296 as:

> ... a city so prosperous and of such trade that it might justly be called another Alexandria, whose riches were the sea and the waters its walls.

It was said that the annual value of the Berwick Customs at this period was about £2,200, while that of the whole of the English ports was only £8,000. Much of this wealth came from the export of wool and skins, particularly from the great monasteries of the Tweed valley and from the supply of corn and salmon to London's domestic market. That Berwick could compete in the corn trade with nearer suppliers in East Anglia testifies to the cost advantage of seaborne over land traffic, before the coming of the railways. Little is known of Berwick's imports at this time, but we can assume that items of general merchandise were brought in. The importation of coal also dates from at least 1265 and the regulation of the sale of imported coal by a Guild Statute of 1294 suggests that it must have been a regular article of trade. A pier or breakwater, known as Holdman Wall, was built at this period and provided with a beacon, probably the earliest such structure in the north of England.

Berwick's lucrative trades were not to last much longer, however. When Edward the Third laid siege to Berwick in 1333 and then defeated the Scots in battle on Halidon Hill, Berwick once more passed into the hands of the English. Initially concerned to continue the town's prosperity, Edward encouraged local and potential merchants to remain with the town by offering to retain the existing duty on the export of Scottish wool, which was only one quarter of that paid on English wool at English ports; enterprise combined with cunning led Northumbrian farmers and wool merchants to smuggle their wool and skins across the border for export from Berwick as 'Scottish' products. After about 20 years of this illegality, during which time Berwick probably became even wealthier, an overreaction by the King resulted in measures which effectively sealed the port. New statutes decreed that wool and skins were not permitted to be carried across the border, nor to be exported through Berwick, and the sale of wool and skins to Scotsmen or to anyone who might carry them across the border was banned, all on pain of death and forfeiture. This draconian law was eventually relaxed when the town became increasingly impoverished as a result of the law and when outcries against the injustice became sufficiently strong, and Berwick was granted a monopoly on the export of all wool produced in Northumberland north of the river Coquet in 1399.

Nevertheless, the damage was done and Berwick had lost the wool export of lowland Scotland to the port of Leith. Fortunately, the establishment of a sizeable garrison in the town provided a new market on its doorstep, or rather within its house, although continued border skirmishes and Scottish attacks on the town prevented a return to a truly ordered commercial existence. Indeed, the town was to pass into Scottish control once more but gifted this time in 1461, in a deal done by Henry the Sixth. Having fled to Scotland during the Wars of the Roses, Henry achieved Scottish support against the Yorkists in return for ceding Berwick to Scotland in 1461. It is unlikely that much, if any, wool was exported from the town while under Scottish control, but salmon were still being salted and exported, and there were also some grain exports. The town was again taken by the English in 1482, at a time when the Scots were in some disarray, and it has remained an English town ever since. Attempts were made to reinvigorate the trade of town and harbour, by a law of 1483 which decreed that all goods passing between England and Scotland should be transhipped at Berwick. It is unlikely that this law could in any way be made totally effective, especially as border hostilities continued to rumble on, culminating in the Scottish disaster at Flodden Hill in 1513; it may be that local confidence increased as a result of this defeat of the Scots, for Thomas Strangwysshe and William Gardyner of Berwick leased a coal mine at Tweedmouth for 30 years at £6 13s 4d per year in the following year.

Still, it was against this background of continued armed aggression, and concerns over a possible French invasion, that Berwick's Elizabethan fortifications were commenced in 1528. Some 30 years later, in 1557, a new and substantial pier was built to replace Holdman Wall; at 1077ft (328m) long and 22ft (6.71m) wide (or 925ft (282m) long and 35ft (10.7m) broad according to different authorities) it was an impressive undertaking and suggests that Berwick was still regarded as an important port and harbour of refuge. With the union of the crowns in 1603, the prospects of a lasting peace seemed to open up and the garrison was disbanded. This was no particular peace dividend for Berwick since the garrison, with perhaps 1,000 men, had provided a ready market for the town's merchants to the tune of some £30,000 yearly. Moreover, the town had virtually abandoned its foreign trade during these years of garrison supply and new markets now had to be found. We can assume that the salmon trade was still yielding worthwhile revenues and it is known that 40 fishermen were resident at Spittal in 1626, some of whom might, however, have been involved in inshore white fishing; the salmon were caught along an 8-mile (12.9km) tidal stretch of the river between the estuary and Norham, as well as inshore.

The town of Berwick was still in a state of decay if Sir William Brereton is to be believed. Visiting the town in June 1635 he noted that there was 'noe trade in this towne, itt is a verye poore towne, many indigent persons, and beggars herein'. As for the harbour, it was 'a most narrow, shallow, barred haven: the worst that I have seen', with only one 40-ton vessel and a few fishing boats belonging to the haven, but he acknowledged that 'itt might bee made good, a brave and secure haven'. He was, of course, impressed by the salmon catches, having been informed by his host that 2,000 had been taken in one draught on the previous Sunday. There were soon to be signs of revitalised trade; some 23 cargoes, of oats, wheat, peas, beef, salt and stockings being despatched to London in 1683, and 10 cargoes returned. About 85 tons of coal were also imported from Newcastle, but only about 3 tons of coal were imported from the Tyne in 1731, possibly because the local Scremerston coal measures had been opened up in the intervening period.

Berwick's salmon continued to be much in demand on the London market during the seventeenth century although, as Daniel Defoe explained in *c*.1700, Newcastle was able to usurp what should have been Berwick's fame:

> You well know, we receive at *London* every Year a great Quantity of Salmon pickled or cured, and sent up in the Pickle in Kits or Tubs, which we call *Newcastle* Salmon; now when I came to *Newcastle*, I expected to see a mighty plenty of Salmon there, but was surprized to find, on the contrary, that there was no great Quantity, and that a good large fresh Salmon was not to be had under five or six Shillings. Upon enquiry I found, that really this Salmon, that we call *Newcastle* Salmon, is taken as far off as the *Tweed*, which is three-score Miles, and is brought by Land on Horses to *Shields*, where it is cur'd, pickl'd, and sent to *London*, as above; so that it ought to be called *Berwick* Salmon, not *Newcastle*.

It does seem surprising that the salmon was brought by road from Berwick and neither pickled nor cured there. Still, stranger things could happen. According to Fuller (1799), one enterprising Berwick man carried salmon to London by road with six horses in the 1730s, and reputedly made a £20 profit on a round trip; he became known as 'London John' in the Billingsgate market. When Defoe came to describe the town of Berwick he marvelled at the bridge, 'a noble, stately work', but as for the town itself it was 'old, decayed, and neither populous nor rich; the chief trade I found here was in corn and salmon'. However, the eighteenth century saw an unsteady growth in trade and in the gross tonnage of ships registered with the port, as corn and salmon exports increased in importance. Only 110 tons of coastal vessels belonged to Berwick in 1709, but this had risen to 350 tons by 1716 and 1,102 tons by 1730. Tonnages owned at Berwick were to fall back to 715 in 1751, but rise again during the second half of the century. These relatively small tonnages do not directly correlate with the extent of Berwick's trade, for it would appear that no vessels in the London salmon trade were actually registered in Berwick at mid-century; rather, the London merchants engaged smacks registered in Harwich and Gravesend for the carriage of salmon. Although these 40-ton sloop-rigged smacks could sometimes reach London in five days, adverse weather could delay arrival by two or three weeks and consequently the salmon were either pickled for the journey or carried live in specially constructed 'wells' within the ships' holds. However, in *c*.1787, Mr Dempster, a Berwick MP, visited a friend who owned a salmon fishery in Perth, and he was informed that it was customary to pack salmon in ice on the Continent to keep the fish fresh on long journeys. This technique had been tried in Berwick, with considerable success by 1788, and ice houses were soon built in Berwick for the storage of ice, some 7,600 cart-loads of ice eventually being collected locally each winter.

There were other important developments around the middle of the eighteenth century. Firstly, Arthur Byram began the Tweed's first shipbuilding yard, at Berwick in 1751; little is known of Byram's early vessels, but the 147-ton *Concorde* and the 145-ton *Francis & Sally* were launched in 1764. The yard seems to have remained in near-continuous production until the 1970s, being kept within the Byram family until 1878. Secondly, the Bucktonburn & Berwick Roads Turnpike was established under a Local Act of 1753, clearly aimed at bolstering the trade of the town and port; unusually, it consisted of a series of radial routes out towards Foulden, Paxton, Coldstream, Duddo and Lowick, as well as a section of the Great North Road between Bucktonburn to the south and Lamberton to the north. It was evidently hoped that these roads would facilitate the export of agricultural products from Tweeddale and Glendale, as well as the easier distribution of imports; the chief exports at this time were still corn, wool and salmon, whilst the imports were mainly timber and deals from Norway and the Baltic, and probably some bar iron from Sweden and Russia. Thirdly, a coal mine had been opened on Ord Moor, some 2.5 miles (4km) south-west of Berwick's bridge, by 1764 and was sending coal to the Tweedmouth shore on a horse-drawn waggonway; isolated sections of its embankment can still be seen. Fourthly, the town's first shipping company, the 'Berwick [Old] Shipping Company' was formed in the same year. Established by local coopers and fishery proprietors, it commenced trading with four vessels, probably built by Byram, but it did much more than mark an advance in the commercialisation of the Tweed salmon industry. The company was able not only to capitalise on Berwick's existing import/export trades, but also on the considerable variety of goods which flowed between London, Glasgow and Edinburgh, for many of these came to be landed at Berwick rather than at Leith, to be carried overland between Berwick and those Scottish towns. There was a rather curious reason for this situation.

Relations between Edinburgh and Leith had never been easy. Described as 'the chief port of all Scotland' in 1656, Leith became the most important Scottish east-coast port of the eighteenth century, principally as an importing port for Edinburgh. But Edinburgh, as the only Royal Burgh in Midlothian, was able to exercise monopoly trading rights over an area which stretched well beyond its own boundaries to include Leith. Thus the principal port of east-coast Scotland, which served also as the granary and warehouse for its capital town, was effectively controlled by that capital. Improvements at Leith harbour, which began in 1717, were financed by Edinburgh's corporation; its 'town debt' at their completion by c.1730 was thereby doubled to £50,000. These improvements were, however, insufficiently far-sighted, and the immense increase in shipping wishing to use the port after 1745 brought acute problems. As a result, it would seem, many Edinburgh merchants preferred to haul their goods back and forth by road from Berwick rather than use Leith, a journey perhaps made somewhat easier after the Great North Road was turnpiked into Scotland in the 1750s. In fact, many of the merchant ships which continued to work out of Leith in the London trade called at Berwick to collect extra cargoes, but the Glasgow trade was lost to both ports when the Forth & Clyde ship canal opened in 1790. Still, to capitalise on passenger revenues between London and Edinburgh, the Leith and Berwick Shipping Company established its headquarters in Leith in 1791. Their small, fasts smacks soon attracted considerable numbers of passengers, but also frequently called at Berwick to collect salmon. Another company, the Berwick Union Shipping Company, was formed in 1794 and for a while it also operated land-carriage services, both for goods and passengers, between Berwick and Edinburgh. By 1799, the Old Shipping Company was operating 10 smacks out of Berwick, while the Union Company, having given up the land carriage business, still traded out of Berwick and Leith with 11 smacks; most of these vessels ranged between 70 and 140 tons burthen. In that same year John Rennie drew up extensive plans for remodelling Leith harbour and it had two wet docks and three graving docks by 1817; Berwick was never again to offer a cheaper alternative to Leith.

The Tweed salmon fisheries continued to be remunerative and, according to Dr John Fuller (1799), some 300 men and about 80 boats were involved in this activity in 1799. The rental for the short stretch of river involved was £10,000 in that year, but it had doubled by 1817; none of the salmon catches were brought to the Berwick market, but were sold direct to the 32 'salmon coopers' of Berwick. Another lucrative, if somewhat unusual, export trade in the eighteenth and nineteenth centuries, but possibly commencing much earlier, was in eggs, sent to London for, according to Hutchinson (1778), the use of sugar refiners. 'Egglers' brought huge quantities of eggs by packhorse and cart from farms as far away as Selkirk, sold them to exporting Berwick grocers and bought groceries in return. The eggs were checked and packed into special crates for the sea voyage to London. Mackenzie (1825) noted that the egg packers checked the condition of each egg with a candle placed in the centre of the chest, before laying the eggs broad end down in rows, with straw packing between each row. He observed that the packers could check and fill a chest of 1600 eggs in just one hour, and that although they were not counted during the packing, a mistake in the total number of eggs rarely occurred. He added that once the eggs were packed in salt or rubbed with butter or tallow, or steeped in alkali to preserve them during carriage, they were also then steeped in lime water. Some £20,000 worth of eggs were said to have been sold in Berwick in 1799 and about 5,000 chests of eggs with a value of £30,000 were sent to London in 1816. That this trade continued well into the nineteenth century is evidenced by the many large hen houses constructed on farms around Berwick in the middle years of that century.

Other articles of export during the latter years of the eighteenth century included wool, corn, potatoes, salted pork, butter, tallow, candles, paper, leather, canvas, sacking and herrings, almost all shipped coastwise to London. There had formerly been an extensive foreign trade, mainly in corn and salted fish, but this had declined during the second half of the eighteenth century as the London market became increasingly dominant. However, some small-scale foreign imports continued − wine from Portugal, oak bark from Germany, timber and iron from Scandinavia and the Baltic, flax from Holland and Russia, tar from Russia, and wheat, barley and oats from Prussia (possibly for re-export to London). Great Britain had ceased to be a net grain exporter in the 1780s and, in these and successive years, grain imports were generally several times larger than exports. It was claimed, however, that Berwick's foreign trade might have been greater had it not been for the 'laxity' of its freemen, who enjoyed the privilege of exclusive rights in the trade and sought to maintain their monopoly by discouraging any potential outsider entrepreneurs. Even so, an average of 40 foreign ships entered and left the port during each of the years 1791 to 1794, and Fuller felt able to pronounce that:

> Without contradiction, there is not such a regular and ready communication between any two places [Berwick and London] of equal distance [apart] in the whole kingdom, nor perhaps in the whole world.

Fuller, who provided a fairly comprehensive picture of industry and trade in the estuarial communities in the 1790s, indicated that activities typical of a small port had developed on both sides of the river. In addition to Byram's shipyard in Berwick (then known as 'Gowans' and later as 'Byram Gowans'), there was another in Tweedmouth owned by Mr Bruce, and both employed about 25 journeymen and apprentices, building about eight vessels per year between them. The largest ship thus far built in Berwick, a brig of 375 tons burthen, had been launched from Bruce's yard on 15 March 1799, while Gowan's had launched a brig of 300 tons for the Berwick brewers Burnet, Grieve & Sons on the same day; Joseph Todd & Company had commenced shipbuilding in Tweedmouth in the same year. Bruce's yard may not have lasted long, for an Admiralty survey of April 1804 recorded only a yard under Mrs Gowan with six craftsmen and 23 apprentices, and another under Todd with 17 craftsmen and 27 apprentices; the dependency on a youthful workforce, none were over 50 years of age, is self-evident, but was not unusual for shipyards of the period. Todd's yard was later to supply the Admiralty with naval vessels, such as the 12-gun *Forward* and the 18-gun *Rover* in 1805 and 1808 respectively, presumably intended to play their part in the Napoleonic wars; a total of 117 ships with an aggregate tonnage of 12,828 tons were launched into the Tweed between 1786 and 1813. Also, according to Fuller, there were two builders of the famous Berwick smacks in the Berwick-Tweedmouth area, as well as sail manufacturers and several roperies. Eight boats, each with a five-man crew, were involved in white fishing, except in the herring season when they devoted their energies to catching herring; the manufacture of red herring had started at the east end of Tweedmouth in 1797. A nearby mill processed tobacco and snuff (presumably from imported raw materials) and there were several small-scale textile industries.

Tweedmouth and Spittal had indeed undergone much change during the eighteenth century and although both depended mainly upon fishing, their several industrial developments meant that they could no longer be described as hamlets. Although the salmon fishery remained its greatest employer, Tweedmouth also had a tannery, a brewery, a boiler works, a soap works and a rope works, in addition to its boatyards and herring houses. The old chapel at Tweedmouth had been rebuilt in 1780, a Presbyterian meeting house opened in 1783, and several fine houses had been built. Spittal, about a mile (1.6km) to the east had, according to Mackenzie (1825), formerly been 'the rendezvous of vagabonds and smugglers', but having lost their lurking place when the adjoining common was enclosed and divided, they had moved elsewhere or perhaps into more legitimate occupations. Spittal, mainly inhabited by fishermen and pitmen, also had its Presbyterian meeting house, opened in 1752, and some new dwelling houses had been erected in the 1790s. As might be expected, there was a large curing house for red and white herrings, but the earliest manufactory at Spittal seems to have produced prussian blue, oil of vitriol and yellow ochre, although only blue was being made by the 1790s. Spittal's medicinal well apparently attracted people from all parts of the country but, according to Fuller, a lack of decent accommodation limited its use and likewise the good opportunities for sea-bathing.

All this industrial activity, and concomitant growth in trade, was reflected in the operations of the Berwick Custom House which employed 31 people in 1799, including 6 'tide waiters', 12 'coast waiters and preventative officers along the coast' and one 'depute searcher at Alemouth'. Custom revenues had increased from £1000 in 1782 to £6000 in 1798. But not all was well in the still largely natural harbour, for the entrance channel was narrow and unprotected, its

Elizabethan pier having long been in decay. According to Fuller, the difficulties in getting out to sea in adverse weather had led the white fishermen to drive a cut from the river to Meadow Haven; this natural basin just to the north of the river's mouth was protected on three sides by rock outcrops but offered two natural outlets which were more suitable than the river mouth in difficult weather.

Some 62 ships belonged to the port of Berwick at the beginning of the nineteenth century with a total of 5,150 registered tons. A dry dock capable of taking five smacks had been incorporated into the Berwick quay, and there was also a ballast quay, but the town quay was very short and the greater part of the shore alongside it dried out at low tide; moreover, there was only 5ft (1.5m) of water on the bar at low water. Consequently, larger ships could not use the town quay and most ships were seeking refuge elsewhere in bad weather. The Tweedmouth side of the river was, however, much better, for the naturally deeper water there allowed vessels drawing up to 18ft (5.5m) to lie at all states of the tide without beaching. But Berwick was not yet ready to concede to any suggestions for harbour development on the south side of the river, even as the north side became less and less able to meet the demands being put upon it, and as trade was being lost to Leith.

It may have been as a response to this situation and also to the high grain prices of the Napoleonic war period that consideration was given, in 1807, to the building of a horse-drawn railway between Berwick and Kelso, some 20 miles (32km) west in the Scottish borders. This would allow for much cheaper carriage of coal and lime from the Berwick area into Tweeddale, and also cheaper carriage of agricultural produce from the latter to Berwick's harbour, but its projected cost of £70,000 probably meant that insufficient public subscriptions were forthcoming at this time: a similar problem had arisen in 1790, after Robert Whitworth had surveyed the line of a proposed canal between the same towns. Still, in anticipation that the proposed railway would be built, an Act of Parliament was sought which would place the port of Berwick under the care of harbour commissioners rather than the Corporation of Berwick. The Petition was presented and read before Parliament on 15 February 1808, the Mayor, Bailiffs, and Burgesses arguing that:

> ... the Harbour of Berwick is a place of considerable and increasing resort for Ships and Vessels trading to and from the same: and that the Pier formerly built to shelter the Harbour from storms and to keep the River Tweed within its channel, is of late years gone to decay; and if powers were given to rebuild the said Pier, and otherwise to improve the Harbour, the same might be rendered capable of admitting Merchant Vessels of the largest size that frequent those seas, and even Ships of War of large dimensions.

The Act gained the Royal Assent on 9 June 1808, more than 40 years before a similar transition of powers occurred with respect to the Tyne. The Berwick

Harbour Commissioners' threefold brief was to improve the harbour, firstly by building a new pier on the Berwick side of the Tweed to the design of John Rennie, and estimated to cost £40,000; secondly to extend the Berwick quay; and thirdly to construct a stone jetty on the Spittal side of the river at Carr Rock. Work on the half-mile (0.8km) long pier commenced in 1810 and it appears to have been built, at least in part, on the foundations of the Elizabethan pier. The foundation stone for the pier was laid amidst considerable celebrations on 27 February 1810:

> A grand masonic procession took place at Berwick, on the occasion of laying the foundation stone of a new pier for that harbour; the day was ushered in by the ringing of bells etc. The different lodges of freemasons from the neighbouring towns joining that of Berwick, assembled on the morning, at the town-hall, along with the magistrates, commissioners, and a number of respectable inhabitants, from thence they walked to the church in due order, where an excellent sermon was preached on the occasion by ... vicar of Berwick. After the

1 Carr Rock jetty on the south side of the Tweed estuary at Spittal. Sailing ships are loading/ unloading by means of horse and cart; salmon fishing cobles to the foreground, the Spittal chemical works to the rear. *Courtesy Berwick Record Office*

2 A salmon coble by Carr Rock Jetty, 1973

service, they proceeded (attended by the band, and a guard of the Forfarshire militia then lying there), to lay the foundation stone. After ... a short prayer, the stone in which was deposited a bottle, containing all the different coins of George III with several medals, and two plates, with suitable inscriptions on them, was laid down amidst the acclamations of an immense concourse of people. When the ceremony, which was honoured by a royal salute from the cannon on the ramparts, followed by the ships of the harbour, who displayed their flags on the occasion, was over, the procession returned to the town-hall, where the lodge of St. George dined; the other lodges dined at their respective rooms, and the day concluded with the greatest harmony.

Nevertheless, the commissioners must have witnessed with some nervousness a proposal then under discussion, to build a horse-drawn iron railway from Berwick to Glasgow. None other than Thomas Telford, the most celebrated road, bridge and canal engineer of his time, prepared the report and recommended its acceptance. With a length of 125 miles (201km) it would have exceeded by 15 times any railway then in existence, but its objects were the reverse of the earlier Berwick to Kelso plan. Coal and lime would be carried west on this proposed railway from Lanarkshire to the Scottish border counties, while grain would travel in the opposite direction; it is difficult to see how this line and intent would benefit Berwick, even though it was proposed that the line should run from the Berwick quay. Telford estimated that the venture would cost £365,700 but that it should yield a return of 12 per cent to its proprietors. It was not proceeded with. However, the Royal Assent was granted to the earlier proposed Berwick to Kelso line in 1811; interestingly, this Act contained a clause relating to the carriage of passengers, the first time that such provision had ever been made, but in the event this proposed line was not built.

Work continued on the new Berwick pier using stone from quarries just down the coast from Spittal and brought by a horse-drawn railway to the south side of the Tweed near Carr Rock, to be shipped across to the pier workings. The pier was complete by 1825, and was 'a most noble monument of the spirit and enlightened policy of the inhabitants of Berwick' according to Mackenzie, who also noted that the corporation had generously vested the shore dues in the hands of the commissioners, and had also voluntarily given up their previous exemption from the payment of such dues – 'Such an honourable display of public spirit seldom occurs.'

Admiral Stow laid the foundation stone for a lighthouse at the end of the pier on 15 February 1826, and the structure was completed later that year to the

3 The weather-worn sandstone parapet of Berwick pier, April 1991

design of Joseph Nelson who had also been responsible for the lights on Inner Farne (1809-10) and Longstone (1826). The other harbour works were also duly completed, but they failed to herald a new dawn in the port's fortunes. One commentator, simply known as 'A Tourist' (1826) noted that:

> ... this pier, which promised so much to improve the harbour, has lessened the trade of the place, by the harbour dues being increased to defray the expense of its erection.

He was also more critical of the Berwick Corporation than Mackenzie had been, noting that:

> The revenue of the borough is considerable; but like that of most corporations, conduces more to individual corruption than public utility.

The same writer, after noting that a good deal of timber was imported from Canada and the Baltic, and that one or two whalers sailed from the port, remarked on the decline in the salmon catch in recent years. In fact, many had argued that the new pier, by reducing the natural entrance to the river, would discourage the salmon from entering and thereby imperil the salmon fishery. This prophecy soon appeared to be justified as the quantity of salmon exported fell from around 350 ton per annum in the first decade of the nineteenth century to around 240 ton per annum by the 1830s; the yearly rental for the fishery had fallen to £9,000 by 1836. The formerly huge catches, such as that which saw more than 10,000 salmon in the Berwick market on 1 September 1814, seemed destined never to return. Some commentators, however, believed that the fall in catch was due to over-fishing, while others no doubt blamed poachers or seals. Various Tweed Acts had been obtained to prohibit poaching and an elaborate system of watchers and constables set up to enforce their provisions. But this was never an easy task and systematic poaching continued through the nineteenth century. As one noble lord was later to assert, 'not one man in a hundred believes himself to be violating any moral law when he offends against the Tweed Acts'.

The 1820s were difficult years for the Berwick traders. French suppliers began to gain control of the London egg trade and Leith merchants gained more and more of Berwick's general east-coast trade. Moreover, the post-Napoleonic war depression saw a considerable fall in wheat prices, although barley had held its price quite well. In spite of these changes, Berwick was able to pick up some new business. When the new harbour of Helmsdale was developed in Sutherland in an attempt to provide work for some Highlanders displaced in the infamous 'Clearances', Berwick was one port to make use of the new opportunity for trade. In 1819, it was the sole supplier by sea to Helmsdale of iron hoops (presumably for barrels), potatoes, leather, soap, dressed hemp, tobacco, snuff, molasses, hops and hulled barley; it was also the major supplier of biscuits and dressed lint. The tonnages exported from Berwick to Helmsdale were quite small when compared with the vast amounts of salt imported into Helmsdale from several Scottish ports and especially from Liverpool, or with the amount of alcohol imported from Leith, but any new Berwick trade must have been most welcome. The Berwick–Helmsdale connection may have been fostered by the presence of Berwick fish curers in Helmsdale; according to James Loch the superintendent to the Sutherland Estate, 'particular circumstances' led him to provide a new and well-equipped curing station at Helmsdale for Messrs Landles & Calder of Berwick, at a cost of £2,100 in *c.*1814; by 1820 a curing yard had also been built for a Mr Redpath of Berwick.

The town's fishing industry came to generate an import which was probably unwelcome but occasionally necessary. The 'Berwick Shipping Co.' had been founded in 1820 with £20,000 capital in £1 shares, to replace the two earlier shipping companies. With more than 20 smacks for passengers and goods, the company initially maintained a regular service between the Metropolis and southern Scotland, but soon succumbed to competition from Leith. Its fleet had dwindled to only seven or eight trading smacks in regular service by 1828, but during the mild winters of 1822, 1833/4, and 1837, the company imported hundreds of tons of ice from Norway to supplement inadequate local supplies for fish packing. Another shipping company, known as The General Shipping Company of Berwick, was also operating in the 1820s, although it was in the hands of trustees by the following decade, presumably after failure. The number of ships registered at Berwick in 1829 was 57, with a total register admeasurement of 4,984 tons, but trade generally appears to have been fairly stagnant. Many of Berwick's ships were owned by local merchants and people involved in the fishing and maritime industries: master mariners, ironmongers, coopers, fish curers, sailmakers and grocers all found shipowning, in whole or in part, to be a worthwhile investment. Berwick also had at least one whaling boat, the *Norfolk*, which arrived back from one trip in January 1836 after great difficulties, the crew having been on short rations for about 13 weeks. Yet another attempt was made, in the same year, to revive the Berwick to Kelso railway scheme in the hope of attracting more trade, but the sponsoring company was moribund and was formally dissolved early in 1838.

Berwick's inshore fishing fleet was also entering a difficult period, probably through over-fishing and a resultant depletion of inshore resources. To counter this, some Berwickshire fishermen were obliged to seek offshore supplies at a time when the offshore herring boom was just getting underway. The herring fishery in the Firth of Forth had been one of the most important in north Britain from the 1790s, and later the fisheries off the north-east coast of Scotland were developed; Northumberland's fishermen were finding catches as far north as Shetland by the 1820s. Much of the herring catch was destined for markets in Europe and exports had built up rapidly following the conclusion of the Napoleonic wars. The herring fishery off north-east England was being developed by the 1840s, partly to satisfy the new inland markets opened up by the spread of the nation's railway network, and the Tweed's native herring fleet was gradually expanded; the number of 'stranger' vessels using the port also increased greatly. Much of this activity was concentrated at Spittal where, in the season, hundreds of men and women could find employment. A large curing station had been established in the village by Boston Bros in *c*.1844, and thousands of barrels of herring were soon being despatched annually to continental markets; the same firm also held leases on salmon fisheries on the Tweed and a branch business in Yarmouth.

It was also at Spittal that, in 1835, the Tweed's first lifeboat was stationed, although a house was not provided for it until 1859. After occupying various locations, on both sides of the river, the station was eventually settled by the Carr Rock at Spittal. Its first lifeboat may well have been built on the Tweed, for the ship and boatyards were still active. Indeed, the output of boats in the 1840s suggests some degree of economic regeneration. Shipbuilding on the Tweed had been dominated by the Byram Gowan yard at Berwick from the beginning of the century, sloop-rigged smacks and schooners being launched in almost equal numbers. The yards at Tweedmouth and Spittal presumably concentrated on the building of fishing boats and cobles, with only a very rare foray into schooner building; almost all the fishing boats registered at Eyemouth in Scotland before 1841 had been built on the Tweed, even though Eyemouth's own shipyard had commenced in 1827. The Byram Gowan yard built its first snow in 1837, the 176-ton *Ocean*, for a shipowner on Holy Island, and its first brig in 1839, the 117-ton *Border Chieftain*. The 341-ton barque *Berwick Castle* was launched for James Forster, a Berwick merchant, in 1842, while in 1852 the 450-ton barque *Lord Delaval* was built for Carr & Company, merchants of Berwick. A new shipping company, The Mediterranean Shipping Company of Berwick, had the 177-ton brig *Dromo* built at Gowan's in 1842, while George Lee, the shipbuilder of Tweedmouth, built one smack and two schooners for his sole ownership in the 1840s. Arthur Byram Gowan also owned ships, in his own right or in part, from the 1820s, but seems to have intensified his personal shipping operations between 1832 and 1846, building no less than eight vessels comprising three schooners, three smacks, a ketch and a brig, for his sole or part ownership. These were signs of recovery as Berwick and, more importantly, Tweedmouth and Spittal, saw continued, if small-scale, industrial development, while the richly productive agricultural hinterland continued to produce grain surpluses. Berwick was officially declared an English port on 1 June 1848, its authority extending from St Abbs Head, Scotland, in the north, to the river Aln in Northumberland to the south.

But there were now to be two threats to the port's regained prosperity. Firstly, the railway between Newcastle and Edinburgh, which opened throughout in 1850 with a branch from Tweedmouth to Kelso opening in the following year, took away much of Berwick's coastal traffic; the Berwick Shipping Company Ltd, which had been incorporated in 1856, was an early casualty to the railway, and it increasingly concentrated on its salmon fisheries as its shipping trade declined. Secondly, the development of steam shipping looked set to bypass Berwick with its inadequate and still largely natural harbour. Even so, new businesses which were likely to place additional demands for shipping accommodation were being commenced at the mouth of the river. One such was the 1868 Spittal Point fertiliser works of Crossman & Paulin, two men who had been partners in the schooner *Maggie* since 1862.

In addition to the 60 or so fishing boats based at Berwick at this period, some 200 stranger herring boats regularly used the harbour during the season. Salmon fishing remained important but continued to attract the attentions of the poachers. One anonymous writer noted that some 327 people had been accused of violations of the Tweed Acts in the year 1872-73; 164 had been fined, 41 were imprisoned, 44 had absconded while 60 were acquitted; in all, some 235 'engines of capture' had been confiscated. He further observed that:

> On the Tweed and its many tributaries there is a considerable population, many of whom have but a slight knowledge of 'mine and thine', and all of whom have a taste for salmon and a strong desire for gain.

The pressures on space in the harbour due to the increase in all shipping and fishing activities, and hopes of an expanded coal export trade (50 tons exported coastwise and 407 tons foreign in 1855), finally led to positive steps for significant harbour development. A second Harbour Act had been obtained on 3 June 1862, which allowed for the election of 15 harbour commissioners, and a third Act of 13 May 1872 empowered the commissioners to undertake major harbour improvement works in the form of a wet dock at Tweedmouth, an embankment and parallel road from the southern end of Berwick bridge to the jetty at Carr Rock, and some coal staiths; they were also authorised to seek agreement with the North Eastern Railway (NER) for the construction of a branch line to the proposed dock; the NER had taken over the Newcastle to Berwick line in 1854. The belated decision to concentrate harbour facilities on the south bank of the Tweed made much sense, for it was there that the deepest water was always to be found. Detailed plans for the works were drawn up by Messrs David & Thomas Stevenson of Edinburgh, perhaps better known as lighthouse builders through their position as engineers to the Commissioners for Northern Lighthouses. David and Thomas, together with their brother Alan, had in this respect followed in the footsteps of their father Robert and grandfather Thomas Smith, the one and only dynasty of lighthouse builders; Thomas Stevenson's son, Robert Louis, also joined the family firm, but soon found an alternative outlet for his energies as a writer.

Work on the new structures began in 1873, after Messrs A. Morrison & Sons of Edinburgh won the contract with a tender price of £37,961 12s 0d, and the new 'Tweed Dock' was officially opened, amidst much celebration, on 4 October

1876, although it had been in partial use for a few weeks. Even if the dock had actually cost £60,000 as was later claimed, this failed to dampen the spirits of its promoters. The Mayor declared an official half-day holiday in the town, and the opening ceremonies began with the ringing of the Town Hall bells. This was followed by a civic march from the Town Hall to the harbour office on Berwick Quay whence the entire company boarded the steam tug *Tweed* for a trip to Spittal before returning to the new dock. After the opening speech by the Recorder of Berwick, wine and cake were partaken at a blacksmith's shop before the return to Berwick was made on foot. In the evening a special dinner was held for 110 gentlemen in the Kings Arms assembly rooms where many optimistic speeches were made.

The new dock, its floor puddled with 'blue' clay, comprised 3.5 acres (1.4ha) of water enclosed by 1,550ft (473m) of granite-faced concrete quay, and it offered a water depth of 21ft (6.4m) in the dock at ordinary spring tides; the sill at the entrance lock gates, however, reduced the entrance depth to 19ft (5.8m). The entrance was 40ft (12.2m) wide and contained a pair of mitred

4 The entrance lock to Tweed Dock, with the former Spittal chemical works in the distance. The hand capstans by the dock entrance were for opening and closing the dock gates the 'Armstrong patent', September 1990

5 *Regina* tied up in Tweed Dock, with Mute swans in attendance, May 1998

lock gates operated by hand capstans (dubbed the 'Armstrong Patent' system by today's operators who now have the benefit of hydraulic power). An approach channel was excavated from the dock to the main river course, being marked by a timber pier along its south side. The dock was also fitted with a slipway, a steam-powered crane and a coal staith for the Scremerston collieries. This was a considerable improvement to the harbour facilities on the Tweed, and although a second wet dock was anticipated, this proved not to be necessary. Thus it is that Tweed Dock is the only wet dock ever constructed on the Northumberland coast, the eighteenth-century cut at Seaton Sluice apart. The NER opened its Tweedmouth Dock branch in 16 October 1878, running from the Tweedmouth Station goods yard down to the dock on a zigzag course with two viaducts, descending some 100ft (30.5m) along its 0.75-mile (1.2km) length.

From the beginning it was anticipated that coal exports would form one of the main activities at the dock and, indeed, some of the first vessels to use it were colliers, but it is highly probable that shipments of grain, salmon and barrelled herring, became the mainstay exports. By the turn of the century the main export was undoubtedly herring, and the main imports were wood, fertilisers and oil-seed cake, but also some pyrites for sulphuric acid manufacture. The latter was associated with the manufacture of fertilisers at Spittal, notably by Messrs James R. Black & Company. James Black had taken over the works established in 1868 by Crossman & Paulin in 1886, and by 1894 the company had installed steam-powered bone and phosphate mills. The imported phosphate was converted to superphosphate fertiliser by the action of sulphuric acid made on the premises from the pyrites; the company was the first in Britain to import phosphate from the famous Constantine mine in Algeria. Another manufacturer of similar products was Johnson & Co. of the Enfield works, Spittal, and these two firms must have accounted for a considerable proportion of the imports to the dock in the early decades of the twentieth century; esparto grass for the paper mills at Chirnside was another import at this period. The First World War brought the herring fisheries to a standstill, and the dock saw very few, if any, exports, although imports held up. Barrelled herring resumed a position of dominance in the dock's exports after the war, and until the outbreak of the Second World War, herring was just about the only regular export. The mouth of the Tweed unfortunately saw some enemy action during the Second World War, with houses and shops destroyed or damaged early in August 1941, while later in that month an enemy plane was fired upon by two naval patrol boats which were lying in Tweed Dock with the result that the plane then attempted to bomb the boats.

Timber from northern Europe dominated the dock's imports from 1945 up to the 1960s, the vast bulk of it being destined for the Allan Bros wood yard in Tweedmouth, while the import of raw materials for the fertiliser manufacture ceased in the 1950s when Fisons and H.G. McCreath, the successors of the earlier firms, abandoned production at Spittal; the import of ready prepared fertilisers became increasingly important, however. There were very few outward shipments from 1945 until 1952 when barley became the leading export, a situation helped in recent decades by the increased demand for lager. Thus, barley shipped to northern Ireland and Germany for lager brewing remained a significant export and with Simpson's Malt Ltd, one of the North's leading companies, firmly rooted in Tweedmouth, malted barley exports should continue from Tweed Dock for many years to come. Some grains also continued to be imported, notably maize for H.O. Short & Son, whose grain mill stood near the dock. Cement had been imported for quite a long period but, by one of those economic quirks which seem so common in shipping, it became an export trade in 1964, when Dunbar cement began to be brought in by road to Berwick before being shipped to destinations such as the Shetlands. Oil was imported from 1915 to the 1950s, and pipe clay for Tennants factory in Tweedmouth was another small-scale import; a more unusual dock activity was the holding of swimming galas in the years leading up to the Second World War.

Tweed Dock was sometimes as busy as at any time in its past in the period 1970 to 1990, despite the loss of its railway connection, a rock bar, shifting sandbanks and a harbour entrance which restricted access by ships of more than 1,000 dead weight tonnage. An example of what could happen with larger vessels was witnessed late in 1989, when the 1,000 ton *Ursa Minor* grounded on a sandbank while approaching the dock with a cargo of phosphates from France. Barley, cement, stone, peas and beans have been the main exports in the last few decades, while the principal imports have been wheat, oats, malted barley, timber, phosphates and fertilisers. Some 58 ships used the dock in 1964-65 and the total tonnage of cargoes was 22,458 tons. The equivalent figures for 1975 were 278 ships and 169,162 tons, while for 1990 they were 177 ships and 142,000 tons; stone and cement exports accounted for almost one half the total tonnage throughput. For a while it was the second largest Northumbrian port, handling in excess of 150,000 tons of cargo and around 200 shipping movements annually. The shipment of live sheep in 2003, some 60 years after the last live cattle and sheep exports, proved to be much more contentious.

The Tweed's fishing industries, salmon fishing apart, are much less important than formerly. In common with most ports on the Northumberland coast, Berwick's herring fleet had already declined during the second half of the nineteenth century, from 64 native fishing boats in 1855 to only 8 or 9 by 1905, and remained in single figures thereafter, although the harbour continued to host larger numbers of stranger boats. The Berwick shipyard, after a few years of uncertainty, closed early in 1979, its last vessel being the sumptuously fitted three-masted schooner *Au-dela*, destined for the West Indies, but the yard was temporarily re-opened in 1991 in association with the boatyard at Eyemouth. The last of the nearby collieries closed down in the 1950s, the first in Britain to be closed after nationalisation, and long before these closures the textile, rope and sail factories had gone, although a close relation of the latter, in the form of marquee manufacture, continued in converted maltings in Pier Road, Berwick. The grain mill by the harbour is no longer in use, and planning permission is being sought for its conversion to flats. Salmon fishing remains important, although, much to the anger of some fishermen, this was restricted in recent years under a disputed scheme imposed by the Atlantic Salmon Conservation Trust. The Berwick Salmon Fisheries plc, the successor company to the Berwick Shipping Company, was the first concern in Britain to register as a plc, while the Berwick Shellfish Company, formed in 1969, exported live lobsters to France, Belgium and Holland.

Although Tweed Dock has seen many changes in its main trades over the years since it opened, it still mainly handles grains, timber and fertilisers, but it recently lost its gravel trade to Blyth. It trades with several northern European ports, including the Baltic, the Mediterranean and beyond. Recent harbour improvements have included the widening of the dock entrance in 1993, together with a strengthening of the harbour walls and an extensive dredging programme

6 The Berwick shipyard erecting yard and slip in August 1973. The yard had little work at the time, and not much more thereafter, closing in 1979

7 Above The Berwick shipyard offices, fitting shop, stores etc. in August 1973

8 Left A Tweed salmon catch near Union Bridge, 1973

to enable larger vessel movements into and within the now tidal dock; it can now handle ships of 3,000 tons dead weight which means fewer ship movements but potentially larger tonnage throughputs. A much larger project, and one in keeping with the much changed times, is the recent completion of a pontoon on the Berwick Quay, with the aim of promoting the port to cruise ships.

Tweed Dock has continued to perform its function reliably, a tribute perhaps to those who had the foresight to plan it and those who have subsequently operated it, but its future cannot be predicted with any degree of certainty, given the ever-present vagaries of seaborne trades. Berwick was never to be a second Alexandria again, but the three Tweed estuary communities still retain a rich heritage relating to their former port-based industries in the curing houses, maltings, ice houses, Custom House, factory buildings, pier, lighthouse and dock. To find, study and enjoy these within the context of the town which Nicholas Pevsner described as 'one of the most exciting towns in England' is richly rewarding.

9 Part of the Berwick riverside frontage, with a former electricity power station at centre, and the outer quay of Tweed Dock in the foreground, December 1990

3

Warenmouth and Budle bay

There is at this day no place or towne of that name [Warenmouth], that we can know.
(Exchequer Deposition, 1575)

Budle bay, some 4 miles (6.4km) south of Holy Island, is entirely tidal, the ebb tide leaving only the Waren and Ross Low burns to run over the exposed Warnham Flats. It may seem, therefore, to offer little in the way of a harbour and yet, according to the *Northumberland County History*, a once flourishing port for Bamburgh, called Warenmouth, was located near the present farm of Newtown on the south side of Budle Bay. The castle at Bamburgh was commenced in the twelfth century, but the whinstone rock on which it stands was occupied in the late pre-Roman period, and it lies just 2 miles (3.2km) south of Budle Point, which itself stands at the south–eastern point of Budle Bay, close to the Black Rocks lighthouse. At times when Berwick was possessed by Scotland, Warenmouth was the most northerly harbour in England. The name 'Warenmouth' ceased to be used sometime during the fourteenth century, however, and thereafter its location was known simply as 'Newtown'; the precise location of the port seems to have been quite forgotten by 1575. Warenmouth must have been essentially a fishing harbour, although other provisions were presumably imported for Bamburgh and some grains may have been exported. It always remained possible, however, for small vessels to pass up Budle Bay, for an advertisement in the *Newcastle Courant* of August 1770 refers to a large granary and kiln for drying wheat for exportation from Budle Bay; a granary is shown near Heather House on the first edition of the Ordnance Survey, *c.*1856, together with a pier, quay and dolphins. Furthermore, an 1805 report on the Waren water corn mill situated at the east end of the bay noted that:

The Waren Mill establishment is a very complete one, was erected in 1783, is situated near the sea and communicating with it by a creek, along which craft are navigated close to the mill, corn, meal and other articles are received and delivered without being subject to land carriage.

In fact the mill site has been in use at least since the twelfth century, but was clearly rebuilt in the early 1780s. When the mill was offered to be let in 1858, an advertisement again noted that it had means of shipping on the premises and, indeed, a small quay could recently be seen to the seaward side of the mill. A coastguard house had been established near the farm of Heather House by that time, with a granary just to the north-east and a limekiln was working at Kiln Point. Later still, whinstone was being shipped from Budle Bay; a footpath which leads across the golf course follows the alignment of the narrow gauge railway along which the stone was carried to a small pier or jetty at the edge of the bay, probably at the site of the granary pier. One of the last maritime activities on Budle Bay was an attempt to cultivate mussels. Mussel beds were laid down by Mr A.H. Browne of Callaly Castle in 1890, and 100 tons of mussels were sold from the bay in 1896/7, but although output was almost doubled in the following year, it seems to have declined thereafter.

As late as 1948, mariners were being advised that they could still enter Budle Bay, even though the 'Warnham Bar' offered only a 13ft (4m) depth at high water; they were, however, warned that this should never be attempted without the assistance of a pilot from Holy Island or Seahouses. Budle Bay remains a strangely beautiful and evocative place, both to mariners and landlubbers, but with little indication of its former role as a port, albeit a relatively minor one.

4

Holy Island harbour

... a place much necessarye to be defended and preserved, for there is a harboroughe sufficient for a great navye of shippes to rest safely in, and very aptlye for the warrs towards Scotland. (Report to Crown, 1550)

The Holy Island of Lindisfarne, only about 1.5 square miles in area, some 10 miles (16.1km) south-east of Berwick, is one of the best known and loved parts of Northumberland. A slightly elevated plain, connected to the mainland at low tide by a causeway 1 mile (1.6km) long, its land was occupied long before it was an island, for flint working has been identified dating over the long period c.8000 to 1500 BC. The island's main historical associations, with St Aidan and St Cuthbert, are too well known to require notice here, but the role of its harbour and its trading activities are perhaps less appreciated.

The only settlement on the island stands at its south-west corner, overlooking a large natural harbour which is set amongst more than 5,000 acres (2,025ha) of tidal sands and mud slakes close southward of the island; the harbour is secure and well sheltered, appearing extensive at high water but in reality quite small; even at low water there is a 9ft (2.7m) depth at the bar, and 24ft (7.3m) at high water. It has long offered a safe harbour of refuge when adverse weather was the enemy, but not sufficiently safe for its inhabitants when the Danes were terrorising the island in the eighth and ninth centuries. At the same time its natural harbour of refuge could also be adventitious to the islanders, especially when trading vessels just failed to make the safe waters. It was reported that such situations were anticipated and encouraged by prayer in the seventeenth century:

The common people ther do pray for shippes which they sie in danger. They al sit downe upon their knees and hold up their handes and say very devotely, Lord, send her to us, God send her to us ... They pray, not God to sauve you, or send you to the port, but to send you to them by shipwrack, that they may gette the spoils of her ... if the shippe come wel to porte ... they gette up in anger, crying, the Devil stick her, she is away from us.

Was such the inheritance of St Aidan and St Cuthbert? The islanders were involved in fishing from as early as 1372, for accounts for that year include expenditure on the construction of ships, fishing boats and herring nets. In addition, the monks of Holy Island possessed an oyster dredge for gathering the shellfish from Fenham Flats, just south-west of the island, in 1394-95. Limestone was being quarried on the island in the fourteenth century – an activity which was also being pursued more than 500 years later – for the monastery accounts for 1344-45 include 57.5 chaldrons of coal 'for the brewhouse, limekiln, hall, [and] prior's chamber'. It is doubtful whether this coal was mined on the island, although some coal was present there, but much more likely that it was brought by land and causeway from Holburn, about 7 miles (11.2km) to the south-west on the mainland.

In 1539, just two years after the dissolution of the monasteries, it was ordered that all 'Havens should be fenced with bulwarks and blockhouses against the Scots', and by fortunate coincidence the upstanding whinstone crag of Beblow at the east end of the inner harbour, and overlooking the sea entrance to it, provided a superb foundation for such a defence work on the island and also a fine vantage point for safeguarding the harbour. An earth and timber defence work was completed some 10 years later, but the garrison commander was not entirely happy with such flimsy protection. A report to the Crown in 1550 stressed the usefulness of the harbour to the navy, and noted that the island had storehouses and brewhouses 'sufficient to furnish the said navye withall', but all was not well, for part of the roof of the great storehouse, 'that was the church of the Priory', had fallen in and a wall of the brewhouse, made of timber, was expected to fall at any minute. This report also noted that the only mills on the island were horse powered (the island is devoid of streams for water power), and that the provision of a tide mill should be considered. In all probability, the tide mill was never built, as Fenham corn mill, on the mainland, had formed part of the properties of the monks of Holy Island at least from the thirteenth century. But other improvements were made and a stone castle replaced the earth and timber defences on Beblow Crag between 1565 and 1571. The western end of the inner harbour was also defended, by the construction of 'Osborne's Fort' in the 1670s.

The village on Holy Island seems to have decayed somewhat during the sixteenth and seventeenth centuries, even if the harbour was a much frequented refuge for merchant and naval vessels. John Aston, who visited the island in 1639, noted that, 'noe part of it [is] tilled nor affoording any thing but conies' but he also witnessed '20 sayle under the command of Marquisse Hammilton' which had landed two regiments of foot soldiers. The islanders themselves has acquired a reputation (and perhaps a habit) for lawlessness,

10 *Above* Lindisfarne Castle, Holy Island, overlooks the natural harbour drying out at low tide, September 1990

11 *Below* How to beach a large boat, seemingly one registered in Caernarvon, in the dried-out harbour on Holy Island, September 1990

smuggling and wreck plundering, but the herring fishery seems to have survived all that. Having been an important island activity at least from the fourteenth century we can safely assume that this continued to be so during the following centuries, albeit with booms and slumps. Some 27 fisherman were said to reside on the island in 1626 and Hutchinson (1776) noted that although the village consisted of a few irregular houses, two or more of which were inns but the rest occupied by fishermen, some new 'tenements' had recently been built and the island had become 'a place of great resort'. Holy Island had seemingly recovered a degree of prosperity. There were then 10 to 12 herring boats, each with a crew of three or four men, numbers which were to remain remarkably constant for several decades, catching cod, ling, haddock and lobsters out of season. The village clearly expanded considerably over the next 50 years, for Mackenzie (1825) tells that there were then 100 houses on the island and seven inns or public houses, 'some of them very convenient and respectable'. He added that:

> The shore is, in many parts, excellent for bathing, and the situation is at once healthy and romantic: it has, therefore, of late years, become a place of great resort, and is much praised for the beauties that grace its solemn walks. The new houses which have been recently erected, give to the place a neat and comfortable appearance.

The island had clearly become what it is today – a popular tourist destination – but it still retained its profitable coney warren and its thriving fishery. The village people then included two shoe makers, three farmers, a tailor, a baker, three grocers, a blacksmith, a joiner, a butcher, a school master, a curate and a parish clerk. The population of the island was said to number 836 in 1831 (although this may refer to the population of the parish which included the mainland townships of Fenham and Goswick), with most of the men being involved in fishing, but two thirds of them were also licensed by Newcastle Trinity House to act as pilots for their own harbour and others on the adjoining coast. Herring fishing continued to be important, the main grounds lying just south of the Staple, one of the Farne Islands to the east, and between the Farnes and the mainland; the season lasted from about 20 July to the first week in September. There were still about a dozen deckless herring boats, each 30 to 36ft (9.2 to 11m) long with two lug sails, 12 nets and a crew of four; most of the catch was then cured at Berwick before being dispatched to Newcastle, Hull or London. In addition, some 60 cobles, each about 26ft (8m) long and with a single lug sail, were active in catching cod, ling and haddock; these fish, like the lobsters and crabs caught out of the herring season, were carried to London in smacks engaged by fishmongers in the metropolis.

That the island continued to attract the discerning visitor, is evidenced by an advertisement in the *Newcastle Courant* of 3 June 1842:

Bathing Quarters: The mansion House at Holy Island having undergone a thorough repair, has been elegantly furnished, and is now ready for the reception of visitors. NB Hot, Cold, and Shower Baths, with a plentiful supply of Sea and Fresh water brought into the House.

The island's first lifeboat was launched in 1829 and a second was stationed in the island's first lifeboat house, built in 1839 at the Snook, at the extreme north-western point of the island; its replacement at the same location was constructed some 30 years later. The fishing industry had expanded considerably during those decades, as had the size of boats used. Some 36 large herring boats were working out of Holy Island harbour by the 1860s, although it seems likely that the majority of these were manned by non-islanders coming in for the season, and there was now a newly-built smoke house down by the harbour. It is also apparent that the fishery was attracting many foreign vessels, for as many as 100 French boats plus many coasting vessels might be anchored in the harbour at any one time. White fishing, salmon netting, winkle gathering, lobster and crab catching all continued to be profitable enterprises and an expansion in the lime-burning business, to be outlined later, added to the island's overall prosperity.

Such activities could be seen as noisome by the more sensitive observer. Walter White (1859) contrasted the 'numerous large and ornamental gravestones and the elaborate tombs' in the churchyard with the unsavoury nature of the 'abodes of the living' on the island:

> … you will perhaps think that the pains bestowed on memorials of the dead would be better employed within the village, or 'the town' as the natives fondly call it. There is a square bestrewn with unsavoury rubbish, and the condition of the streets accords therewith, implying that public cleanliness has not yet grown into a habit. The spring is a good way off. Whitewashed cottages, some of them retaining the primitive thatch, constitute the bulk of the dwellings, while among those of better style appear nine inns or public-houses. In the last census returns the population of the island is given as 908, of whom 458 are males; hence, excluding the boys, we may form a notion as to the number of customers to each public house.

Even so, White was able to demonstrate the typical enthusiasms of many a Victorian *voyeur*:

> We saw 'the town' under its busy aspect, preparing for the herring fishery; nets lay in heaps, or stretched out fifty or sixty yards, while men and boys disentangle their mazy folds and tie the loops; around almost every door lies a heap of floats, and lines, and queer-looking oil-skin garments, and ample sou'westers hang on the walls. And at times a few men, wearing thick seagoing jackets, and boots up to their hips, take their way down to the beach with a pile of gear on their shoulders. They will sail ere long, for rumour says the herrings are in the offing....
>
> On our way [to the castle] we passed the beach where the fishing-boats come in, and saw the huge wooden vat — if vat it be — round which the women stand to clean the herrings,

and on the other side of the road fourteen hundred herring-barrels in piles and rows, and two men industrious over their final preparation. 'There wouldn't be any too many' they said, 'nor yet half enough, if the boats did but have luck'. While re-crossing the herring beach, we had a pretty sight in the departure of a number of the boats. The tide served, evening was coming on, and one after another they hoisted sail, stood out of the bay, made a tack, some two tacks, and then away to the open sea, perhaps for five-and-twenty miles.

In fact the island's fishery was approaching its high-water mark and it may never have been so busy again. As the Fisheries Commissioners were to note in 1866, the previous 20 years had witnessed a constant increase in the number of fishermen, the size of their boats and the quantity of nets and other gear, at Holy Island, Newbiggin, North Sunderland and Cullercoats as the spread of the inland railway network in the 1840s and 1850s, providing easier access to the London and other markets, resulted in an intensification of inshore fishing. But a depletion of inshore stocks was already becoming apparent and the same report also noted the impact of sailing trawlers which had made their appearance in Northumberland waters within the previous seven years. These trawlers came to the Northumberland coast in considerable numbers from Scarborough and Hartlepool, to trawl about 4 to 6 miles (6.4 to 9.7km) off shore between Cullercoats and Newbiggin in the south of the county, but it was said that they thereby disturbed the spawning grounds along the whole of the coast and thus contributed still further to inshore stock depletion.

The cumulative effects of these changes, the intensification of inshore fishing and the emergence of trawlers, were to increase the need to fish in more distant waters and to reduce the importance of inshore fisheries such as that of Holy Island, a decline which would be accelerated by the introduction of steam trawlers after 1877. Only those harbours with deep water facilities, and those fishermen of sufficient means, could hope to capitalise on these changes, and as Eyemouth, Seahouses and North Shields advanced, so the smaller fishing harbours declined. The decline was not, however, immediate at Holy Island. Its native herring fleet remained at 12 herring boats in 1875, and Bulmer noted in 1887 that 'the little port is chiefly visited by fishing boats, and in the season presents a lively scene, if not always a pleasant odour'; 17 men were still listed as being pilots. It is also clear that the earlier prosperous times had brought a measure of social advance, for there was a Fishermen's Brass Band, a reading room and library, and three carriers operating between the island and Beal Railway Station on the mainland, some 4 miles (6.4km) west of the village.

This prosperity had been generated as much by the rocks and minerals of the island as by the harvest of the sea. At periods during the eighteenth century the Carron Iron Company of Falkirk had shipped ironstone nodules from the island to their furnaces in Scotland; apparently the nodules could only be extracted on the ebbing tide, for they were found in shales which outcropped below the high-water mark. But the island's main economic mineral resource was the limestone with which it was well endowed in the deposits known as the 'Sanbanks' and the 'Acre' which were extensively quarried, while the 'Eelwell' limestone was only exposed at low tide; these strata were all mainly exposed around the north shore. But carboniferous limestones have little economic value unless burned to give lime for use in mortar or as a neutraliser of acid soils, and fuel was needed for that process to be carried out. Perry claimed that the monks of the island were quarrying limestone at least from 1344, although their purpose in so doing is uncertain. He further suggested that:

> Ever since the old days of Priory overlordship the Islanders had been accustomed to quarry their own limestone at the Snook, burning it with kilns at the Snook and the Lower Kennedy with coal from their own workings.

There is, however, little documentary evidence to support the suggestion of such a long continued island-based activity. Certainly some coal deposits exist on the island, as a series of test borings between 1792 and 1840 showed; the site of these borings is marked by a stumpy tower at the Snook. It is also known that a thin coal seam was worked by islanders during the General Strike of 1926, but the coal seams were generally thin and poor, the best being only 18in (46cm) thick. Indeed, it must have been the inadequacy of local coal deposits which led to thoughts of importing coal for lime burning on the island, and of exporting limestone by sea for burning elsewhere. The building of at least two large ships on the island during the second half of the eighteenth century may relate to a realisation of such trades. The *Sally* built by Mr Edward Byram and described as 'a very handsome vessel of 25 keels of coals' (i.e. about 525 tons), was launched from Holy Island harbour on 8 October 1763. The 365-ton *Kent* was also built on the island, in 1766. It seems likely that vessels of such large size were intended for bulky cargoes such as coal or limestone.

More positive evidence for coal and limestone traffic emerges from a document dated June 1789, which enumerated the costs involved in bringing coal to the island from the river Tyne but also seems to have considered the cost of transporting limestone to the Tyne to be burnt there:

Price of small coals ['per chaldron' deleted]	5s – 0
Duke of Richmond's	1s – 0
Custom House Charges (about)	1s – 1
Town Dues per chaldron	= 5
	7s – 6d
Limestone at Lemington [on Tyne] per ton	2s – 7d

NB   A chaldron of coals is equal to three fothers containing 8 bolls coal measure which is rather more than 12 Bolls by Winchester measure, and is as much as is usually carried with a cart and three horses. These coals will burn 2 fother of Clot or shell lime for one fother of Coals – and rather better. The freight for bringing limestone to Lemington or to Whitle point, [probably near Whitley where there were coal mines and limekilns by the 1680s – see chapter on Cullercoats] and carrying Coals back to Holy Island to be considered – the size of vessel will make a little difference to the price of carriage.

The significance of the above seems clear, although the outcome is not. It was intended to bring coal from Lemington or 'Whitle' to Holy Island for lime burning and to take limestone back to the Tyne as a return cargo. An advertisement in the *Newcastle Chronicle* for 9 February 1793, indicates that part of this traffic had indeed been established:

> Stone Boats
> Wanted immediately, a Number of Stone boats, to carry Limestone from Holy Island to North Shields, Agreement to be made per Ton. Apply to Mr. Selby, Swansfield, near Alnwick; or to Mr. Taylor, of Newburn near Newcastle.

There is no reference here to return cargoes of coal, but this does not of itself imply that there was no lime-burning on the island at this time and certainly a Parliamentary Bill of 1791, which proposed the enclosure of common land on the island, recognised the need to allow for the quarrying of limestone and the operation of a lime kiln. According to Perry:

> In 1791 the provisions of a Bill for Enclosing the Common Land if the Island (carried through by tampering with the Vote, and made Law two year later) throw further light on the state of the Island at this time and previously. The Lord of the Manor – his residence was the old Priory brewery, which together with the bakehouse, had been removed to the 'Pallace' on the East side of the village – was to have the liberty of hawking, hunting, fishing and fowling over the Island: but the Freeholders or Stallengers ... and the owners of burgages, messuages, tenements and garths were entitled to Right of Common or Eatage, and Stinted Pasture; Right of Seawood or ware or driven wreck: but not more than two acres of Freestone and Limestone Quarries among them, and only one kiln at a time.

The first edition of the Ordnance Survey, published in 1866, shows two lime-burning sites on the island. One lay to the north of Snook House on the North Shore, a single kiln near the tower marking the site of the coal boring; there appear to be no surviving kiln remains above ground at this site. The second site, at Lower Kennedy, was a much more complex affair, for the Ordnance Survey shows three banks of 'limekilns'. The most northerly group consisted of two kilns, side by side, having curved frontages and single pots; these were probably the oldest kilns of the group for they were bisected by a tramway which could bring limestone to the kilns from quarries at Coves Bay to the north. The tramway also continued beyond these kilns, presumably to carry burnt lime past Chare

Ends to a jetty west of the village near Tripping Chare; the same tramway could have been used to bring coal from the jetty back up to the kilns. The fact that the limekilns were bisected by the tramway suggests that this was a modification to enable limestone to be brought straight through to supply another bank of kilns which was located about 300 yards further south, by the side of the tramway – the most southerly bank of kilns of the Lower Kennedy Works. Between these two kiln banks, the Ordnance Survey shows another structure marked 'lime kilns' although the plan-form on the map is most unusual. It is, however, of interest, that an undated and unattributed map in Perry, shows 'Kelp Pits' at this location, and certainly kelp burning was a long established activity on Holy Island; other structures here were a crane, a smithy and a cottage. The Lower Kennedy site is probably that referred to by the Cartwrights, who noted that permission was given to erect a large limeworks and to develop brick and tile making in 1846. To this end they suggest that a c.1840 pier near Chare Ends was extended and new lengths of tramway constructed; the planned brick and tile works apparently came to naught. Several of the Lower Kennedy kilns and other structures are still recognisable although greatly decayed. The scale of this limeworks indicates that its product was not simply for local consumption but for export, and it is appropriate here to say a little about the carriage of limestone and quicklime by sea.

Carrying limestone by sea presented no particular problem, but there were potential dangers in carrying quicklime by sea, for there was always the risk of contact between the quicklime and sea water, and therefore of an exothermic reaction between the two, causing fire; carrying slaked lime, a powder, would present difficulties in handling. Evidence on the sea transport of lime is scarce, but there is one helpful account of shipments both of limestone and lime from the river Wear in April 1829, when that neighbourhood suffered a violent storm which, according to the local newspapers, occasioned considerable damage:

> The sloop *Bee*, of Blyth, laden with limestone, from Sunderland to Blyth, was obliged to put back for Sunderland … having lost the whole of her canvass at sea, in a most tremendous gale …. On returning, she struck upon the bar, drove amongst the framework, and soon after went to pieces. …The schooner *George and Henrys* of Sunderland, laden with lime, for Scotland, went to sea the same time as the *Bee*, and was obliged to put back. She made for the harbour, when, there not being sufficient water for her, she struck upon the bar and sprung a leak; the water then getting to the lime, she took fire, and afterwards drove up into the harbour mouth, where she sunk.

Clearly, the schooner was carrying quicklime with unfortunate, but perhaps predictable, results. It was at the time of this activity on Holy Island that the two leading marks or 'beacons', the slender obelisks on Old Law (Guile Point), were built to facilitate navigation for the coal and lime trades; they were designed by John Dobson, the famous Newcastle architect, for Trinity House, and built between 1820 and 1840. There is no lighthouse on Holy Island, but another beacon on the Heugh between the village and harbour was established before 1836. A flag was hoisted from this beacon at times when ships might safely enter the harbour in bad weather, even if the local pilots could not get to them – a practice which still applied over a century later. Subsequently, a further beacon, a 48ft (14.6m) high white-painted stone pyramid, was provided on Emmanuel Head at the north-easterly point on the island, to assist with the approach to the harbour from the north, while the Old Law beacons, the 'East' being 70ft (21.4m) high and the 'West' being 83ft (25.3m) high led towards the harbour. With the Old Law Beacons in line, vessels were steered on this line until the Heugh Beacon aligned with the belfry of St Mary's Church, at which point the course was quickly altered to keep within the narrow channel which led to the anchorage.

A major new lime-burning enterprise was carried out by a Dundee firm in the 1860s, by the erection of a huge limekiln bank on Castle Point immediately east of the castle; a new horse-drawn waggonway system linked the kilns with limestone quarries at the north shore, and a pair of new jetties were built just west of the castle; the waggonway rails were presumably of iron, possibly supplied by the Carron Iron Works, giving rise to *The Iron Rails* public house on the

12 Emmanuel Head Beacon, Holy Island, September 1990

island. As the waggonway from the quarries approached the kiln bank, it curved sharply round a slight eminence to approach the kiln-head from the west. The burnt lime drawn from the base of the kilns was then taken by waggonway under the quarry line and around the north side of the castle to the pair of jetties west of the castle, where some fragmentary wooden stakes remain. The kiln structure, one of the largest in Northumberland, has six kiln pots, each with three or four draw arches, a tunnel through the structure giving access to some of the internal draw arches; the presence of firebricks in the kilns marked 'Glenboig' is further evidence of the Scottish nature of this enterprise. The Dundee company was said to have constantly plied five ships between Fife and Holy Island, bringing coal down and taking burnt lime back. It seems likely that all of the older kilns on the island were closed once the new ones were in production, and the industry thereby rationalised.

According to Perry, the Dundee Company introduced Irishmen to supplement the 30 or 40 islanders working at the quarries and kilns. The Cartwrights, however, indicate that while some 39 men - 20 per cent of the adult population - were employed in lime working and carting by 1861, this figure had fallen to 14 per cent by 1871, figures presumably based on a little-changed overall population. Although the lime works was to be closed down before 1896, these were

13 Fragmentary remains of the lime jetty on Holy Island; the leading marks in the distance on the left, September 1990

14 The limekiln block of the 1860s at Castle Point, Holy Island, July 1978

probably the busiest years in the island's modern history, present-day tourism apart. As Perry noted:

> There can have been little peace on the Island during the last half of the nineteenth century. The tramway embankments from the quarries at the Coves to the kilns at the Castle and the Lower Kennedy almost encircled the body of the Island, and many of the 'foreign' workmen had cottages outside the Village: five being at the Lower Kennedy a few hundred yards north of the kiln, and two more in the sandy crater behind Sandon dunes. The works joiner and the blacksmith lived in these two, the latter being remembered more especially because his wife wore a single garment of sacking. There were ten or eleven inns to cope with the demand for liquor, and if this be thought a tall story I can name nine of them – The *Ship Inn*, the *Britannia*, the *Fisherman's Arms*, the *Selby Arms*, the *Plough Inn*, the *Iron Rails*, the *Northumberland Arms*, the *Castle Hotel*, and the *Crown and Anchor* – and can verify the site of a tenth, the *Cambridge House*. Doors opened at six o'clock in the morning, when the fishermen came in for their drams of whiskey (at 3d a half) or rum (at 4d a noggin), before going off to their fishing. Street and inn brawls were frequent, but there was no doctor on the Island, and no policeman could be induced to stay for any length of time – for it is still recalled how, when Constable Joe Smoke clapped in jail one of the brawlers – grandfather of one of the present Islanders – the inhabitants broke the windows of the

jail, which was on the east side of the Market Square, and so terrified the constable, that he took to the roof of the jail and sought refuge with the parson; and how next day twenty mounted police from Berwick came riding across the sands.

But the twentieth century was to witness a drastic change in the island's basic economic foundation. The demise of the island's fishery had been heralded in the closing decades of the nineteenth century and the native fishing fleet went into decline. There were only four sailing vessels in the herring fleet by 1905, and not one coble involved in line and crab fishing, but 15 'mules', small keeled boats intended to be crewed by four men, were still active. Several of the larger sailing boats had been laid up, some to be upturned on land and converted to boat stores and sheds for the remaining line and lobster fishermen. The introduction of steam drifters along the Northumberland coast from 1907 finished off the remaining inshore herring shoals and Holy Island's last sailing herring boat was laid up in 1914. Although there was a slight recovery during the 1914-18 war years, when the offshore steam trawlers were less active and whitefish stocks consequently increased, the post-war years saw the trawlers and drifters return to their former dominance. Similar effects attended the Second World War, when trawling was virtually prohibited and the islanders could take reasonable amounts of whitefish again, but the former prosperity of the Holy Island fisheries was never to return.

15 The last of the Holy Island herring boats, upturned for use as stores, the former curing station behind on the right, September 1990

There had been little economic use for the harbour after the failure of the herring fleet and the closure of the lime works, although it continued to serve as a harbour of refuge. A few islanders continued to catch crabs and lobsters, but the main occupation for most eventually became focused on tourism; no tourist today should leave the island without tasting a crabmeat sandwich. Walter White had discussed some of the problems of increasing tourism in 1859:

> It is said that if good lodgings were available the Island would be more visited than it is by sea-bathers; but the difficulty of access and the want of pleasant scenery are perhaps the chief reasons against immigration.

That situation was to change radically in the twentieth century as both the scenery and modes of transport were improved. Sir Edwin Lutyens transformed the near-derelict castle on Beblow Crag into its present form in 1902, as a holiday home for Edward Hudson, the then proprietor of *Country Life*; Gertrude Jekyll laid out a walled garden for the castle in 1911, and work began on the conservation of the dramatic remains of the priory in 1913. The publicity which the island gained from these development attracted even more tourists. One who witnessed some of these changes was the great Scottish architect and designer Charles Rennie Mackintosh (1868-1928), who stayed on Holy Island in 1901, 1906 and 1913, the first visit being, perhaps, his honeymoon. Never without his sketch book, he used it to full advantage on these trips; exquisite colour drawings of Sea Pinks; a complex sketch of a kitchen range in a cobbler's cottage; dramatic views of the castle before the Lutyens additions, which are strongly reminiscent of his 1897 designs for the Glasgow School of Art – perhaps he had visited the island on an earlier occasion.

The development of motorised transport from the 1920s enabled even more people to visit the island's attractions, the demand for 'bed and breakfast' facilities enhanced by the fact that the island is cut off from the mainland for 5.5 out of every 12 hours. Small-scale industry returned to Holy Island with the establishment of the Lindisfarne Liqueur Company in 1961; after difficulties which saw it in receivership in 1966, the company was reconstituted and continued successfully. But in recognition, perhaps, that Holy Island now has no significant maritime trades, its lifeboat was withdrawn by the RNLI in 1968 and the former curing station has been converted into dwellings.

Although the population of the island fell through the early decades of the twentieth century, it had begun to pick up again by 1940 when it stood at 243 people. But the population fell again after the end of the Second World War such that there were only 182 inhabitants by 1972, over half of them beyond retirement age; the population had fallen by a further two by 1990. Throughout these decades the island was regularly inundated by up to 5,000 visitors on a sunny Summer day, but it virtually keeps itself to itself between October and Easter. That, perhaps, is the best time to see the kilns, the railway embankments, the upturned boats, the beacons and the fragmentary remains of the lime jetty, which rank alongside the monastery, the castle and the vestiges of Osborne's fort, as poignant reminders of the island's past. The living of the few remaining fishermen is more precarious than ever, as catches of lobsters and crabs continue to fall, perhaps though over fishing; Malcolm Patterson, a fisherman on the island for 20 years, abandoned the sea in 1991, to take over the village post office.

5

North Sunderland Seahouses

A small, common-looking town, squalid in places ... Signs of trade are, however, manifest.
(White, 1859)

North Sunderland is an ancient village, about 1 mile (1.6km) from the sea, and 7.5 miles (12km) south-east of Holy Island. The sea journey between the two places could be fraught with danger, for the Farne Islands stand on the most obvious route. It was possible to navigate to the west of the islands, easily the shorter route, and coasting and fishing vessels would do so, but appropriate knowledge and fine weather were always advisable along these lanes. The route to the east of the islands could also be problematical, for the outer extremity of the Farnes, marked by the Longstone light, was bedevilled by sunken rocks; it was here that Grace Darling participated in rescuing crew members of the *Forfarshire* in 1838.

To the south of the Farnes, a small rocky haven served as a natural harbour for North Sunderland. Seemingly the ancient name for the settlement was 'Sutherlannland', implying 'land south of Bamburgh', but the 'North' prefix was added to distinguish it from Sunderland on the river Wear, some 48 miles (77.3km) south on the County Durham coast. Thus, the attempt to avoid possible confusion resulted in a name which actually meant 'North South Land'. The associated village which developed around the haven came to be called 'North Sunderland Sea Houses', but it is now more commonly known simply as 'Seahouses'.

It is not known how long there has been a fishing community at North Sunderland Sea Houses, but 'Shoreston and North Sunderland' had seven resident fishermen in 1626; it can be presumed that the haven was still in its natural state, apart from the possibility of a small timber jetty. Later in the seventeenth century, Lord Crewe, Bishop of Durham, acquired the North Sunderland estate by marriage, together with those of Bamburgh to the north and Blanchland in southern Northumberland. By his will of 1720, he formed a charitable trust whereby the profits of his estates were to be used for educational purposes and for distressed clergymen. The developments at North Sunderland and Seahouses were thereafter to be the responsibility of the Crewe Trustees, duties which they performed, not always with alacrity, until 1935.

Before c.1786, the haven for North Sunderland was merely a narrow channel through the rocks, presumably accessible only to small fishing boats. There was, however, a small lime-burning business by that time, for extensive beds of the Eelwell limestone, and the associated Snook Top coal seam, outcropped on the foreshore to the south of the haven, running inland from Snook Point. There were also similar deposits to the north of the village and these were being worked by John Pringle by 1767/68, under a seven-year lease from the Crewe Trustees. When William Brown of Throckley, the eminent Tyneside colliery viewer and Newcomen engine builder, visited the mines in 1768, the coals appear to have been won from shafts and from a 400-yards long cliff face level. It seems likely that some of the burnt lime was being shipped from North Sunderland at this time, as it most certainly was by 1775, probably to Scotland. Messrs Robinson & Henderson now held leases on a farm, colliery and limekiln, at North Sunderland, at rents of £24, £15 and £34 6s 6d respectively, and a statement for 1775 noted:

Lime sold at North Sunderland by Mess Robinson and Henderson in the year 1775:

2137 Cart loads Ship
1047 ditto Sold to land

In all 3184 Cart loads at 3d   £39-16-0

It would seem that Robinson & Henderson only operated a single kiln, probably somewhere near the haven, but perhaps in the hope of expanding the lime business, and of course the fishing trade, Robert Cramond of North Sunderland was employed in c.1786, to build a pier at the expense of the Crewe Trustees; the word 'pier' as used at this time can be misleading, in that it might actually imply a small harbour. This Cramond was almost certainly the 'Cramond of Dunbar' who had carried out work to a John Smeaton design for Eyemouth harbour in Scotland in 1773, and he was also to be later involved at Beadnell to the south of North Sunderland. He was said to be possessed of spectacular strength, stopping an enraged bull with nothing but a steely stare before beating it off with a pick. The harbour thereby created at North Sunderland was quite small, being only a little larger than its near contemporary at Beadnell. The present inner south pier at North Sunderland shows well the form of Cramond's construction, utilising large, squared blocks of red and grey sandstone, some of which were won by quarrying within the harbour area itself, and appear to have been lifted into place with lifting dogs rather than Lewis bolts. Cramond did not set these stones level, but on an inclination down towards the inner core of the pier, as Smeaton had recommended at Eyemouth. Some thought this 'an abuse of Gravity' but no problems appear to have arisen over the following half century; part of the inner north pier, which was modified in the 1880s, is rather similar in its construction. Cramond's new harbour, essentially the present inner harbour, was soon being frequented by fishing vessels and a few schooners in the corn trade with London.

John Robinson of Tuggal took a new lease on a colliery at North Sunderland in 1800, evidently in anticipation of a steady trade. The lime trade certainly expanded, for by 1825 Messrs Robson & Skelly were working a bank of four limekilns on the harbour quayside, each with a capacity of about 80 fothers, the lime being carried in small coasters to Scotland. (It is notoriously difficult to translate the kiln capacity into tonnage, for the fother in Northumberland, like the boll, was a volumetric measure; traditionally a fother of lime was the amount carried by a two-horse cart; generally there were six bolls to the fother.) Corn and fish were also still being exported and the inhabitants of North Sunderland Seahouses were said to 'display considerable activity and industry'. There were other evidences of growing prosperity as the population of North Sunderland grew from 401 in 1801, to 860 in 1831. The Blue Bell, 'a new and commodious Inn', augmented an existing public house, a Presbyterian Meeting House had been built in 1810, and a lifeboat station was established in 1827.

A rope-worked railway was constructed by Robson & Skelly at some time before 1858, leading from the quarry at Snook Point to the kiln heads at the harbour. Walter White saw the system operating:

> Then we came to a huge gap, a limestone quarry, running in half a mile or more from the
> sea; and men hewing and blasting, and loading wagons; and trains hauled up tramways by
> a rope from the engine-house above, and there sent speeding down a long incline to the
> kilns by the port.

The railway probably also carried coal from the pits to the north and south of the quarry, and part of its alignment can be traced from the now-flooded Snook quarries, across the golf course and on towards the limekiln bank. The amount of limestone extracted can be gauged from the extent of the abandoned quarry running from the Beadnell road across to the foreshore; another section of the quarry which was of comparable size to that on the west of the road has been filled in. Some of the burnt lime produced was for the use of the Crewe Trustees' estate and some for its tenants, but considerable amounts were shipped through the harbour throughout the 1840s and into the 1850s, mainly destined for Dundee, Perth, Arbroath etc., although a merchant in Blyth also received North Sunderland lime during this period. The coasters in the lime trade seem to have had a maximum cargo of between 144 and 580 bolls, and the round trip to Dundee took anything between nine days and three weeks. The Crewe Trustee Papers show the lime exports at this time to be:

	Shipments	Bolls
1841	111	35,624
1842	91	29,812
1843	70	25,040
1844	79	27,044
1846		36,752
1848		46,000
1849	105	42,111
1850		21,602
1851		23,188
1852		22,240

It may not be coincidence that lime shipments peaked in the year after the full opening of the railway from Newcastle to Tweedmouth, which passed 4.5 miles (7.2km) west of North Sunderland; by 1850 this line formed part of the link between London and Edinburgh. The railway may have damaged the lime trade of North Sunderland by enabling lime from elsewhere in the North East to be easily distributed throughout Northumberland and into Scotland. For example, the huge lime works at Littlemill, near Craster in Northumberland, were a direct result of expansion after the railway passed the very edge of its quarry. On the other hand, the equally huge kilns established in the 1860s by the Dundee company on Holy Island, were based on coastal carriage of both coal and lime.

North Sunderland's population reached its nineteenth-century peak at this time. It had grown to 1,103 by 1841 and reached 1,208 in 1851, but thereafter it fell to 1,008 in 1861 and 953 in 1871. Walter White, who visited the town mainly in order to take a boat to the Farnes, was not particularly impressed with what he saw in 1858:

> ... a small, common-looking town, squalid in places, with shops that are also living-rooms and bed-rooms, and a general appearance of not caring very much for the fitness of things. Signs of trade are, however, manifest: two stone piers, all wasted and water-worn, with wide gaping joints from the shock of the sea, form a small harbour, into which vessels of three hundred tons may enter. Lime is the principal article of trade; and the kilns are built close to the harbour for convenience of loading, and for the inconvenience of the town, which gets well smothered with the smoke whenever the wind blows from the sea.

The lime trade ceased soon after White's visit, the decision being taken in 1858 and brought about within the following two years. This must have been a mixed blessing for the village of 'Seahouses', situated around the harbour and set apart from its older sister community of North Sunderland. The village would be cleaner but potentially poorer, for the harbour had lost an important article of trade. Fortunately the fishing industry had been expanding from the 1840s, and the Newcastle to Berwick railway had no immediate adverse effect on that. Some 52 herring boats were based at the harbour by 1855 and the herring boom of the 1860s brought much work to fishermen during the July to mid-September season, but also to the girls and women, some who followed the stranger herring fleets from the highlands and islands of Scotland, employed in the preparation, curing and packing of fish. As Bulmer noted in 1887:

> Female labour is chiefly employed in the work, and such marvellous dexterity do they attain, that a clever girl not unfrequently earns as much as ten shillings a day.

He also noted that there were 10 separate fish curing businesses in the town, including that of John Woodger & Sons. John Woodger may well have been John, the brother of Thomas and Edward Woodger, who commenced fish curing in Newcastle in 1846. John had left the partnership in 1853 and perhaps went to Seahouses. Another brother, William, claimed to have been the originator of the kippered herring (c.1860). Although the word 'kipper' actually derives from the name given to male salmon after spawning, at which stage they are not particularly tasty unless smoked, the word 'kippering' came to be used for the smoke-curing of herring. The extent of the curing business can be seen in the abandoned and converted curing houses and stores in South Street and Union Street at Seahouses. A group of such buildings surrounding a large cobbled yard behind Horncliffe House on Union Street have been converted into domestic accommodation and some fishermen's houses still remain, in the delightful Craster Square off South Street.

It is clear from White's description, that the harbour piers were in poor shape; the entrance channel between them was only 59ft (18m) wide and they embraced only about 1 acre (0.4ha) of water which dried out at low tide. Even so, it was not until 1886, rather too late in the day, that the Crewe Trustees embarked on a programme of improvement. Doubtless this move was partly prompted by the steady increase in the size of vessels wishing to use Seahouses harbour – a trend which saw a reduction in the number of herring boats, but without a fall in overall capacity – and partly from a desire to expand the fishing business. The new harbour, to plans by Sir John Coode and Mr J. Watt Sandeman, and estimated to cost £25,000, would be some five times larger than the old one which it would embrace; Sandeman, a well-known civil engineer of Newcastle upon Tyne, was also involved at the Craster and Beadnell harbours at this time. A new pier with a terminal lighthouse would be constructed on the north-west side of the existing harbour and part of the existing north pier would be removed to give a slightly larger inner harbour with a wider entrance channel; these alterations can be observed in the materials of construction, the masonry work of c.1786 merging with the concrete facings of a century later.

The new pier was to be 875ft (267m) long with an upper width of 37ft (11.3m), formed with a rubble core but faced with Portland cement concrete. Its new lighthouse was to be a fairly modest affair: a hexagonal section, concrete tower, some 27ft (8.2m) high and probably painted white from the very beginning. A new mass-concrete breakwater would also be built, running north–west from Pace Hill, amongst the rocks at the east of the harbour, towards the pier; it was to be 874ft (267m) long and give an entrance channel some 120ft (36.6m) wide. Work commenced in July 1886 and the new harbour was opened on 25 June 1889. The new harbour must have given Seahouses a considerable boost, although even the outer harbour was tidal and consequently it could only be used by light-draught vessels which could be laid aground, and even then only in good sea conditions.

The absence of a railway connecting directly with the harbour was seen as a great disadvantage. Although Chathill Station on the Newcastle to Berwick line was just over 4 miles (6.4km) away, only rough un-metalled roads linked it with Seahouses, and the cost of overland carriage between the harbour and Chathill, plus the railway tariff, left little profit to any fish merchant who chose to use that route for the export of their catches. Approaches were made to the NER for a branch line between Chathill and the harbour but, understandably, the

16 A quiet time at Seahouses harbour, from a postcard postmarked 1913

17 Seahouses north pier and outer harbour, dry at low tide, probably in the 1940s; note the two fishing boats propped against one another to the right. The fishing boat to the left has a Kirkcaldy registration

railway company did not regard this as an economically rewarding proposition. Local interests pressed on with a scheme of their own, in the hope that rail access would enable them to enter London and other southern markets, and also encourage summer visitors to Seahouses. Consequently, a public meeting held in the Drill Hall in Seahouses in April 1891 decided to place a Bill before Parliament; surprisingly perhaps, the Act for the 'North Sunderland Railway' gained the Royal Assent in 1892, as a totally independent railway. However, its directors had considerable problems in raising the necessary capital for the work, even after Lord Armstrong, the great Tyneside industrialist, offered to join the board with a plan to extend the line to Bamburgh, whose castle he had bought in *c*.1890. Construction of the new line to Seahouses was underway by 1896, but the company then obtained a Light Railway Order in 1898, which authorised the operation of the original line as a 'light railway', as well as an extension to Bamburgh. The provisions of the general Light Railway Act of 1896 had enabled new railways to be constructed to somewhat lower standards, and therefore lower costs, than standard railways, but also restricted their operational speeds to a maximum of 25mph, reduced to 10mph on sharper curves; in fact, the North Sunderland Railway locomotives were run at a maximum speed of 16mph. The North Sunderland Railway, which opened on 1 August 1898 for goods traffic, and on 18 December 1898 for passengers, was one of the first to be built under the Light Railway Act. The line terminated at 'North Sunderland' Station, a few hundred yards short of the harbour quayside, which was probably seen as a minor inconvenience at the time. The extension to Bamburgh was never constructed, perhaps because Lord Armstrong died in 1900.

Eight large herring boats were permanently based at Seahouses by 1905, but more than 140 stranger boats, from the Firth of Forth, Berwickshire and Cornwall, made the harbour their temporary base for the herring season. So fishing continued to remain important to Seahouses, for it was well situated for

18 Seahouses harbour, from a postcard postmarked 1956 but the image was probably made in the late 1940s. The fishing fleet is tied up by the south pier of the inner harbour; the disused limekiln bank is at top right

some of the richest fishing grounds off the Northumberland coast. On some occasions fishing boats were laid alongside, right across the inner harbour, a situation which was only possible in a tidal harbour when all the boats using it had very nearly the same draught. Seahouses's position as a fishing port seemed well assured, for it had a considerable trade in barrelled herrings with several Baltic ports as well as its London and inland markets, now more easily served by its railway connection to the main line. But the railway did not bring the anticipated benefits.

Promoted in the hope that the Seahouses fish merchants would gain better communication with more lucrative inland markets, the impact of the North Sunderland Railway seems to have been marginal. Having been spurned by the NER, the railway was again kept out of the fold at the railway grouping of 1923. Although it did carry considerable fish traffic at the height of the herring season and some special trains were run with fish wagons destined for London or Birmingham, especially during the Second World War, the railway company rarely made a profit; between the years 1937 and 1951, profits were only made in 1943 and 1944, at £305 and £65 respectively. It is hardly surprising that the North Sunderland Railway was not nationalised in 1948, for it was clear that its days were numbered, and it was closed down in 1951, still technically independent, although effectively run by British Rail staff; the company was liquidated in the following year. The official receiver attributed its failure to under-capitalisation from the outset, to the failure of the harbour to sufficiently develop its fishing industry and to the lack of interest in promoting Seahouses as a holiday resort. Ironically, the site of North Sunderland Railway Station is now used as a car park and tourism and holiday-making now provide the economic base for the town.

The harbour must have been in need of further improvement by 1929, for a local shipowner, Walter Runciman, offered a loan of £100,000 towards any such upgrading. This offer was not taken up, perhaps because the Crewe Trustees felt that they would be incapable of repaying Runciman. Indeed, when the outer breakwater was breached in 1935, the trustees felt unable to meet the expense of its repair on their own, but this potentially damaging situation was resolved when the then Ministry of Agriculture and Fisheries took over the harbour and appointed commissioners to act on its behalf. Typically those commissioners included members of the Northumberland County Council and Berwick Council as well as three representatives elected by the local fishermen and one by the Crewe Trustees.

The North Sunderland Harbour Commissioners must have carried out the necessary repairs, and they undertook significant improvement works again in 1974, deepening the harbour to provide faster turnaround times for the existing fishing boats and any larger fishing vessels which might wish to use Seahouses. This was achieved by dredging the accumulated silt and ripping out the rocky floor of the harbour; the tidal nature of the harbour meant that it was possible to carry out this work using normal civil engineering plant at low tide. The work

19 Mending fishing nets at Seahouses, September *1967*

was financed by the commissioners out of their harbour and landing dues, and carried out by Thomas Muckle & Sons of Rothbury. A new launching ramp was also built, partly to benefit the long-established boat-building yard at Seahouses of R. Dawson & Sons, the only such yard then left in Northumberland. Dawson's had long specialised in traditional wooden-built vessels and, until the early 1980s, these were still being constructed in the open air, using techniques which any eighteenth-century shipwright would recognise – a keel fashioned from a single piece of oak, oak framing and larch skin. This was a dying craft and, unfortunately, Dawson's closed in the 1990s.

When the Dawson-built, 16-tonne *Britannia II* was launched in June 1989, as a pleasure boat for Farne Island trips but doubling up as a fishing boat for the winter season, the harbour commissioners decided that no further boats could be accommodated within the harbour, for it was then at full capacity. Although no other harbour in Northumberland, and few if any in the country, could make that claim, it resulted from the fact that the effective capacity of the harbour had been reduced; with so many boats of differing draught using Seahouses, it was no longer possible to lay them alongside across the tidal harbour. Moreover, whilst

20 Quiet time at Seahouses in 1981. The launching ramp built for Dawson's boatyard is at bottom left

21 and 22 Dawson's boatyard, Seahouses, August 1974

the mixture of fishing boats, Farnes passenger boats, and the increasing numbers of pleasure boats gave the harbour a certain vitality, their differing requirements and varied leaving times presented difficulties of organisation. Seahouses was once more undergoing a process of change.

These changes are apparent in the town, with the increased facilities for tourists and day trippers. As already noted, the car park lies on the site of the railway station and its track bed is now a walkway. The head of the lime kiln bank is now a very pleasant pub garden and a marine life and fishing heritage centre have opened. Moreover, the North Sunderland Harbour Commissioners, with a Trust Port in their care, have begun the process of making the harbour fit for the twenty-first century, one which will essentially serve leisure interests rather than a fishing industry. The evolution of Seahouses over the last 150 years or so can be seen in microcosm in the lifeboat house. Although a lifeboat station was established at Seahouses in 1827 by the Crewe Trustees, the first RNLI lifeboat, the *Joseph Anstice*, arrived in 1865. In 1936 the service obtained its first motor lifeboat, the *WRA*, for which a new house had been built in the previous year. This boathouse lasted until 1991, after another one had been built to take a new 'Mersey Class' boat. The new boathouse holds the records of the callouts and rescues over the years, from schooners, herring boats and cobles in the early

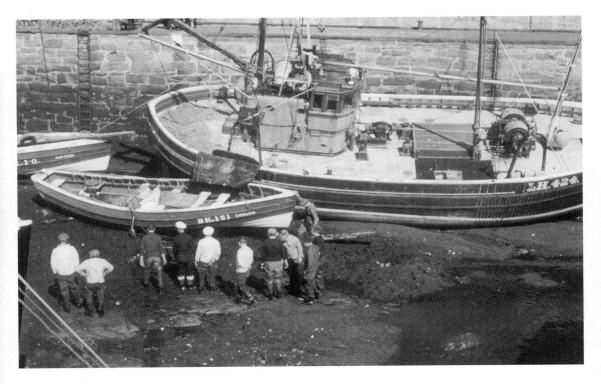

23 Unidentified problem in the dried-out harbour at Seahouses, September 1967

years, and the arrival of motor boats and even an aeroplane in the middle years. The service has increasingly come to the assistance of cabin cruisers in recent years; nowadays it is most often called out to assist and rescue skindivers and windsurfers!

24 Busy times at Seahouses on a fine day in April 1991, a mix of business and leisure

6

Beadnell harbour

... a populous and flourishing village ... it has altogether a different appearance from the dirty and wretched-looking hamlets so frequently found upon the coast. ('A Tourist', 1826)

Beadnell harbour lies some 2.5 miles (4km) south-east of Seahouses, the coast between the two places being low-lying, and the foreshore rocky. Beadnell Bay, however, with its fine sandy foreshore stretching near 2 miles (3.2km) southwards from Beadnell Point (also known as 'Ebbe's Nook' and sometimes as 'Ebbe's Snook'), to Snook Point (not to be confused with Snook Point on Holy Island, nor Snook Point at Seahouses) offered a natural haven and refuge which, according to the 'Tourist' of 1826, was 'so spacious that in it, half the navy of England might ride at anchor'. Stretching for about 1 mile (1.6km) north of the bay, alternating strata of coals, shales, limestone and sandstones outcrop on the foreshore, and the washout of some of the softer strata has left several natural inlets through this rocky seaside, notably Lady's Hole (sometimes called 'Ladys Washing Hole'), Nacker Hole, Beadnell Haven and Collith Hole. These inlets, rather than the bay itself, seem to have provided the earliest fishing havens, although the largest of them, Nacker Hole, was partly obstructed by a whinstone dyke. These strata, plus the fish and salt of the sea, were to provide the basis for Beadnell's modest eighteenth-century settlement and harbour development; their irrelevance today helps to explain Beadnell's role as a minor resort and pleasant place of domicile.

In common with most of Northumberland's natural havens, Beadnell had an early fishing industry. An entry in the accounts of the Proctor of Norham for 1408 relates to the hire of a horse to carry 'Bidnelfysh' to Durham and the tithes paid on fish landed at Beadnell were a useful source of revenue to the Augustinian cell at Bamburgh. Beadnell's importance as a fishing community in the early seventeenth century is evidenced by the fact that it was said to have 14 resident fisherman in 1626, compared with only seven at North Sunderland.

The village of Beadnell, just a few hundred yards in from the sea, grew around its tower house of the fifteenth or sixteenth century and, by c.1700, the settlement comprised two rows of houses on either side of a green; there were stocks, a pinfold and a windmill at Delf Point immediately east of the village, possibly for water pumping. St Ebba's Chapel, built in 1745 and replacing an earlier chapel on Ebbe's Nook, stood on the green. Indeed, the origins of Beadnell may date to an early Christian settlement, since both chapels were dedicated to St Ebba, the sister of King Oswald, who died in 683. The chapel on Ebbe's Nook was thought to be of the thirteenth century when it was excavated in 1853. It now survives as a disarray of earth mounds with some exposed stonework.

Although Beadnell was owned by just five landowners in the early eighteenth century and was mainly an agricultural village, it was also obviously still involved in fishing. In fact, the village must have stank of fish for, in 1721, the Bamburgh Manor Court ordered that:

> ... none of the inhabitants of Beadnell shall boil or extract oil out of fish in the town streets or within their houses there, the same being not only noisome and offensive but also dangerous to the neighbourhood.

But soon another form of air pollution was to make its presence more strongly felt at Beadnell. Traditionally, the landowners of Beadnell had liberty to win and use whatever stones they wished from the foreshore, and this might explain the finding of the remains of a limekiln at Ebbe's Nook in 1994, believed to have been last used in the late fifteenth or early sixteenth century. There is nothing to indicate the continued practice of lime burning at Beadnell from that time, but when John Wood of Presson bought the two largest properties in Beadnell for his son Thomas in 1735, exploitation of their rocks and minerals was set to be put on a commercial basis through the mining of coal to support the making of salt from sea water, and lime from the Beadnell limestones. In 1747, Thomas awarded George Turnbull of Cambois a 30-year lease at £5 per annum, to quarry limestone from the cliffs and rocky foreshore between Delf Point and Ebbe's Nook, and to erect limekilns; he could win whatever freestone he required to build the kilns. To facilitate the export of lime and limestone, the lease also allowed Turnbull to:

> ... cutt away any rock ... as he shall think most Necessary and Convenient in order to make a Commodious harbour for the safety and more Conveniency of Ships or other Vessels [probably at Nacker Hole] to take in and deliver on board the said Loding of Lymestone or Lyme.

Both Wood and Turnbull clearly saw considerable potential for this enterprise, for there were four limekilns on the south side of Delf Point by 1759. Two coal mines had been sunk between the kilns and the village and these were being worked for Wood, who had salt pans near Delf Point, and also, presumably, for Turnbull's kilns. It would appear that Turnbull also improved Nacker Hole by quarrying through the whinstone dyke, thereby creating a small 'Key'.

Nacker Hole, or perhaps the bay itself, seems also to have provided a haven for smugglers, although it proved no refuge in September 1762, when some 2,700 gallons of brandy, 400 gallons of rum and geneva, 23 hogsheads of wine, tea and other articles were confiscated from Scottish smugglers.

George Turnbull seems to have disappeared from the scene by 1764, perhaps having met with financial or health problems and in 1766, the year of or before his death, Wood allowed the remaining nine years of Turnbull's original lease to pass to Job Bulman, so that both he and Wood were shipping limestones from the 'whinstone rock in Beadnell Harbour' – presumably Nacker Hole. However, differences had arisen between the two men over priority of use. These were resolved by an external arbitration which decreed that they should land or ship their respective products in alternate months, provided that they had sufficient limestones to ship; neither party was to leave any limestones on the rock at the end of their month. But the continued quarrying at Delf Point soon threatened the improved haven, kilns and salt pans, for as more and more of the Point was removed, so the sea broke in more easily during north-east gales. Nevertheless, Nacker Hole must have continued to be used until relatively recently, as evidenced by the two rusting crab winches (hand winches) which still stand on a small patch of grass set back from the sea wall.

Wood gave up direct involvement in salt making when, in September 1764, he leased the coal mines, with their wind engine, ropes, tubs, smith's forge and other utensils, to Alexander Long of Sheerness, Kent, for 21 years at £45 per annum, with liberty to make salt. Long was also given permission to win stones for any necessary buildings and he appears to have rented a farm of 4 acres (1.6ha), at £6 per annum, at the same time. Long, now described as being of Brunton, Northumberland, then secured another 21-year lease from Wood, signed in June 1766 but backdated to November 1764, which allowed him the use of all the havens and harbours at Beadnell including, it would seem, the bay itself, for he was granted:

> ... the sole liberty of shipping and vending by sea, salt etc. and all other commodities whatsoever and also the sole liberty of laying ships on the main shore there to load and unload all such goods, and also the liberty of erecting wharfs, keys, ports, jetties, cran[e]s, docks and landing places on any place near the said harbour ... and building houses granaries and other conveniences there for the more effectually carrying on foreign export or co[a]st trade from Beadnell.

Long did not, however, have a total monopoly on the use of Beadnell's havens, for Joseph Bullman Job Bulman(?), Richard Pemberton, John Williehay(?) and Wood himself were to be allowed to continue shipping as before. Long's rent for the above liberties was a mere 5s 0d per annum and he soon had five salt pans at work; at some time before 1770 he was also winning clay and making bricks, perhaps for his own building works.

Long apparently introduced a new way of salt making to the area, although one which was common elsewhere, especially in localities where coal was expensive, and he may have been familiar with this process from his time spent in the south. The method involved concentrating sea water by natural evaporation, before crystallising out its salt in a salt pan. His method was described in 1770 as follows:

> The common way of making Sea Salt in this Country is by making a large pitt or Recevoir near the full sea mark, which is made to Communicate with the Sea and may be filled by the Sea at any time when it is High Water – and from this pitt the Sea Water is pumped and Conveyed with Troughs into salt Pans or Boilers where it is made into Salt by the Force of Fire – But the said Alexr Long not only makes Salt in this manner, but he makes several shallow pitts or Receivoirs above the High water mark ... into which (after standing some time and being strenthed or Made Salter by the watery particles being in some degree evaporated by the Heat of the Sun) is afterwards Conveyed from thence into the Salt Pans and made into Salt.

As far as is known, Long's method was not widely copied in the North East, for most salt makers were able to obtain cheap 'pan coal' from the local collieries. John Wood succeeded his father Thomas in 1767, and he sought to take back to himself the enterprises which had been leased to Bulman and Long, finally achieving this in 1775. He also attempted to put the fishing business onto a more commercial footing, firstly by building a new square of fishermen's houses above Beadnell Haven in 1777, each cottage having two rooms with a storage loft above; as the village's population built up, he constructed more buildings just outside the village. Secondly, in 1788, Wood formed the Northumberland branch of the 'British Fishery', a co-partnership arrangement which collectively bought boats, nets and other fishing tackle, and collectively disposed of all fish caught or purchased. Initially, the British Fishery concern was to be jointly based at Ullapool in north-west Scotland and at Beadnell where it traded under the name of John Wood Esq & Co. Wood also owned at least one sloop, the *Tarter*, and it can be presumed that he was engaged in some export and import trades.

It was probably the creation of the British Fishery branch at Beadnell, that encouraged Wood to consider providing better harbour provision at Beadnell, and to decide that such improvement should be designed by a experienced engineer. Alternatively, the inspiration may have come from developments at Sunderland in County Durham for, according to Craster (1956), Wood had contracted with Joseph Robson, possibly a son of the Sunderland harbour engineer of the same name, to ship fallen stone from near the face of Ebbe's Nook for the building of Sunderland North Pier in 1788. Whatever the reason, Wood approached Robert

Cramond of 'N[orth] Sunderland' to provide an estimate for a new harbour at Ebbe's Nook; Cramond was, as we have seen, then active at North Sunderland harbour, but he thought that the bay by Ebbe's Nook, just a mile (1.6km) south of the village, was the 'most eligible' situation for a harbour of most places he had seen, being in effect land-locked on all sides. In fact a pier had already been constructed at this location, but it was simply described as 'old' by 1759. Cramond reported, on 16 May 1788, that the bay was:

> ... by nature defended from the direct action of the North and North-east winds, which raises the highest storms on this Coast so that there is nothing to fear but the recoil of these north and north east storms comming [sic] over the rocks at the outside of the pier .... But what I look on as a great advantage of this place is having such a spacious entrance and deep water, that a ship may run into it in the very worst weather; altho, the sea was running so high, that no Boat could go to her assistance, and at the same time, it will contain a good many vessels of considerable burthen.

Cramond recommended that a pier should be built without specifying its length, but advised that it be built to 3ft (0.9m) above high-water mark, with a 6ft (1.8m) high parapet. It should also be 21ft (6.4m) broad from the inside of the parapet, forming a 'Key (or warf [sic]) on the inside of the Pier', to allow carts to be able to turn when goods were being shipped or landed. His estimate for the work was £8,395, possibly beyond Wood's means or inclinations, and the plan did not proceed. However, Cramond produced a much cheaper scheme for the pier early in 1790, effectively a limestone breakwater which could later be faced with ashlar. It would be 690ft (210m) long, 22ft (6.7m) broad at the foundations, 10ft (3m) broad at the top at a mean height of 18ft (5.5m), the whole to cost £2,942. Cramond seems to have estimated the Beadnell work at somewhat more per linear yard of pier than at North Sunderland, but he advised Wood that the several reasons for this were 'too tedious to mention here'. He did, however, explain that the stone needed for construction at North Sunderland was all to be found within the harbour, which greatly reduced the cost of the work there, but that Beadnell had no such advantage. Wood was clearly uncertain whether to proceed with this proposal, for he wrote to a William Forster at Maryport, Cumbria, about the matter. In a very long and detailed reply, Forster sent details and sketches of piers at Maryport and Whitehaven. He also commented on the pier then being built by Cramond at North Sunderland, and was critical of the manner in which the stones were being laid. Wood had also been concerned about the projected cost, and asked Forster whether anyone near Maryport would do the job. He was advised, however, that there was 'no likelihood of procuring a person here [Maryport] to Execute the work, besides Workmen have higher wages here than with you'.

We can only presume that the work on a new Beadnell harbour began along lines suggested by Cramond, but perhaps based upon a third scheme which has not survived in any documents, for it was certainly not carried out to any of his extant specifications; the present harbour, with its two piers and quayside, does comprise about 230 yards of mooring, and the arrangement was rather similar to that which Cramond devised for North Sunderland. Each harbour had one straight and one dog-legged pier, while the form of construction, still evident at Beadnell, is consistent with a late eighteenth-century build, being of massive dry-stone blocks, now mainly capped in concrete. Curiously, but advantageously for an east-coast harbour, the entrance channel between the Beadnell piers faces west towards the shore.

Before his new harbour was complete, and possibly before work on it had commenced, Wood granted a lease in November 1794 to Jno. Ormston and Jno. Brown for a field, link, warren, house and stable, with liberty to make kelp, for three years at £20 per annum, together with a limestone quarry north of the 'Ladies washing hole' at a rent of 4d per ton of stone won and shipped. He followed this up by awarding a 15-year lease on his coals and limestones to Richard Pringle in November 1798 – perhaps a relative of John Pringle who had the North Sunderland kilns in the 1760s. It is clear that the new harbour was not yet finished, for Wood agreed, as part of the lease, to 'finish the Harbour now begun' and to maintain it during the term of the lease. The lease was fairly complex, with a range of covenants and obligations covering the operation of the lime and coal businesses. Pringle was allowed to construct a limekiln on the pier and, rather unusually, his memorandum of agreement stipulated the precise dimensions of the kiln to be built; it also ordered that this work was to begin immediately so that it might be ready for the next burning season. Pringle was also allowed to build whatever roads and sheds might be needed for the business and these, and the new kiln, were to be financed out of the profits of the first 4,000 loads of limestone burnt, on which output Pringle would pay no rent. Thereafter, Pringle would pay Wood 9d for every load of lime shipped and 6d for every load sold direct 'to the Country', provided that he shipped at least 1,000 loads to ensure a yearly rental income to Wood of £37 10s; Pringle was not, however, allowed to ship or sell limestone. He would not be required to pay rent for any coal which he won specifically for lime burning, but if he intended to sell any surplus coal, then Wood was to be first served; the rent to be paid for any coal sold would be determined by two 'indifferent persons'. If, on the other hand, Pringle chose not to mine coal for sale, then Wood could do so himself, provided that there was always sufficient made available for lime burning. Wood would let whatever houses Pringle needed for his workmen at the going rent and likewise he would let two grass fields if Pringle required them.

Pringle's lime business soon built up and additional kilns were built at Wood's expense as allowed under the lease. The extant kiln block at Beadnell harbour is quite complex and, due to partial collapse and subsequent stabilisation, difficult to fully interpret, but it is apparent that the first kiln block was extended until there were three kilns in the block, all essentially built of limestone but with

25 Beadnell Harbour and its limekiln block, viewed from the shoreline, April 1990

sandstone dressings; this suggests considerable expansion of the lime trade from the harbour in the early years of the nineteenth century. Another limekiln at Beadnell, set amongst splendid rigg (ridge) and furrow just to the south-east of Beadnell school, may have closed down at this time, although no direct evidence has been found to support this suggestion. Certainly it had ceased to function by the middle of the nineteenth century, but the large, part infilled and part flooded quarry, stretching north-east from the kiln towards the sea, suggests a long period of use.

Beadnell's herring fishery had grown in importance since 1788 and a large herring house with sheds, stables, warehouses and salt cellars had been built by 1800. In that year Wood leased his herring house and all utensils to Messrs Ramsay & Bogue, both coopers of Berwick, for seven years at £31 10s. The schedule of utensils included four spiting trays, 4,000 good spits, seven bundles of common spits, six water spouts, eight tressels, various weights, four candlesticks and a culling board. The herring business seems to have expanded quickly, but there must have been a concomitant decline in the lime business for, in 1821, Wood allowed two Berwick men, Thomas Hill, a cooper and John Ormston, a former custom officer but possibly the same man involved in the kelp manufacture, to use one of the kilns for the curing of herrings until he had further need of it – an interesting case of 'adaptive re-use'. The lease was for 35 years and the rent £6 per annum, but, oddly, Hill and Ormston were also charged with using the harbour dues, of 5s 0d per stranger vessel or any vessel belonging to themselves, to maintain the harbour; Wood himself could use the harbour free of all dues. Hill and Ormston's occupancy of one of the limekilns was perhaps only short-lived, for they built the herring yards in 1827 which lasted as a going concern until *c*.1900.

The harbour-side kilns seem never to have been used again. The loading ramp to the rear of the extant kilns suggests that the limestones had been won from the shallow cliffs and reefs around Ebbe's Nook, and it may be that these became unprofitable to work. Alternatively, since a wall has been built on the shore to the north-east of the limekilns at some stage, presumably to protect them from high seas, it may be that problems with such seas had caused the kilns to be abandoned at a fairly early stage.

The abandonment of lime burning at Beadnell harbour must have improved the local environment and certainly the 'Tourist' in Beadnell in 1826, was quite enamoured of the place:

26 Beadnell harbour and its limekiln block, viewed from the north pier, April 1990

27 Beadnell harbour quay with vertically set stonework, presumably by Cramond, April 1990

Beadnell ... has altogether a different appearance from the dirty and wretched-looking hamlets so frequently found upon the coast. The inhabitants are chiefly fishers; and numerous boats, when the weather permits, may be seen plying in the bay. ... During the herring season, many of the fishers sail in their own boats to the northern coast of Scotland; and their departure causes the greatest bustle in the village. Not an inhabitant but is interested in one or other of the adventurers; and a stranger cannot look unmoved upon a scene in which care and hilarity are frequently most ludicrously contrasted. Brave as our seamen are in battle, and cool as they are in the tempest hour, their courage is never more evinced than when they deliberately become dwellers on the deep, in such a frail habitation as a fishers skiff.

But the fishing activities at Beadnell were more complicated than this suggests. For many decades, boats from the east coast of Scotland and as far away as St Ives in Cornwall, came each year to Beadnell for the herring season, and Scottish women often came down to work at gutting and curing, following the herring fleets southwards down the coast. Clearly there could be occasions when the area was thronged with fishing boats as, for example, in 1828, when Wood wrote to Trinity House about a rain storm with gale-force winds which had resulted in 'near one thousand poor fishermen in open boats not daring to near the shore ... til a large coal light was raised on Beadnell Point, when nearly one hundred boats run in and all got safe'. Trinity House, regarding Beadnell as a central point for the herring fishery, allowed Wood to display a lantern on the Point during the season.

John Wood died in November of that year and was succeeded by his eldest son Thomas, who then inherited the Craster estate in 1837 and took the name Craster in the following year by Royal Licence; Beadnell harbour was to remain with the Craster family until 1949. Craster was still letting his limestone quarries in 1834, and was to do so for several more decades. The takers in 1834 were William Dickinson of Cockle Park Tower and John Shanks of Amble, who obtained a 12-year lease but were specifically prevented from working northwards from Delf Point; as their rent was 4d per ton, we can presume that the limestone was not being burned, but was perhaps being shipped as stone. The continued extraction of limestone from the foreshore below high-water mark was to cause some friction between Craster and the Board of Trade, but Craster answered their criticisms by claiming that he and his predecessors had always exercised these rights. No action seems to have been taken by the Board, but they would not concede that the foreshore at Beadnell was not vested in the Crown.

Thomas Hill the fish curer had died in 1831. His will contained no specific bequests concerning the Beadnell premises, but did refer to the stock held there. Thomas Gilchrist, a solicitor of Berwick and one of the inheritors under the will, eventually persuaded Ormston that he had the right to certain utensils at the herring yard (10,940 spits, 398 tenters, four tubs, two ladders etc.) and these, together with Hill's share of the unexpired lease, seem to have been assigned to Gilchrist in 1834. Craster purchased the surrender of the lease of the herring yard and the equipment belonging to it in 1841 for £150 and then, or soon after, leased it to Alexander Ewing who was also the tenant of Bent Hall farm at Beadnell. Thus, the herring trade continued to be the main beneficiary of the harbour, and the quite large herring yard continued to attract several stranger boats to Beadnell. White fishing, crab and lobster catching also remained significant, but these activities may well have remained centred on the 'holes' to the north of the bay rather than on the harbour itself. Beadnell's situation at mid-century was described by Walter White:

> Next Beadnel or Beadlen, as the fishermen call it, appears in sight at the end of a sandy bay. Coming to the Point, we find reefs and beds of sandstone sloping up from the beach .... Here are more of the amphibious edifices, half boat and half hovel, receptacles for yarns and lines; and fishing gear and lobster pots lie about in heaps; and the big caldron, fixed with a stumpy chimney, shows where the tar is heated [in 'barking pots' for tarring fishing nets]. One of the men tells me that the village owns nineteen boats, and has subscribed to buy a barometer.

Ewing re-leased the herring yard in 1857, but was in considerable debt by 1870, and the business and farm were taken over by James Gilroy, a merchant of Berwick, and James Ewing, Alexander's cousin, himself a fish curer and potato merchant of North Sunderland. Alexander was now an old man, lame in the left arm and 'quite unfit to earn his living by manual labour', but James wished to take the tenancy of both farm and herring yard so that his cousin and family could stay on at Bent Hall, to which they were 'much attached'. James Ewing and Gilroy then obtained a further eight-year lease in 1872, but something clearly went wrong with this arrangement, for within two years Andrew Ewing, also of Bent Hall, had offered to take the herring yard from year to year at £25 per annum. In the event, the yard seems to have been taken by Henry Cowe, a fish curer of Leith, at £8 per annum, although the associated cottage, then occupied as a cooper's house, was not included. This all suggests that the curing business was in some decline, perhaps because the harbour was not suitable for the larger herring boats now fishing along the coast. Although there were still two fish curers at Beadnell by 1884 – Davidson, Pirie & Co of Leith, with John Cowe as their man on the spot and J.C. Edminson – harbour traffic figures suggest the probability of a declining importance in Beadnell's herring fishery, partly as a result of better harbour facilities elsewhere. In that year Davidson Pirie received only two shipments of empty barrels, three of herrings, and one or two of salt into the harbour and shipped out some 2,000 barrels of cured herrings. Edminson imported one load of herrings and sent 300 barrels out. These were the main traffic movements of the harbour in 1884, although two loads of stone and one of gravel were also shipped; most of the activity in the harbour was confined to the months June to September – the herring season. The dues on these cargoes and those on the stranger herring boats which now only made occasional use of the harbour, plus the rental on the curing houses (£4 each), raised the un-princely sum of £14 15s 5d; in addition, there would be about 10 native herring boats paying £2 each per season.

Further decline seemed inevitable and, moreover, the harbour was now in need of repair and modification. It is apparent that the existing piers were only as high as high-water level, at least at their outer ends and that the sea must have regularly washed shingle over the piers, and over the quay wall near the limekilns, into the harbour itself. An attempt had already been made to limit the drift of sand and shingle into the harbour mouth by constructing a short, angled extension to the south pier, but clearly this had not been entirely successful. Accordingly, in August 1885, J. Watt Sandeman of Newcastle reported on the several necessary repairs and improvements. The south pier should be repaired and raised to 4ft (1.2m) above high-water level; the north pier should be raised to 2.5ft (0.76m) above high-water level; a parapet wall should be constructed from the old lime kilns to the east end of the south pier to prevent shingle being washed into the harbour; and the harbour itself should be excavated to its original depth of 7ft (2.1m) below average high-water level at Spring tides at the inner end, and to 12ft (3.7m) at the outer end; some excavation should also take place outside the harbour, to give a 12ft (3.7m) depth at high-water level. Sandeman estimated that all this could be done for £600, a sum which included the wages of a competent superintendent plus £50 for Sandeman's professional services. J.W. Craster seems to have accepted this without question, the work soon being put in hand and completed during 1886. Robert Air & Son of Beadnell, a carrier and, appropriately, a road contractor, carried out the excavation work for £120, while Edward Fordy of Seahouses, mason and contractor, carried out the work on the piers and parapet using a rough dressed limestone for the facings, for about £226. Additional expenses included cement from Johnson's works in Gateshead, the empty sacks having to be returned by rail; 12 mooring rings from Douglas Bros of the Globe Ironworks, Blaydon; the hire and carriage from Jarrow of a 15 cwt crane for three months and a day. In all, the total cost of £598 17s 11d was, amazingly, below estimate, even allowing for some additional works in 1887 when part of the quay surface was concreted and a little extra protection given to the outer end of the south pier.

None of these harbour works had any immediate impact on the harbour's trading figures, the harbour dues for 1887 being much the same as they had been three years earlier, but they probably saved what little traffic still wished to use Beadnell and continued to provide the local fishermen with a safe haven. In fact, Edminson may have gone out of business, for he appears to have paid neither rental nor ships' dues that year, while Davidson Pirie's throughput was much reduced. Small amounts of gravel, sand and stones were exported, as well as 4 tons of bunker coal, presumably from the Beadnell colliery which was certainly still working.

Beadnell's population showed none of the growth to be seen elsewhere in the county during the nineteenth century, only rising from 223 in 1801 to 311 in 1861, then falling back to 217 in 1881. Beadnell still had 14 fishing cobles for line fishing and crab catching in 1905, and nine sailing herring boats, but some 20 stranger herring boats were based in the harbour. In reality, the village had changed little between the early nineteenth century and the beginning of the Second World War, except for the closure of its mines, quarries and lime works, and the demolition of Fishermen's Square in the 1930s. Major changes were to come, however, after the Second World War, as the village and the area around the harbour became increasingly popular for new residential accommodation and as a small holiday resort. This was perhaps presaged by the widowed Lady Delaval of Ford Castle who, in 1816, took a seven-year lease on a house and gardens with a three-stalled stable and coach house on the south side of the village, presumably to be beside the seaside. J.M. Craster gave the harbour to the Beadnell Fishermen's Association in 1949 and it still remains intact, although the entrance channel has been narrowed to about 20ft (6.1m) by an angled concrete extension at the north pier head.

28 Beadnell Harbour: the angled extension to the south pier, April 1990

Today Beadnell Bay offers fine sailing, skin diving, windsurfing, water-skiing and bathing, and it is one of the most popular small holiday areas in Northumberland, but only two or three 30ft (9.2m) cobles now work out of the bay catching lobsters, crabs, sea trout and perhaps some salmon during the season. Not surprisingly there have been conflicts of interest between the remaining fishermen and the water sports enthusiasts. There were only 49 houses in Beadnell in 1920, but there were about 400 houses by 1990, and with plans laid in 2004 for a further 136 houses, the direction in which Beadnell seems to be heading becomes quite clear.

7

Craster harbour

The inhabitants ... maintain themselves chiefly by fishing, and have many characteristics which distinguish them from the agricultural people of the neighbouring villages. A stranger will receive a pleasing impression from the fisherfolk. He will observe their fine physique, their rugged but handsome features, and the peculiar softness of their speech. These traits, in some measure due to the simple and healthy occupation of the people, have been developed by their manner of life. (*Northumberland County History*, 2 (1895))

Craster and its harbour lie almost 6 miles (9.7km) due south of Beadnell and, although it had served as a natural haven for fishermen for centuries, the harbour was the last to be constructed on the Northumberland coast. Whinstone outcrops dominate the foreshore in the vicinity of Craster, most dramatically at Dunstanburgh just a few hundred yards to the north, and several small inlets to the immediate north and south of Craster, 'Hole o' the Dike', 'Black Hole', 'Oxbery Law Holes' and 'Liverpool Hole', which may have provided additional beaching for fishing cobles. The sandy inlet just to the south of Dunstanburgh Castle and known as 'Nova Scotia', must also have provided an occasional haven, but it was the two protecting limestone islets of Little Carr and Muckle (or Great) Carr which made Craster's north-east facing haven the safest on this stretch of the coast, even if it could not be used at all in very bad weather.

The earliest parts of Craster Tower, which stands almost 1 mile (1.6km) to the west of the harbour, were built before 1415, while the neighbouring castle of Dunstanburgh was commenced early in the fourteenth century. Craster is known to have supported eight resident fishermen in 1626 and it is reasonable to suppose that fishing remained its economic mainstay for some centuries after that. The original Craster village lay immediately on the east side of the Tower, but Shafto Craster (the family seems to have taken its name from the settlement, rather than vice versa), provided new houses for the fishing families on a vacant site by the sea in *c*.1780; at first this small settlement was known as 'Craster

Seahouses' in similar fashion to 'North Sunderland Seahouses', but the new village soon became known simply as 'Craster'. This village was on the south side of the small stream which runs into Craster haven, for the Craster family had owned that parcel of land since the twelfth century, while the Tankervilles owned the land to the north.

Alongside its fishing activities, whinstone quarrying appears to have been a significant economic activity at Craster at least from the eighteenth century, the south front of the Georgian part of Craster Tower being constructed of dressed whinstone blocks in 1768. Moreover, in 1772, the fact that the owner or tenant of the quarry was offering employment to men experienced in the dressing of whinstone setts suitable for the paving of streets in London, is perhaps indicative of an existing coastal trade.

Thomas Wood, who had inherited the Beadnell properties in 1828, also inherited the Craster estate in 1837 – his mother and grandmother were both Crasters – and, as already noted, he took the name of Craster by Royal Licence in the following year. This change of ownership made little immediate difference to the fishing village and its haven, and it seems reasonable to suppose that whinstone setts continued to be exported by sea, but this trade, if it still existed, must have been severely reduced by the opening of the Newcastle to Berwick railway in 1847, for this line passed right between the considerable whinstone and limestone deposits at Littlemill, some 2.5 miles (4km) south-west of Craster. Craster was described as being 'occupied chiefly by persons employed in fishing and the fish curing trade' by the 1880s, and Bulmer's directory of 1887 lists four fish curers, including William Archbold who was also a grocer and cod liver oil manufacturer, and Robert Grey who was also victualler at the Jolly Fishermen's Inn; Tomlinson (1889), however, states that Messrs Cormack & Son were the main herring curers. The population was only 272 in 1871, falling to 197 by 1891, largely because of a decrease in its agricultural population, but the village population was sometimes seasonally swollen by fishermen from Scotland and Yarmouth, and by the women who gutted and packed the fish; apparently the fishermen set up tents in which to smoke their catch.

Even though the haven was protected by the Carrs, it could be exceedingly dangerous to enter or leave at certain tides, or in particularly rough seas, for the Carrs became hazards in such situations. Still, it was not until the 1890s that the Craster family appear to have given serious thought to improving the haven for the fishermen. It would seem that the provision of breakwater piers was considered, with advice from J. Watt Sandeman, and a rough estimate of probable harbour dues was made in 1897, presumably to indicate likely revenues after improvement. This schedule suggests a low usage of the haven:

8 Craster Herring boats at £2-10-0	20	0 0
14 Craster cobles at 20/- (winter fishing)	14	0 0
Strange Herring Boats at 2/- per time say	5	0 0
3042 Barrels fresh herring landed at 1½d	19	0 0
2251 Barrels cured herring shipped at 2d	18	6 0
1800 cwt other fish at 1½d (90 tons at 2/6)	11	5 0
1233 cwt crabs and lobsters at 1½d	7	14 0
158 tons salt landed at 6d	3	19 0
Tonnage duties on ships (say)	1	10 0
	100	14 0

It was perhaps in anticipation of such low returns, or because the family had insufficient funds to proceed, that the plan failed to materialise. Clearly there were now problems with the haven, for many of the larger stranger herring boats were reluctant to enter it and would instead lie at sea just off the haven and discharge their catches into smaller craft for subsequent transfer into horse-drawn carts on the small shingle beach. Indeed, many of the Scottish herring boats were abandoning Craster altogether by 1900, fearing damage to their boats on the Carrs and the whinstone outcrops, damage for which they could get no insurance recompense if they chose to use a harbour without appropriate accommodation.

The kippering houses were losing trade as a result of these desertions, but the earlier project to build a harbour was resurrected in 1902/3, with support from the herring curers and fishermen who apparently believed that a new era was dawning on Craster. The plan was to make entry to the haven safer by building two protecting piers and removing some of the dangerous whinstone rocks; the piers would also enable catches to be discharged direct into carts on the pier roadways. In addition, the salt required for curing would be more easily imported, and the kippers could be shipped direct from the harbour instead of having to be sent by road to Littlemill Railway Station. However, for the Craster family to carry out their plan, they had first to acquire the land to the north of the stream from the Tankerville estates, for the north pier would be built from that land.

Thomas William Craster, grandson of Thomas Wood Craster, re-engaged the services of Sandeman & Son to advise on the best way to achieve their plans for a harbour at minimal cost. In fact Sandeman or Craster came up with the ingenious if somewhat improbable idea of a self-financing harbour construction scheme. Such optimism may seem extraordinary given the history of civil engineering projects, but there was some sense in it. Two or three stone merchants had recently approached Craster, seeking permission to open out whinstone quarries on his land, and as Craster presumed that it would not pay them to carry the stone over the 'rough hilly road' to the railhead at Littlemill, their intention must have been to ship from the haven. Consequently, the harbour could be created by quarrying out the whinstone rocks from its foreshore and the proceeds on the sale of this stone would finance the two planned concrete piers. It is unlikely that the Craster family had expected to gain much financial return from this scheme, but if a protected haven could attract stone boats as well as provide safety for fishermen, and if its construction could be made self-financing, then some income would be generated from harbour and landing dues, without any capital outlays on their part. Craster and Sandeman decided to proceed on this basis.

Sandeman drew up the main points of the intended contract for the constructional work, to be carried out to detailed plans and specifications prepared by his company and completed to their satisfaction. These details seem not to have survived, but some notes to be embodied in a contract agreement suggest that, in essence, the plan was to build a quay on the south side of the haven which would lead onto a short north–south pier, together called the 'east pier and quay', to build a short approach road to the latter from the village, and to create a 'harbour entrance', presumably by the building of a north pier. Part of the harbour would be excavated, presumably by low-tide quarrying, and the east quay and road completed, before the harbour entrance was to be made; any buildings which had to be removed to facilitate this work would be subsequently reinstated at the contractor's expense on land freely provided by Craster. The contractor would meet the entire expense of the works, but the quarried stone would be given to him, free of any royalty, to the value of the work done, and the contractor would be required to erect a weigh bridge so that the tonnage of rock extracted (and therefore its value) could be ascertained, and the proper harbour dues of 4d per ton paid on any stone shipped out while work was in progress. The rock excavation in the bottom of the harbour would have to be made finally safe against vessels grounding, by filling in any holes left after the excavation with sand and gravel. Some questions remained, however. Would anyone be prepared to take on the contract to quarry out the foreshore while simultaneously constructing the piers, and would anyone be prepared to ship the quarried stone before the piers were completed?

Craster had opened negotiations for the construction of the harbour with J. Richardson of the nearby Littlemill limestone and whinstone quarries by February 1903, along the lines of Sandeman's plan – that the piers would be constructed on a *quid pro quo* basis for the value of the foreshore stone, on which no royalty would be payable. Richardson was, understandably, reluctant to proceed on this basis, largely because neither he nor any of his workforce had any experience in constructing concrete piers. Neither was he reassured by Sandeman's suggestion that one of his own inspectors would train Richardson's men and supervise the work, nor by the intimation that he could subcontract the pier work out. In fact, Richardson believed that the value of the whinstone to be extracted to make the harbour would not compensate for the cost of getting it, let alone cover the additional cost of building the piers. He was probably correct in this assumption for he was, after all, a quarry owner, of both whinstone and limestone, and therefore better able than Sandeman to properly judge the costs; he may also have anticipated that problems would arise when attempting to quarry in tidal waters. Craster had been anxious to get the work underway by the month of May, and although he clearly hoped that Richardson would eventually co-operate, he was prepared to seek other undertakers if necessary.

As discussions with Richardson dragged on, well beyond the May target date, Sandeman produced his estimates of the cost of building the concrete piers and of excavating the earth and rocks. The 'Sea and Harbour Walls' would cost £2,497, the 'North Breakwater' would cost £996, which, together with £220 for retaining and parapet walls for the road approach, plus £250 for the removal and re-erection of other walls and a few sheds, came to a total of £3,963. Against this, he suggested, could be set the value of 79,000 tons of rock from the excavations needed to create the harbour, and of nearly 11,000 tons of rock to be excavated outside the immediate harbour area. These estimates were sent to Richardson by Charles Percy, a solicitor of Alnwick and Wooler, who was now acting for Craster, but they seem to have finally convinced Richardson that it would be unwise of him to proceed.

Craster was not to be put off, however, and an unsought impetus to continue arose from the death of his brother, John Charles Pulleine Craster, who was killed in action in 1904 with the British forces who were attempting to protect British interests in India by conquering Tibet; the family decided that the new harbour should be his memorial. On a more prosaic level, 12 fishing cobles, nine sail herring boats and 20 stranger boats were now using the haven, while whinstone quarries were already being opened along the coast; it must have seemed that there would never be a better opportunity to make the new harbour pay its way.

A Provisional Order for constructing the harbour was made by the Board of Trade in April 1905 and an appropriate Bill passed safely through Parliament later that year. The north pier would be 210ft (64m) long, running south-east from the end of a newly constructed road along the western edge of the haven; it would have concrete inner and outer walls, with periodic cross walls between them and rubble infilling and, like the south pier, it would terminate at low-water mark of ordinary spring tides, to make a tidal harbour. The mass-concrete south pier would be taken east from the foreshore for 35ft (10.7m) then north-east for 153ft (46.7m), before running north for 70ft (21.4m) to give an entrance channel about 50ft (15.3m) wide; there must have been a subsequent departure from this plan for the south pier does not have this configuration. In addition, about half an acre (0.2ha) of rock and sand would be excavated within the harbour, down to the level of low water at ordinary Spring tides to give 14ft (4.3m) of water at high-water Spring tides. A beacon was to mark Little Carr rock and simple leading lights were to be provided at the harbour.

As Richardson had ruled himself out of contention as contractor for the harbour, agreement was made with 'J. Rowland McLaren and H.G. Prowde (BSc.

Engineering)', of Pilgrim Street Newcastle, who described themselves in 1910 as 'Engineers, Contractors and Whinstone Quarry Owners, Craster and Newcastle-on-Tyne'. Work commenced in 1905 or 1906 – the date of the memorial tablet on the north breakwater and the year in which the first accumulated funds for the works were placed in the bank. But the original plan for a self-financing project had been abandoned and the construction costs were met by grant aid and private subscription. It may indeed have been deemed inappropriate to seek a self-financing memorial to brother John, and five members of the Craster family each contributed £826 2s 6d, equivalent to ten-elevenths of the locally generated funds, while Mr M.J. Osborne, Craster's brother-in-law, contributed £413 1s 3d. A grant of £3,000 was also obtained from the English Board of Trade, and another of £1,000 came from the Scottish Fishery Board. Thus a total sum of £7,686 (which included some interest on money deposited) was available to finance the construction of the harbour.

Construction of the road and piers should have been a fairly simple affair, although working in tidal waters always brings potential complications. The south pier was the easier of the two to construct, but the more complex north pier called for an array of shuttering for the inner walls, outer walls and cross walls. The cavities thereby created after the concrete had been poured, and the shuttering removed, were filled with rubble and sand, and well watered in to give a substantial core. When this fill had reached the top of the walls, it was concreted over, then crossed with steel bars at 1ft (0.3m) intervals, before these in turn were concreted over to form a roadway. The machinery used included a stone crusher, a concrete mixer, and a derrick crane - all steam powered - and a tubway which was extended from the mixer as the piers were progressively built out from the shore. Hopper tubs were filled at the concrete mixer then run out along the completed sections of the pier before being lifted by the derrick crane and swung round to wherever the concrete was needed. The extreme outer end of the north pier presented the greatest difficulties, for work could only be carried out here at the very lowest of Spring tides, and then only for three hours at a time. All this activity was supported by a Heath Robinson arrangement for supplying water to the steam engine boilers and for watering in the core filling. A steam pump took water from the nearby burn and pumped it via a pipe to an old coble, supported on timber staging, which acted as a storage tank. Pipes from the boat then conveyed water to wherever it was needed.

Although McLaren & Prowde were said by the local fishermen to have proceeded in an 'unbusinesslike and pottering manner', work had advanced sufficiently for shipping to use the harbour from early in 1908. In the year ending 31 March 1909, some 2,225 barrels of herring, 780 of white fish, 2,270 cwt of crabs, plus a few tons of salt were landed, giving an income to the harbour owners of £39 0s 0d, and allowing total dividends to be paid to the shareholders of around £20. Stone shipments commenced in the following year, some 3,797 tons being shipped; this raised harbour income to £135, allowing a total dividend payout of some £93. For the year ending March 1912, stone shipments had reached 8,750 tons, income was about £250 and dividends totalled £136. The only expense during these first years appears to have been the harbour master's oddly calculated salary, he being paid at 7.5 per cent of the yearly income, e.g. £2 18s 7d in 1909 and £18 5s 0d in 1912, presumably on the basis that increased traffic brought him an increased workload. However, he also received 'other considerations' which kept his yearly salary between £13 and £30. Stone shipments must have exceeded expectations in the first few years, but the stone handling systems appear to have negated the possibility of a greater throughput, for the stone appears to have been carted down to the harbour, or brought on a railed tubway, before being laboriously loaded on to the waiting boats.

McLaren & Prowde in particular seem to have sensed these difficulties, but also new opportunities even though the harbour works were not yet fully completed, and they decided to re-form their partnership as a private company in 1910-11. They intended to continue as engineers, contractors and quarry owners, but also wished to be able to purchase, charter and manage steam boats or other craft, to contract for haulage and removals, to purchase, lease, or rent and then cultivate land; they had already enquired about obtaining a 125ft (38.1m) long coaster from Thomas Eltringham of South Shields, which would have cost about £2,500, and they may indeed have purchased it. The new company was to be called McLaren & Prowde Ltd and it would be registered with a capital of £10,000. The partnership's assets and business would be transferred to the new company, and McLaren and Prowde would be the first directors; after Charles Percy declined to join them, a Mr A.H. Clarke of Balham, London, became the third director, being paid £160 per annum.

The new company was incorporated on 22 March 1911, although it did not commence business until one month later. The assets of the old partnership were valued at £5,704 and this was satisfied by the allotment of 5,704 shares in the new company to the vendors. Soon McLaren & Prowde Ltd were seeking to have additional quarry land included in their 42-year lease, and they were now anticipating annual outputs of between 20,000 and 100,000 tons of stone. But the planned harbour, still uncompleted, would not permit of such throughputs without modification.

There is no reason to believe that McLaren & Prowde sought to ship all their output through Craster harbour, for there must have been a viable local market. They had their own Foden steam waggon and a tarmacadam plant, both of which suggest a local demand for their products, but clearly they planned to increase coastal shipments. Already by 1911 there could be three steamers engaged in the stone trade in the harbour at any one time and, in occupying both north and south piers, they presented difficulties for the fishermen. To remedy this, Clarke, who was a professional engineer, suggested, in May 1911, that a completely new harbour should be built, quite independent of, and effectively enclosing the harbour then approaching completion. He argued that the Muckle Carr could be used as the basis for a north–south concrete breakwater 486ft (148m) long, and that a stone-shipping timber-built quay of 180ft (55m) length could be built on its inside, to hold storage bins for stone of 4,000 tons capacity. These bins could be fed by an aerial flight from the quarry at a sufficient height, 70ft (21.4m), to clear the highest masts of steamers. A 510ft (156m) long rubble breakwater could be run from the north end of the concrete breakwater to the shore so that the entrance to the harbour would be from the south – particularly advantageous in the more common north-east gales. Then the fishermen could the use either this new, outer harbour, or the existing inner harbour with its north-eastern entrance, as appropriate. Clarke estimated the total expense, including dredging and a fish jetty, at £8,800. His main aim was to develop a harbour able to accommodate vessels with some 500 tons carrying capacity rather than those of 150 to 180 tons to which the inner harbour was presently restricted, and thereby secure the lower freight charge which the larger boats could offer. Craster would no doubt have approved of the plan but not the cost of realising it, unless the Board of Trade could be persuaded to finance it.

It is clear that the scale of possible whinstone shipments had not been foreseen when the harbour plans were first drawn up by Sandeman & Son. According to an undated, but *c*.1911, draft application for grant aid from the Board of Trade, presumably submitted in the hope of obtaining grant aid to enable Clarke's plan to be implemented, it was claimed that two large quarries had been opened up since 1905, employing about 100 men, and that a third was about to open. These quarries, it was exaggeratedly claimed, were already shipping nearly 30,000 tons of stone per year, and were capable of turning out 100,000 tons; these figures bear no resemblance to those in the harbour accounts, but, even so, it is clear that a larger harbour would be at least temporarily beneficial. Although £6,207 had already been spent at Craster Haven, it was argued that a further £6,000 was needed if the harbour was to attract larger vessels and so compete with the Norwegian and German quarries. Optimistically, the application ended by noting that the revenue to be derived from the tonnage and harbour dues of an enlarged harbour would be 'more than ample to insure a permanent maintenance of the harbour'.

Clarke's scheme did not go ahead, presumably because the Board of Trade did not see fit to support the idea, but his proposed aerial flight to storage bins was incorporated into the now near-completed harbour, although even this scheme was not without its detractors. Craster had agreed by June 1911, to allow storage bins to be placed at the end of the east pier, provided that they were only for temporary use and that they would not interfere with the fishing trade. The fishermen, however, or some of them, were certain that the bins would indeed interfere with their trade. Three of them petitioned the Board of Trade 'on behalf of the Craster Fishermen' and objected to the proposal in the strongest possible terms. The bins, they claimed, would interfere with the safe sailing of boats approaching the harbour by causing contrary winds, thereby 'endangering our lives upon the very treacherous rocks at either side'. The pylons supporting the aerial flight would make it dangerous to land cobles in easterly breezes when it was usually necessary to haul them onto the road and beyond. Finally, suggested the petitioners, no one should be thinking of running before they could walk, and no further proposals for the harbour should be considered until the present works were completed and the haven made 'something like a harbour', with all dangerous rocks removed, and the beach 'made as it ought to be for a fishermen's harbour'. As they pointed out, six years of work on the harbour had gone by and yet they were still compelled to run to other harbours to reach safety in a storm. After prompting by Percy, the Craster Pilot Master claimed to have no idea how many of Craster's 35 fishermen actually supported the objectors, for they were 'purposely keeping me in the dark', but Clarke clearly felt it prudent to attempt to allay the fishermen's fears.

Firstly, he informed them, the beach pylon would be more than 70ft (21.4m) inland from the high-water mark at Spring tides, and since its base would only occupy 12ft (3.7m) square, with the central 9ft (2.7m) quite open, cobles could be drawn right through it as well as to either side of it. Secondly, the pier-head bins would not come down solid to the quay but would be supported on a concrete arch to allow a cart to pass beneath, and although this archway was presently intended to be 9ft (2.7m) high, it could be increased to 12ft (3.7m) if it was believed that this would allow a freer passage for the wind. He also argued, however, that the bins would be too small to materially affect the wind direction in such an open space, but added, somewhat unconvincingly, that the boats could be propelled, as they often were for several miles when becalmed, using sweeps. As to the complaints that the harbour was not yet complete, Clarke noted that Sandeman was to make his final inspection at the next Spring tides, and that while it was true that rock removal was not yet finished, it had been agreed that it would be completed within three years.

Clarke actually believed that the chief cause of the fishermen's hostility was the success of the harbour in attracting stone boats, for their presence had certainly denied the fishermen a free and unfettered use of quay space. But sometimes, he claimed, the fishermen wilfully neglected to unload their boats, thereby preventing the stone boats from coming alongside to take their load until after the harbour master had moved the fishing boats out of the way. Clarke pointed out that this problem would cease to exist once the storage bins were in place, as the stone boats would load their 180 tons in one or two hours at the pier head, rather than occupy quay space for up to one day. He concluded, perhaps regretfully, in a letter to Percy:

> The fishermen will not meet with me, regarding us [McLaren & Prowde Ltd] as their natural enemies so I will just press on and design so as not to inconvenience them.

Clarke's assurances to the fisherman may have swayed some opinions, for within a month, eight Craster fishermen let it be known that they, unlike some other fishermen, did not oppose the proposals. Of these men, five had the surname Archbold, as did one of the objectors and the Pilot Master!

McLaren & Prowde Ltd were informed in November 1911, that the Board of Trade were sending a Captain Monroe to report on the revised proposals for the harbour. 'Can Mr. Clarke and the eight supportive fishermen be there when Monroe comes?' asked Percy. Monroe's verdict supported Clarke's plan for the pier-head storage bins, and these and the aerial ropeway were built soon after, the latter running in a north-easterly direction from a crushing plant at the quarry to the pier head, each of its skips carrying 1 cwt of whinstone chippings. Three 90ft (27.5m) high silos were built at the east pier head, being supported on concrete staging – Clarke's 'concrete arch'; perhaps from the beginning, or as a later modification, the silos were given extra stability by struts which raked back to the parapet wall of the pier. The silos themselves were constructed of timber, strapped with 16 steel hoops and topped off with the aerial flight discharger and return wheel. Chutes led from the base of the silos, to discharge into the stone boats alongside within the harbour, although precisely how the boats were reversed out after loading is unclear.

29 Craster harbour and its whinstone silos, disused; part of an aerial flight pylon to the left; fishing nets drying on the pier parapet. Probably in the 1930s

30 Craster harbour and its whinstone silos, disused; Dunstanburgh castle in the distance. Probably in the 1930s

It remains unclear how this latter work was financed, although an expenditure of £431 19s 1d in the harbour accounts for 1913 may refer to part or all of the construction costs. A slight fall in the stone shipments for that year may reflect the difficulties of access during construction, while the increase to 10,245 tons shipped in 1914 probably indicates that the harbour became fully operational in that year. Harbour income reached £386 in 1914, but no dividends were paid to the proprietors on account of the previous year's expenditure. A total of £8,032 had been spent on the entire venture by 1915, but thereafter it was downhill all the way for the harbour and the hopes of its creators. Stone shipments tailed off during the First World War and, in an attempt to rescue the situation, various harbour enlargement schemes were considered, but wisely discarded, between 1915 and 1919. It seems likely that wise counsel, to cut losses during these difficult years, and not to throw good money after bad, had prevailed. Additional expenditure had, however, been necessary in the years 1916-18, which required the harbour proprietors to take a mortgage of £1,116; thereafter negative balances and zero dividends became fixtures on the balance sheets. There were no recorded stone shipments in the years 1918-20 and 1923-31.

Inshore fishing activities had also slumped during the war years, perhaps due to voluntary enlistment, for landings seem to have increased in this period at some other local ports. Landings at Craster reached a record low in the year ending March 1918, when only 163 barrels of herring, 745 of white fish and 296 cwt of crabs were landed. Although catches of herring and crab increased after the war, and remained fairly steady until the 1930s, they were never to equal the relatively high landings of the period 1909-1912. Catches of white fish, however, after falling to 196 cwt in 1913, rose to around 1,000 cwt per annum between 1917 and 1932; through all these years the boat and landing dues combined rarely exceeded the figure of £100 per annum anticipated in 1897. Salt imports quickly tailed off from 164 tons in 1909, to zero in 1911. Likewise, early imports of barrel staves and boxwood had ceased by 1911-12, while the export of salted herrings fell from 1,495 barrels in 1909, to zero in 1914. A few tons of coal were imported during only four years between 1909 and 1938.

McLaren & Prowde Ltd may have abandoned Craster quarry in 1923, but another company, confusingly called McLaren & Co. (Belford) Ltd, opened up the Craster quarry in 1931 on a rent and royalty basis, and recommenced shipping whinstone from Craster. This company was begun in 1923 when the McLaren brothers, who had no known relationship with J. Rowland McLaren, returned to England after many years living in Canada. Initially, they supplied whinstone setts and kerbs to local authorities throughout the North East, mainly distributed by Sentinel steam lorries, but soon they also produced whinstone blocks of between 3 and 10 tons each, for sea defence works such as the Roker breakwater at the port of Sunderland, where about 70,000 tons of stone were used; some of the sea defence blocks were loaded on to lighters at Craster and towed down the coast by tugs. Whinstone chippings were not produced, however, and consequently the silos remained unused during McLaren & Co.'s tenure. Thus, there was a brief resumption of stone shipments in the early 1930s, when as many as 25 different steam and motor vessels might use the harbour in any one year, some calling many times whilst others took only one or two cargoes; the majority of the ships had tonnages between 500 and 600 tons, the smallest being 250 tons and the largest 727 tons. These ships were owned in Barrow in Furness, Middlesbrough, London, Antwerp and Rotterdam, and their visits must have made Craster more cosmopolitan than at any other time in its history. This flurry of activity was, however, brief, for the McLarens sold the quarry lease to the London firm of Crowe Catchpole in 1936, and they shipped whinstone chippings to the south of England in ships with capacities of up to 750 tons; the surviving Craster harbour account book gives no indication of the scale of this activity and in any case terminates at 1938. The silo towers, however, had already been deemed to be unsafe and they were demolished soon after 1936, leaving only the concrete-arch support to indicate their former existence.

31 Craster harbour: aerial flight pylon, cobles and women cleaning and packing fish. Probably in the 1930s

32 The only surviving curing house at Craster, seen here in 1974

33 Craster harbour entrance, with the silo base support at the end of the pier, September 1994

Fishing and herring curing continued at Craster after the Second World War but steadily declined. Of the three curing stations of which Craster could once boast, there is now only one, the others having been either demolished or converted to other purposes. The surviving curing house has flourished under L. Robson & Sons Ltd, and its kippers have been much prized by connoisseurs of that particular breakfast delicacy. Commercial cobles seemed to have deserted the harbour by 1974, when the last two crews joined in a seine net trawling venture at Seahouses, but others replaced them and by the 1980s there were four cobles at work, mainly catching crabs and lobsters, although two or three had licences to catch sea salmon which were smoked at Robsons; in addition, a few non-commercial boats continued to use the limited harbour space available. Robsons came to buy their herring from Mallaig, the Clyde and even Norway during the June to September kippering season, when up to 9,000 herring might be kippered per day. As had always been the case, kippering provided work for women in gutting, soaking, spitting and packing, but thankfully carried out indoors rather than on wooden trestles and benches outdoors on the edge of the harbour foreshore.

Craster's small harbour remains much as it was when newly built by the Craster family. In 1975, Oswin E. Craster inherited the Craster estate from his

34 Craster harbour entrance, with the silo base support at the end of the pier and Dunstanburgh castle in the distance, September 1994

cousin Sir John Craster, and he formed the Craster Harbour Co. Ltd in 1980, to control the harbour's and the family's affairs, not in the expectation of financial reward, but rather to limit the family's liabilities should the harbour works ever be swept away. The family's returns on their original investment had always been modest in the extreme, often with no dividends being paid; any small balances which have been made since the Craster Harbour Company was incorporated have been spent on repairs to the harbour. But perhaps the harbour always was primarily intended to be a memorial to a member of the Craster family and an improved facility for fishermen, rather than a profitable venture. It is equally a memorial to a way of life now all but gone; the fishing industry, often precarious, is once more entering a potentially difficult phase that could mean the end of any commercial fishing from Craster.

8

Alnmouth harbour

... a considerable and well-built village at ye entrance of ye river Alne into ye sea, hath a
small harbour for ships and hath considerable quantity of corn loaded for London, France
etc. On a bank adjoining are standing ye walls of a very large and neat chapell which hath
been in ye figure of a cross. (Warburton M.S. *c.*1715)

The place now known as Alnmouth was, until relatively recently, pronounced
and spelled 'Alemouth'. Mackenzie (1811), quoting a contemporary, noted:

This name may be termed corruption refined. By provincial usage Alnmouth became
Yalnmouth, and, by a natural contraction, Yalmouth. But Yal is Ale; hence Yalmouth is
Alemouth; and such has been its English name!

Be that as it may, the name 'Alnmouth' is used here except in quotations.
Alnmouth lies at the mouth of the river Aln, some 6 miles (9.7km) south of
Craster, but whereas the latter is set within a rocky foreshore, Alnmouth is
surrounded by sandy beaches. The ancient town of Alnwick, standing astride the
Great North Road, is only 5 miles (8km) inland, and Alnmouth was its port.

Although there was a settlement at Alnmouth in the eighth century, which
was a focus for Christian religious activities, and although it seems likely that
a small town existed at or near the present site in the immediate pre-conquest
years, the present form of the town dates from the late twelfth century. It was
created by the deliberate policy of one of the first lords of the manor of Alnwick
to create a new town and harbour. Thereby, according to a survey of 1567, the
burgesses both of Alnmouth and Alnwick could:

... for the comon welthe of the said country bringe all maner of merchandyze by sea and in at
the haven of Aylmouth from diverse and sundry countryes in ther owne ships, crayers, or boates
and likewyse to use the trade of fishing and make sale thereof in Alnewyk accordingly.

Within the quite narrow natural boundaries of the spit of land on which Alnmouth stands, between the river Aln and the North Sea, a typical small medieval town was created whose layout can still be identified. Its houses lined both sides of the road along the promontory with burgage plots and occasional lanes descending towards the river on one side and the sea on the other. On a hill to the south of the town, but on the same promontory, stood an enlarged or rebuilt earlier chapel, which overlooked the mouth of the river as it entered the sea to the south; it became known as St Waleric's chapel. Clearly the new town was successful, and its importance was increased when royal permission was granted in 1208 for the establishment of a port and a Wednesday market, primarily for the sale of fish, mainly herring and cod. The fishery in the Aln was then in the sole ownership of the abbot and convent of Alnwick, who also had the right to tythes on any other fish landed at Alnmouth.

Alnmouth was affording good natural anchorage to foreign vessels as well as its own smaller fishing vessels by the end of the thirteenth century, but the nature of its trades at that time can only be presumed; as the port for Alnwick, general merchandise was probably imported while fish and some agricultural products may have been exported. It is known, however, that some ships which had set sail from Alnmouth in 1314, were seized while carrying skins, and that in 1316, the town bailiff was instructed to provide vessels equipped for a naval expedition. Clearly then, Alnmouth was active in seaborne trades, but if it seemed set fair to become a port of some significance for its rural hinterland, that potential was seriously damaged when it was sacked by the Scots in 1336. This setback, and the subsequent decay and disorder in the town, may have been partially rectified by 1464, when Henry VI gave leave to the burgesses of Alnwick to ship coal, wool and other produce of the area between the rivers Blyth and Tweed, from the port of Alnmouth, but the town and its trade hardly even began to fulfil their early promise – just seven ships paid port dues in 1503.

In an attempt to improve the port's prospects, the Earl of Northumberland agreed to allow the burgesses of Alnwick to create a 'weir' or 'haven' at Alnmouth in 1529. This work may well have been carried out, for an increase in port dues did follow, but all was not well according to a 1567 survey produced for the Earl. About one-third of the population were Scots ('foroners'), and whereas the original plan had been for Alnmouth to be inhabited mainly by fishermen and others who in one way or another supported the fishing industry, there were now only 20 fishermen amongst its 60 householders. Of the rest, excluding the bailiff, the vicar and six other people 'active in their own industry', most either made their living by baking or brewing (which was contrary to the Lord of the Manor's exclusive privilege) and selling their products to the fishermen. But some inhabitants were said to contribute nothing to the common wealth of the town, for not a thing could be left outside of a house for fear of it being stolen by certain of them. An additional problem was that of absentee burgage holders who let their plots fall into decay, and the Earl gave instructions in 1594 that all burgage holders should reside on them in the future. The twelfth-century plan for a fishing town and port was clearly in some disarray, but the Earl sought to restore the town from further decay by 'replenishinge the same with fishers'. This plan, if it was effected, had no long-lasting effect, for another report, of 1614, noted that 'the inhabitants there are very poore and the toune and burrough in great ruine and decay'; even so, there were 19 resident fishermen at Alnmouth in 1626, the fourth highest number along the Northumberland coast.

It would seem that it was not until the late seventeenth century that matters began to improve significantly and the merchants of Alnwick and Alnmouth saw fit to petition the Custom House at London in 1704, requesting that Alnmouth be made a port in its own right, on the basis of its increased trade, rather than merely a 'creek' of the Port of Berwick. As they pointed out:

> ... it is a great trouble and expence to the merchant to go Twice to Berwick which is thirty miles from Aylmouth to procure Custom House despatches, and that during the time of such a journey, they often loos the benefit of the wind to the great Discouragement of the traders of that place.

The London Custom House replied that Alnmouth was indeed only a creek, and that it was not a member of the Port of Berwick, and since creeks had been debarred from being ports of custom by Act of Parliament, it was not in their power to establish Alnmouth as a place of custom. This might, at first, seem an ideal solution to the merchants' problems – as a creek, Alnmouth could neither be a port in its own right, nor was it a member of the Port of Berwick, and consequently perhaps, no one need travel anywhere – except that the situation was much more complicated than that, not only because the Treasury would never contemplate losing any of the revenues which it received from custom duties, but also because designations such as 'member' and 'creek' had legal implications. As a 'head port', Berwick's custom officers had complete authority over its 'members' and 'creeks'. A member port was otherwise independent of the head port, and might have similar trading patterns, while a creek within a head port's jurisdiction would only seldom be involved in the foreign trades. If it was involved in such trades, usually under license from the head port, then the duties payable would have to be made in advance, and if the head port's customs officers chose not to appoint a deputy to the creek in question, then duties would have to be made at the head port. The Custom house at London was, in effect, insisting that the *status quo* should prevail.

Nonetheless, that episode suggests that Alnmouth's trade was increasing and it probably became greater still in the eighteenth century. In fact most English exports increased during the late seventeenth and early eighteenth centuries, and a rising surplus of English grain for export was particularly significant in this expansion of trade during the first half of the latter period. Alnmouth had clearly played its small part in the export of corn from before 1712, for

Quarter Sessions records of that year refer to a 'corn road', a common highway some 2 miles (3.2km) south-east of Alnmouth in High Buston, which had been obstructed by a hedge and locked gate, thereby causing problems to the carriers of corn along that road for shipment from Alnmouth. As High Buston was not on a direct line between Alnwick and Alnmouth, this route must have been only one of several which gave access to the harbour at Alnmouth. It was reported in 1715, that Alnmouth was shipping corn to 'London, France etc.', and its growing trade seems to have been bringing a degree of renewal to the town, as a report for the Earl of Northumberland indicated in 1727. It was claimed that although there were nearly 100 ancient burgages in the town, which was almost depopulated, the inhabitants were now beginning to erect houses and granaries for the shipment of all sorts of grain. Subsequently an improvement in Alnmouth's trade appears to have been quite noticeable, for in Mark's survey of Northumberland of 1730, it was said to have 'a very good harbour for ships, and is the only flourishing place for trade and shipping, except Blythe's Nook, between Newcastle and Berwick'.

In spite of, or perhaps because of, improvements in Alnmouth's prosperity at the middle of the eighteenth century, some of its inhabitants were deemed to be in dire need of spiritual attention. On 19 July 1748 John Wesley rode into Alnmouth, 'a small sea port famous for all kinds of wickedness'; unfortunately Wesley was not specific about the nature of this wickedness. Although he returned three years later to the largest congregation he had ever seen in Northumberland, this initial success failed to secure the early establishment of a Methodist Society at Alnmouth.

The town may have been approaching the height of its prosperity when a turnpike, linking it with Hexham via Alnwick and Rothbury, was established in 1752. The 'Alemouth Turnpike Road' has often been referred to as 'The Corn Road' in twentieth-century publications, and this designation is now widely used by local historians; no eighteenth- or nineteenth-century writers seem to have used this appellation in respect to this turnpike and, indeed, there is extremely little, if any, real evidence to justify so doing. It has been claimed that the turnpike was described as 'The Corn Road' within the Allgood papers, although a search through the relevant documents in this collection has so far failed to demonstrate the use of any such term; nor is any support for the notion of a 'Corn Road' to be found in the surviving records of the Turnpike Trust, where the word 'corn' only appears in passing on a couple of occasions. It may be that some confusion has arisen out of the reference to a 'the corn road' in the 1712 Quarter Sessions referred to earlier, but the High Buston road there mentioned was on quite a different route to the later turnpike.

Even so, in an attempt to justify the use of the term, it has been said by many that the turnpike road was conceived and constructed to give the farmers of west Northumberland and Hexhamshire an exporting outlet for their grain at Alnmouth. What is clear is that Alnmouth did export considerable quantities of corn during the eighteenth century, and that the eastern end of the turnpike served a useful function in this respect in its early years. It also seems likely that corn passed on to the turnpike from around Whittingham Vale to the west of Alnwick, and from the coastal plain to the north and south of Alnwick. However, it is equally apparent from the trust records that there was never any significant through traffic of any kind between Hexham and Alnmouth. Most activity on the road was at its extreme ends, a fact which the trustees clearly acknowledged in 1796 when they noted that 'the principal traffic [was] at the extreme ends' of the turnpike. The turnpike may have made carriage to and from Alnmouth somewhat easier, and may have increased its trade a little, but it is quite impossible to quantify the road's significance for the harbour at Alnmouth, and quite unjustifiable to refer to it as a corn road.

Alnmouth's corn exports and general merchandise imports certainly continued throughout the eighteenth century, but it would seem that the town could only develop further if Alnwick itself progressed, rather more than vice versa. But Bishop Pococke's comments on Alnwick and Alnmouth in 1760 could equally well have described their situation some 50 years earlier:

> The principal support of [Alnwick] is its lying in the great road to the north, the markets, fairs and sessions, also coals; a salmon fishery and an export of corn at Aylmouth where small vessels come in and carry oats etc. to different parts, the salmon goes chiefly pickled to London.

Pococke did, however, note that 'small ships' were being built at Alnmouth, and shipbuilding, no matter how small the scale, generally encourages the creation of associated industries. Thus, a saw mill was established near Waterside, a ropery was opened and on 13 March 1763 the first large ship to be built there was launched, and at 300 tons burthen, this was quite a substantial vessel for the period; it was followed up by the 219-ton *Providence*, launched in 1765. Furthermore, considerable building activity in Alnmouth's hinterland was encouraging still more imports, of blue slates from Scotland and timber and general merchandise from Scandinavia. On occasions pipes of Madeira were also brought into the harbour and advertised for sale.

The last quarter of the eighteenth century saw several offshore skirmishes between merchant, naval and privateer vessels along the Northumberland coast. In August of 1779, a two-hour engagement between two French privateers and the British man-of-war *Content* was viewed by many of the inhabitants of Alnmouth. Although the French out-gunned the British by 42 guns to 20, the French were, apparently, compelled to flee. In the following month, Paul Jones took a brig off Alnmouth before firing a 68-pound cannon shot at the ruins of St Waleric's Church; the shot missed the church but, after bouncing three times, it did demolish the east end of a farmstead. One of Alnmouth's vessels, the *Two Brothers*, was taken by a privateer in 1796. But generally trade remained quite brisk at this time, with corn, eggs and pork being exported from Alnmouth, and as many as 18 vessels might have lain in the harbour at any one time.

A rather curious reference from this period has been taken to imply that the Aln may have been made navigable to Alnwick, even though the tidal limit on the Aln was at Lesbury, just a couple of miles (3.2km) upriver, and there were several low bridges and mill weirs between Lesbury and Alnwick. On 27 February 1782, 'a noted prostitute' named Jane Young was found drowned in 'Alnwick water, near a ship lying there'. The ship is apparently shown on Stadlar's 1805 engraving of Alnwick Castle, lying between the Lion and Denwick bridges, but we can be fairly certain that this 'ship' was an ornamental landscape feature of the castle grounds rather than a trading vessel.

The port of Alnmouth had always been as nature had created it but, and as is sometimes the way of things, the same agency was to greatly alter it. On Christmas day 1806 a 'furious storm of wind from the west' was experienced in the North East and at about noon, accompanied with rain, 'it became an absolute hurricane'. This storm caused the Aln's floodwaters to cut a new channel to the sea at Alnmouth by breaking through the promontory between the town and Church Hill. Now, instead of flowing round the south side of the hill to enter the sea as it had done from time immemorial, the river passed its north. Church Hill, with its ruined church further damaged by the gale, a granary, guano sheds and other buildings were now isolated from the town. The effectiveness of Alnmouth

35 Alnmouth from the air. The river Aln enters the sea on the left, along the new course formed in the 1806 flood

as a harbour soon began to gradually deteriorate, although it is by no means certain that the altered channel was directly responsible for this decline.

Certainly the port continued to trade long after 1806, but the wars with the French were exerting their toll on trade, as well as on captured ships. Mackenzie described Alnmouth's situation in 1811:

> ... a pretty little town containing eighty-eight well-built houses, while several large granaries contribute to give it a respectable appearance, It may properly be considered the port to Alnwick, whose merchants employ several small vessels in conveying their merchandise to London etc. A considerable quantity of timber, for the purpose of building, is also imported from Norway and Holland; but this trade in consequence of the continental disturbances, is now nearly annihilated. The exports are principally corn, of which immense quantities were lately shipped for the London market; but this branch of trade has recently experienced a rapid decrease .... The harbour is extremely inconvenient, but it is capable of much improvement; and being so excellently situated for trade, it is to be hoped that effective measures will be adopted, on the return to peace, to revive and extend the trade of the place....

He added, without further comment, that Alnmouth had 'several convenient lodging houses, always filled in the bathing season', and someone with perhaps a greater degree of percipience might have been tempted to prophesy about Alnmouth's new future; someone like, for example, the landlord of the *Schooner* who, by 1842, had:

> ... attached to his House a Hot and Cold Bath, supplied with Salt or Fresh water, which may be had at all Times, on the shortest possible Notice, and on moderate Terms.

In fact, as Mackenzie was writing, Alnmouth was still shipping considerable amounts of eggs and pork to the metropolis, and of wool to Yorkshire manufacturers; it was also one of the few Northumberland ports that was still shipping grain. In 1813, for example, Alnmouth shipped a total of 44,266 quarters of grain, mainly oats (32,370qrs) and wheat (11,7612qrs); in the same year Berwick exported twice as much grain as Alnmouth, while Newcastle shipped just over half the Alnmouth total. Although it is difficult to be certain, given the complications of units of measure at that time, Alnmouth's grain export could have been the product of some 9,000 acres (3645ha) of corn cultivation, a relatively small area of arable land, easily to be found in Alnwick's hinterland. Mackenzie reported again on the port in 1825, when there were 'ten vessels, from 50 to 150 tons burthen' belonging to the port, besides 'many others that visit it occasionally'. The nature of its imports and exports were more or less as before but, according to Mackenzie, 'all the branches of this trade have lately suffered a rapid decrease'; presumably the smuggling which Mackenzie noted as having previously been pursued with 'singular dexterity, boldness and success' had also declined. But there were to be no harbour improvements, for there was no one to instigate them, and Alnmouth was never to recover its former trading significance. Its population figures reflect Alnmouth's stagnation at this period, from 406 inhabitants in 1821, rising to only 488 by 1851.

Even so, a few schooners and the odd brig, those which could cope with the shallow bar, plied regular trades with London and as far away as Gothenburg, and even if it was gradually losing most of its former import and export trades, Alnmouth continued to provide a safe harbour for small fishing boats. Indeed, the fishing industry, together with the building of cobles, remained important to the town up to the middle of the nineteenth century, while the oyster ponds on the tidal banks of the river to the west of the town continued to yield their particular delicacy. But a new change in Alnmouth's fortunes had occurred by then, one which relied less on its natural harbour and more on its sandy links and the coming of the railway. With the opening of the Newcastle & Berwick Railway between Morpeth and Chathill in 1847, which allowed through working between Newcastle and Tweedmouth, followed in 1850 by the opening of the Alnwick Branch from the main line at Bilton, Alnmouth's new destiny, primarily as a seaside resort, was assured; its death as a trading harbour was equally signalled.

Alnmouth was not directly on the main railway line, but an attractive railway station was provided nearby at nearby Bilton – still one of the prettiest on the line. However, an improved connecting road was needed between Bilton to Alnmouth if the best use of this new opportunity was to be realised. Although this railway station was only about 1 mile (1.6km) from Alnmouth 'as the crow flies', the only road to avoid difficult fords across the Aln estuary first led to Lesbury, with its turnpike gate, and then passed along the turnpike to Alnmouth, a total distance of just over 2.5 miles (3.2km). This route had to be used at least until 1864, but a new, direct road between Bilton Station and Alnmouth was under construction by 1856. It can only be presumed that the county authorities were responsible for financing the new road, but it is apparent the county had no intention to bridge the Aln, that provision was left to philanthropy in the shape of the then Duchess of Northumberland, as a plaque on the bridge parapet records:

> To Eleanor, Duchess of Northumberland, the public are greatly indebted for this stone bridge and footpath to the Station AD MDCCCLXIV.

Road traffic between Bilton Station and Alnmouth could now bypass the Lesbury turnpike gate completely and legitimately. Although the turnpike was discontinued in 1872, its narrow and twisting route along the north bank of the Aln to Alnmouth remains open, but most of today's travellers prefer the less adventurous but wider and direct 'new road' to Alnmouth across the Duchess Bridge.

In 1887, according to Bulmer's *Directory*, about 40 Alnmouth men out of a total population of 535 were employed in the fishing trade (with about 20 cobles at work), and there were still some imports of timber and slates from Holland and other places, but social and economic changes were much in evidence as indicated by Alnmouth's varied inhabitants and its social and service provisions. There was, by then, a 'Club and Reading Room', an 'Alemouth Gas and Bath Co.', 17 lodging houses, a hotel and a golf club. The inhabitants included the usual trades people – blacksmith, draper, tailor, butcher, baker and cabinet maker – but also people like Major Browne of Callaly Castle, and the businessmen John William Pease of Newcastle, who had second homes at Alnmouth; the town even boasted two artists in residence.

Alnmouth was now seen as one of the most picturesque and popular watering places on the Northumberland coast, its destiny was sealed as a possible rival to Cullercoats. Many of its former granaries had been converted into large dwelling houses, some of which, in Prospect Place for example, remain in use as such today; these early changes of use, which were to be echoed in the so-called 'marina village' developments of the late twentieth century, were, according to Tomlinson (1889), 'not without a certain picturesque incongruity'; one former granary was serving as the parish Sunday school by 1889, while another boasted the Alnmouth Academy. The town managed to retain its medieval plan, but new villas, their blue slate roofs contrasting with the older red pantiles, soon

36 Alnmouth as a seaside resort. Probably in the 1930s

occupied vacant plots. This intermingling of the 'better class' houses with those of the fishermen and their cobles served only to enhance the town's picturesque appeal. Amongst the dunes, near the edge of the links, bathing boxes of various hues stood alongside the lifeboat and its house presented by the fourth Duke of Northumberland in the 1850s, and the 'Bather's Life-Saving Boat House' presented by the Pease family. What more could the discerning visitor require? A writer in the *Monthly Chronicle of North-Country Lore and Legend* for September 1889 waxed lyrical:

> Alnmouth, as seen under azure skies through a sunny and crystalline atmosphere, may truly be described as the prettiest watering-place on the coast of Northumberland.

Although some consideration was now actually given to improving the harbour, with an application made, presumably by Alnwick interests, to the Board of Trade in 1897, for permission to construct a pier and a locked dam across the river, Alnmouth's days as a port were well and truly over, and only four fishing cobles were operating from the harbour by 1905; there were only one or two plus a few small pleasure boats in 1948 and today there are pleasure boats only. The change from active port to seaside resort is now complete and Alnmouth remains an ideal spot for golfing, fishing, swimming, paddling, or walking along the miles of sandy beaches. But also, through its buildings and silted harbour, Alnmouth presents a superb field archive of 800 years of history.

9

Warkworth (Amble) harbour

Warkworth can scarcely be called a harbour at present but its breakwater piers when finished will give it a claim to the name and on the principle of 'any port in a storm' I think the harbour when completed will occasionally be useful, particularly for small vessels running into it when the tide is in. (James Walker, 1841)

Warkworth lies on the river Coquet about 1.5 miles (2.4km) from its present mouth, which lies some 4 sandy miles (6.4km) down the coast from Alnmouth. The small Coquet Island stands just over a mile (1.6km) to the east, the Coquet Road between the island and the mainland being useable by vessels except in strong north and north-east winds. Prehistoric sites and relics have been found in the Warkworth area, but little is known of permanent settlement there until the founding of its Saxon church which, with the town itself, was granted to the monks of Lindisfarne in the eighth century by the King of Northumbria. The present church is essentially Norman and around it the town retains its early medieval form, with clearly marked burgage plots, the whole dominated by the castle, a Percy stronghold from the thirteenth and fourteenth centuries. All of this is strategically located on a sharp loop in the Coquet, making Warkworth a smaller version of the heart of Durham city. Its only bridge, which may be of the fourteenth century, still retains its defence tower, but was pedestrianised when a new road bridge was opened alongside in 1965.

The Coquet is tidal to about 1 mile (1.6km) above Warkworth's bridge, and the river may have served as a trading harbour from as early as the twelfth century, for the monks of Brinkburn Abbey were granted the right, in 1178, to make salt (from sea water) by the Gildean Burn, a small tributary stream which ran into the Coquet near its mouth, where the town of Amble would later be created; there was coal in the neighbourhood of Warkworth, but it cannot be said with any certainty that this was used as fuel for the salt pans. Amble's salt output in the twelfth century may only have been consumed locally, but the river certainly saw some seaborne trade when the town had a garrison and a market in the thirteenth century, for there are infrequent references to shipping during that and the following centuries. For example, one Stephen of Frisem had his ship seized at Amble in 1280, and all vessels at Warkworth capable of carrying at least 40 tons were ordered to join the royal fleet under the command of the King's admiral in 1326. Salt making clearly continued, for an inquisition of 1310 valued two salt pans at Warkworth at 10s per annum, and the sea and Coquet fisheries there at £6 13s 4d.

It is not until the sixteenth and seventeenth centuries that we get any specific information concerning the trade at Warkworth harbour. Coal and grindstones were being exported from the haven at 'Newtown', directly east of the Warkworth, in 1567, but we can only surmise the general nature of trade from the Coquet at this period, possibly some salt, grain, coal and salmon exports, and general merchandise imports, and it is likely that these remained the chief trades until the eighteenth century. Eight fishermen were said to reside at Warkworth in 1626, and nine at nearby Hauxley, while a Royal Commission of 1611 noted coal mining and salt making in the area, the mines and salt pans being let or worked together. The pans at 'Ambell' were worth 4s 0d per annum in 1628, and the coal mine £2 1s 0d, but they were let together for £20 per annum a century later. It was suggested, however, that the tenants were making £200 per annum from the mines and pans, and that these activities could be advantageously expanded by creating a harbour 'for a very small charge, and as many pans as you want'. But then a seemingly significant change in Warkworth's fortunes stemmed from an apparent misfortune caused by the forces of nature. A contemporary account of this event, taken from *Sykes Local Records,* reads:

> The quantity of snow, sleet and rain, which fell this month [March 1765], swelled the rivers to an alarming degree. The river Coquet … left its old course below the village of Warkworth, and forced its way between two sandy hills … that had obstructed its passage for ages, by which it opened a passage into the sea above a mile nearer than its former channel.

There may have been other, earlier changes in the river's direction between Warkworth and the sea, as an examination of large-scale Ordnance Maps will suggest, but the present parish boundaries may well follow the line taken by the Coquet before 1765. These boundaries, together with riverbed remnants, indicate that the river had performed another tight loop below Warkworth, embracing what is now known as the 'Braid', then headed north-west before turning to the sea due east of Warkworth. The new river channel broke across this loop to its north and entered the sea directly in an easterly direction, thereby reducing the total river passage from Warkworth to the sea by about 1 mile (1.6km). Moreover, as a *Newcastle Courant* of 1772, quoted by Hutchinson, indicated, this new channel below Warkworth was quite straight, and the river was:

… now settled in a very deep channel, with a fine clay bottom, which makes it navigable for small craft. It is said there is upwards of 14ft of water upon the bar at full sea, and continues that depth very near the town; so that with a little assistance of art, it might be made to admit ships of a considerable burthen; and as Coquet Island is situated a little to the southwards, forms a fine bay at the very mouth of the river. The grounds adjoining thereto abound with a fine seam of coal; and so plentiful is corn, that few counties can equal its fertility. From these considerations, what pity it is that Warkworth was not made a sea-port, since nature has almost half finished the design.

Both the *Newcastle Courant* and Hutchinson were correct in their suggestion that the change in the river's direction and nature could be used to advantage in the creation of a sea port, but no harbour developments of significance were to take place for another 60 years. Even so, the naturally improved river was attracting other export trades during the second half of the eighteenth century. The *Newcastle Courant* of 1772 again:

Contiguous to the bridge [at Warkworth] is a large free-stone quarry, the stones of which are so much esteemed, that great quantities thereof are shipped for London. The salmon fishery here is carried to a very great extent, so that at the mouth of the Coquet, in the summer season, as well as in the river itself, are some thousands caught, which gives employment to a number of hands.

But another more spectacular, if more speculative industry was to be created on the banks of the Coquet in the 1770s when, according to the *Northumberland County History*:

The rural calm of Acklington Park was broken in the year 1775, [when] a group of speculators, attracted by the unfailing water power of the Coquet, acquired a lease of land from the Duke of Northumberland with liberty to erect a foundry for the manufacture of tin and iron.

It may well be thought that only the most foolhardy entrepreneur would attempt to develop a tin foundry in Northumberland, where no tin ores occur naturally, but the men behind the plan were no ordinary speculators. They were, in fact, members of the Kendall family dynasty, originally a Warwickshire family, who became involved in a large number of iron works in Wales and throughout the north of England, from Cheshire to Northumberland, in the eighteenth century; locally they were particularly associated with the Cookson ironworks at Chester le Street in County Durham, and at the Little Clifton furnace in Cumbria. No doubt intending nothing but the best for their new works by the Coquet, some 6 miles (9.7km) upriver of Warkworth, the Kendalls engaged the services of John Smeaton to design the necessary works, including its waterwheels which would power the tin-rolling mills, and a magnificent horse-shoe weir to impound the river water. Smeaton's plans were ready by September 1776 and construction of the works was soon underway, going into production under the superintendence of George Kendall himself. It is not known how successful the works was in a commercial sense, suffice it to say that the Kendalls offered it for sale in 1791, with 45 years of the lease unexpired.

It was almost certainly too ambitious an undertaking, for Acklington Park's location was far from ideal for such an enterprise. All the necessary raw materials must have been brought by sea to the mouth of the Coquet and up to Warkworth, before being transferred into carts, or conceivably pack horses, for carriage to the foundry. Likewise those finished products which could not be sold locally, would make a similar return journey for export. The 1791 sale notice informed would-be purchasers of the works that there was an associated warehouse and shipping place at Warkworth, presumably developed by the Kendalls, where vessels of 8-9ft (2.4-2.7m) draught could be accommodated at spring tides. In the

37 Smeaton's weir for the Coquet Ironworks, April 1973

event, the works was purchased by a Newcastle woollen draper who converted the premises into a woollen mill. His trade was clearly more successful than the tin and iron foundry had been, for the main mill building eventually had four storeys whereas the foundry would almost certainly have been single-storied; the heightening of the original foundry structure remains evident today. The concern was then sold to a Galashiels textile manufacturer in 1828, and the mill continued to function until 1884. It is not known whether the Coquet was important as a harbour to these latter textile concerns, but it is unlikely that all of the raw material supplies and subsequent sales were strictly local.

The weir designed by Smeaton for the foundry seems to have brought problems for the salmon population of the river for its 11ft (3.4m) height defeated many of them. Still without a fish pass in the nineteenth century, the eccentric surgeon and naturalist Frank Buckland, who was appointed Inspector to HM Salmon Fisheries in 1867, erected a hand-written notice for the benefit of any literate salmon which might find their way into the river, advising them of a diversionary route:

> No road at present over this weir. Go downstream, take the first turn to the right and you will find good travelling water upstream and no jumping required. F T B.

In spite of the promise held out in the eighteenth century, there was no real impetus for harbour development at the mouth of the Coquet until the opening out of the adjacent coalfield in the townships of Hauxley and East Chevington. As already noted, coal had been won in the area at least from the sixteenth century, and a staith had been built for Togston coals by 1826, but it was not until the 1830s that the possibility of expanding the coal trade, through the agency of an improved harbour, was seriously considered. A plan to create an entirely artificial harbour, independent of the river with piers and a wharf, was drawn up in 1832 by Hamilton Fulton, a man already experienced in harbour and canal work elsewhere, but no action followed. However, after Messrs Kingscote & Co. obtained mineral leases at Hauxley and began to open up Radcliffe Colliery in 1835 (named after the family name of the Earl of Newburgh, owner of the royalty), the quest for improved shipping facilities was engaged in earnest. Having built a railway from their pit to a new staith, apparently on the north side of the river and accessed via a trestle bridge over it, Kingscote & Co. now led the arguments for an expansion of trade by means of a better harbour.

A new harbour improvement plan, which would involve the excavation of a new river channel and the building of breakwaters, was drawn up by Robert Nicholson (better known as a railway and bridge engineer), and this plan was used as the basis of an Act of Parliament of June 1837, for the establishment of the Warkworth Harbour commissioners. The passing of this Warkworth Harbour Act was celebrated with great optimism and style:

... by illuminations and rejoicings. The town presented an animated appearance, being thronged to excess with people from the adjacent parts, all of whom seemed to participate in one joyous feeling.

The commissioners were to comprise the Earl of Newburgh and the trustees of his estate, two lessees of the newly opened Radcliffe Colliery which had begun shipping coal from Warkworth in that year, a representative of the Greys of Howick who owned the nearby Broomhill Colliery, and 12 others, three of whom would be nominated by the Duke of Northumberland. The Duke was to have powers of veto over any actions which the commissioners might pursue, provided that such actions could be deemed to adversely affect his Warkworth and Amble Stell fisheries. The Act limited the dues which the commissioners could exact, and prevented any dues being taken until £3,500 had been expended on improvements; as the commissioners' borrowing powers were set at £100,000, they clearly would not be required to carry out much work before they could begin to obtain returns. A flurry of pre-construction plans now ensued.

The commissioners already had two possible improvement plans, Fulton's for a new harbour and Nicholson's based on a new channel. John Murray, the engineer to the river Wear Commissioners from 1832 to 1859, who would shortly be responsible for one of the most popular engineering events of Victorian Britain – 'the lighthouse which moved' – was asked to examine these quite different schemes. Murray found fault with both plans, but made an alternative proposal, and recommended that the commissioners seek an opinion from Sir John Rennie, a famous son of a famous father, and both engineers of national repute. But before Rennie got to work on the problem himself, James Leslie, the harbour engineer for Dundee and, like Fulton, a colleague of Rennie's, was asked to pronounce on the three plans now on the table. Leslie thought Fulton's plan was a possibility, but did not approve of Nicholson's plan, and suggested two possible but radical alterations to Murray's plan. Rennie had submitted his own report by 1838, and although he believed that Fulton's plan for a new harbour had much to recommend it, he was worried that it might too easily silt up. He deemed Nicholson's plan to be impracticable, Murray's inadequate without alterations and Leslie's inappropriate; these differing opinions, on how best to proceed, illustrate the uncertainties inherent in harbour design. Rennie's own preferred scheme embraced features of all of the earlier plans except Fulton's, and after further modifications to his plan, contracts for construction were let in May 1838. In Rennie's view, the natural river imposed an upper limit of 80 tons burthen on vessels seeking to trade at Warkworth harbour, and he argued that the fundamental objective of improvement should be to ensure that vessels of 200 ton burthen could use the harbour safely and commodiously. The main obstacle at present, in his view, arose out of the crooked, irregular and shallow channel of the natural river, and the exposed nature of its mouth, the periodic silting up of which had caused shifting alignments of the entrance channel. Consequently, his plan would be to redirect and restrain the channel by virtue of a massive north pier, which would also provide protection for the harbour in heavy seas; a breakwater, built near due north from Pan Hill on the south side of the river mouth towards the pier, would give an entrance channel of 250ft (76m), and this would complete the necessary outer works. New quays for staiths would be provided within the protected harbour and these would also serve to straighten out the river's present circuitous route.

Curiously, but perhaps to ensure completion of the work, the contract for building the new harbour was let to Kingscote & Browne, the Radcliffe colliery lessees, who then subcontracted the work out to John and James Welch; this was the beginning of a convoluted affair which was to have troublesome complications. According to McAndrews (1912), the contractors soon built a 'pretentious domicile' at a location which overlooked the proposed works, which also incorporated a 'Tommy Shop' and a large room for religious worship. Moreover, in an unfortunately familiar fashion, the estimated costs of the harbour works had to be revised upwards from the original estimate of £46,200, even before any work had commenced. Firstly, the Duke argued that his fishing interests would indeed be imperilled by the new works and consequently £10,000 had to be set aside just in case his concern proved valid. Then unanticipated and unspecified problems added a further £20,000 to the expected costs, and the commissioners were therefore obliged to seek grant aid from the Exchequer to meet their expected shortfall. James Walker, another engineer with nationwide experience of harbour and canal building, was asked to report on the situation for the benefit of the Exchequer Loans Commissioners, and to advise accordingly. He was not sanguine regarding the possibilities, primarily because he found it difficult to argue that the proposed works could be said to be in the national interest; on the other hand, he seemed to argue, the Loans Commissioners could just about justify support for the proposals as offering a harbour of refuge:

> Warkworth Harbour, when finished as proposed, will not be entitled to the high character which the word 'National' seems to convey; but that, nevertheless in connection with the roadstead, it will, when completed, be useful to the public ... Warkworth can scarcely be called a harbour at present but its breakwater piers when finished will give it a claim to the name and on the principle of 'any port in a storm' I think the harbour when completed will occasionally be useful, particularly for small vessels running into it when the tide is in ... Warkworth [is] deserving of the notice of the Commissioners for the Loan of Exchequer Bills; supposing always a security for the repayment of any advances, to be good, independently of the harbour; for I do not consider that dependence for repayment can be placed on the returns from the harbour.

In the event the Loans Commissioners, reflecting the unenthusiastic tone of Walker's advice, decided against making the loan. Even so, the harbour commissioners now gave consideration to an even more ambitious modification to the existing plans, one which would incorporate wet-dock provision. This plan was stillborn, for the commissioners' finances were utterly inadequate for such an undertaking; however, a rescue package then materialised.

Messrs Ladbroke & Brown had taken over the lease on Radcliffe Colliery in 1841. They remodelled Radcliffe village, provided a school, and offered to advance all the necessary monies for the completion of the harbour works – not a purely magnanimous gesture, for the colliery's trading strength would clearly benefit from an improved harbour. The Welch partnership now found itself in what must have been an unenviable position; they were sub-contractors for Kingscote & Browne, the former lessees of Radcliffe Colliery, who were meant to supply all the necessary building materials; the harbour works were now being effectively financed by Robert Ladbroke, while the whole undertaking was, nominally, under the supervision of Rennie and Murray. The Welchs sought to be relieved of their contract in 1842 – the year in which the work had originally been scheduled for completion – but not before they had indulged in further speculative building in the town. Another Harbour Act was needed, for the first one had called for work to be completed within five years; there were further suggested modifications to the harbour plans, and yet more unanticipated expenses. Some works, however, must have been completed, for coal was being shipped by 1844.

The harbour commissioners now decided that their deteriorating situation might be arrested by forming a Joint Stock Company to oversee harbour developments. The company would have a capital of £100,000 and borrowing powers of £50,000, but although debentures valued at some £60,000 were immediately issued, the proposal collapsed. However, another Act was obtained in 1847, giving the commissioners powers to raise capital and loans of up to £200,000, to enable the harbour works to be completed within five years. Unusually, the works were finished within that period, but when Rennie certified the works complete in 1849, almost £120,000 had been expended on the piers alone. The north pier, almost 2,000ft (610m) long, had been a particularly expensive work, partly on account of the storm damage it suffered during construction; this had accounted for more than £100,000. Even so, it soon proved to be defective both in its design and the materials used. First constructed in local sandstone quarried from the Pan Rocks and Cliff Quarry just to the south of the river mouth, and carried across the estuary on a temporary bridge, it had to be extensively re-constructed in the vastly superior Aberdeen granite. Construction of the quays and staiths had cost about £50,000, but they had usefully fixed the formerly circuitous river into a direct channel about 83 yards wide.

The harbour works at Amble were at last complete, and the harbour's promise was seemingly enhanced by the opening of a goods and minerals branch line to the emerging town of Amble from the Newcastle & Berwick line in 1849; the line did not serve passengers until 1874. But the harbour was essentially dependent on the coals of only two collieries, Radcliffe and Broomhill, the latter leased to Burdon, Barkass & Co. at least from 1853, and being served by the new branch line. The 78,000 tons of coal which were being shipped per year from the harbour by 1854 were quite insufficient to make it profitable, the harbour revenues in that year amounting to a mere £1,262, on a capital expenditure by then of nearly £184,000. In the same year John & Joseph Harrison of Newcastle took over Radcliffe Colliery, and John, the senior partner, was appointed to the Harbour Commission in the following year. Harrison had already held discussions with the Sunderland Dock Company about the possibility of shipping his coals from the river Wear, some 30 miles (48.3km) to the south in County Durham, but on becoming a Warkworth commissioner, he immediately pressed for a new coal-shipping berth at Amble, and then for the building of a wet dock within the harbour; the new berth seems to have been constructed, but the dock proposal again fell, presumably through lack of funds. Although the Harrisons captured some new overseas coal markets, coastal coal shipments fell dramatically, so that the coal trade grew only very slowly overall. This was partly due to lower than estimated outputs from the collieries, but it was also apparent that there was an insufficient depth of water in the harbour, particularly at the Radcliffe Colliery staiths. Hopes of further improvements again foundered on the lack of funds, although a new dredger was acquired in 1863, suggesting a determination to provide deeper water within the harbour.

In a further attempt to stabilise a deteriorating financial situation, the embattled harbour commissioners offered the harbour to an utterly disinterested NER, and the bondholders later sold their entire interest to the owners of Radcliffe Colliery for only £8,000. It had all been a costly and unprofitable undertaking and coal shipments were falling, from 88,000 tons in 1860 to 42,000 tons in 1869. In the latter year the entire debenture stock of the harbour was acquired by Hugh Andrews, a Belfast merchant, who became a managing partner in Broomhill Colliery in 1871. Andrews was reported to have doubled the colliery's output within a very short time and it was perhaps he who instigated the Broomhill Collieries' firebrick works, sited just behind the Radcliffe Quay, burning clays dug from the local mines to produce a wide range of fireclay products under the brand name 'Radcliffe'. The works was in production by the 1870s, and its products were despatched by rail and sea as far as the Baltic and Mediterranean ports.

The harbour's still precarious situation was only slowly rescued after the appointment of Meik & Nesbit as consulting engineers. Thomas Meik was midway through a 20-year stint as engineer to Blyth harbour at this time, and had also spent a decade in the same capacity at Sunderland; he was clearly a very competent harbour engineer, and he embarked on a strategy of steady improvement at Amble at minimum cost – it was time to stop throwing good money after bad. Extensive dredging gave 8ft (2.4m) of water at low tide, the piers were strengthened (the south pier was practically rebuilt), the river line above the berths was straightened to generate a better natural scour in the harbour, and a new fish dock was constructed in the upper part of the harbour; by 1878, Meik was satisfied that significant improvements had been made to the harbour. Some 187,000 tons of coal were shipped in 1880, and 79 ships were registered under local owners. Other exports that year included 700,000 bricks, 1,787 barrels of herring and 620 tons of stone, while imports included 3,450 loads of timber, 182 tons of flour and 200 tons of salt; the latter may imply that the local salt pans were now engaged in refining rock salt. Some iron was also exported around this period and occasional cargoes of slates and empty barrels were brought in. Meanwhile, the Harrisons had sold their interest in Radcliffe Colliery to Messrs Haggie, Smith & Co.

Meik was anxious to maintain the momentum of gradual improvement of the harbour, and there was a pressing need to do so, for he recognised that harbour provision here and elsewhere would soon be unable to accommodate the larger colliers now being built. Consequently, the Warkworth commissioners again sought a new Act, one which would allow the north pier to be extended, a new south pier to be built and enable the necessary borrowing requirements to be met. The Bill was, however, withdrawn in 1884, a year when coal shipments from Amble had reached 226,000 tons, carried on 691 vessels of which 361 were UK registered steam colliers and 184 were UK registered sailing colliers. Although the quantity of coal shipped from Amble had trebled since 1856, the aggregate amounts were still quite small when compared with some other coal ports of the North East and harbour revenues remained stubbornly low, a mere £5,111 in 1884, leaving a working profit of only £3,840, a poor reward for the high capital outlays of the previous years.

Another abortive scheme of this period was the proposal that a 'Harbour of Refuge' might be constructed at Amble. While the nineteenth century generally witnessed a tremendous investment in port and harbour facilities directed towards aiding trade by reducing turnaround times, there was also considerable interest in reducing the dangers to shipping at sea. Much of this interest had been generated by those with interests in the north-east coal trade, people who were led by a desire to determine in what ways many coastal wrecks could be prevented and many lives saved. Recommendations were made for more and superior lighthouses and lifeboat stations, for closer control over the loading of vessels, for better-trained ship's officers and for additional 'harbours of refuge'. The idea of harbours of refuge was not a new one. They had been defined by a sixteenth-century Act as:

> ... sanctuaries at all tides and at every full sea, to ships, boats and vessels, in any adversity, tempest or peril.

Many east-coast ports like Whitby, Scarborough and Bridlington, had long been designated harbours of refuge and could, therefore, levy 'passing tolls' on all craft which might at some time benefit from their existence. But there were no officially designated harbours of refuge along the Northumberland coast, nor along that of County Durham. They had been suggested on several occasions, in 1789, for example, when the merchants of the Scottish Forth ports pleaded for a refuge at Beadnell 'as a place of safety for ships on that dangerous coast'. But it was not until the nineteenth century, when statistics for the numbers of wrecks and lives lost were better recorded, that national pressures for harbours of refuge, financed by the public purse and maintained by passing tolls, became strong. There were some 780 deaths per annum from coastal wrecks between 1852 and 1857 and a single gale could cause havoc. A severe storm in October 1824 caused 37 vessels to be driven ashore at Redcar on the north Yorkshire coast, and in January 1854, a year in which coastal wrecks resulted in a total of 1,549 deaths, a hurricane created mayhem along the north-east coast with as many as 180 ships being wrecked, including 10 at Amble. Again, in January 1857, a 'fearful storm' drove 94 ships, mostly colliers, ashore on the north-east coast; many went down with all hands, seven vessels being lost between Amble and North Sunderland.

In the latter year, stung by the annual death toll in the coastal trades, Parliament appointed a select committee to inquire into the provision of additional harbours of refuge. Henry George Liddell (later Baron Ravensworth), then Member of Parliament for South Northumberland, and a leading representative of the north-east coal trade, served on the committee and he, supported by other north-eastern MPs such as George Hudson and William Schaw Lindsay, pressed for a harbour of refuge on the north-east coast. The committee reported favourably, but laissez-faire attitudes baulked at the notion that state funds should be used to support private shipping and trading interests. Nevertheless, a Royal Commission was appointed and it reported in 1859, recommending that government grants should be made available to help create a number of new harbours of refuge, including one on the Tyne and another at Hartlepool in County Durham. The report also noted, however, that there were no simple causes of wrecks, for some, the Commission observed, had been the direct result of a degree of inebriation amongst ships' crews 'in excess of what even hearty tars could cope with'. A change of government, following soon after publication of the report, effectively ensured that nothing came of the report's recommendations.

The idea was not allowed to die, however, and even though the steady replacement of sailing vessels by steam ships arguably reduced the need for harbours of refuge, north-eastern MPs in particular continued to press for them. Three such harbours had been constructed along the south coast of England by 1883, and in that year the Warkworth Harbour Commissioners attempted to re-activate a suggestion made some 36 years earlier, that a breakwater connecting Coquet Island with the mainland would form a very secure harbour of refuge. Meik prepared such a plan in 1883, in the hope that it would be sufficiently attractive to gain the support of Parliament and the shipping interests. But it was a massive scheme, one which could only be justified by a truly national interest and only financed by central government funding. Two breakwaters, commencing on the mainland over 2 miles (3.2km) apart, with Warkworth harbour located almost centrally between them, would curve out into the sea to provide an entrance channel almost half a mile (0.8km) wide at about 2 miles (3.2km) from the river mouth. The north breakwater would be about 1.7 miles (2.7km) long while the south breakwater would incorporate Coquet Island and give a total protected length of 1.9 miles (3km). The huge scale of this plan can be envisaged by comparing its proposed breakwaters with the piers at Tynemouth (which in fact became the only officially designated 'Port of Refuge' between the Humber and the Forth), where the longest pier, that on the south side, is less than 1 mile (1.6km) long. The Warkworth plan was estimated to cost £1.5 million, but it was suggested that this figure could be reduced by one sixth if convict labour were to be used; to this end temporary convict workshops and a prison could be established on the island. It hardly needs noting that the proposal failed to gain the necessary support and Northumberland never got its 'Alcatraz'.

As the population of Amble had grown quite rapidly from 247 in 1831, to 1,040 in 1851 and 2,016 in 1881, several public and social facilities had been developed in the new town. As usually happened in the new industrial towns and villages, the non-conformists were the first to provide places of religious worship. The town had a Congregational chapel in 1848, a Wesleyan Methodist chapel in 1863, followed by an Anglican church in 1870. A committee was established to provide for the education of young people in 1854 and the Alnwick Rural Sanitation Authority agreed to carry out a sewerage scheme for Amble in 1875, although widespread dissatisfaction with their approach soon led to the formation of the Amble Local Board District to oversee such works. A private gas works, which had been erected in 1846, was incorporated in 1865, but the 'Amble & Warkworth Gas, Light & Cable Co. Ltd' was formed in opposition to this venture and bought it out in 1879. The town appeared prosperous by 1887, despite the poor trading performance of its harbour. There was a Custom House, a reading room and a masonic hall, and the town was well served by tradesmen, retailers and hoteliers. It even hosted a 'Vice Consul for the German Empire, Denmark, Sweden and Norway'. A salt works was still operating at Pan Rocks, while a fish-curing establishment, a steam saw mill and the boatyard of J & J Harrison, were all active.

Harrison's yard, established in 1870, maintained something of a tradition stretching intermittently back into the eighteenth century, for it is said that a vessel named the *Chevington Oak* was launched into the Coquet from near the old granary on the Warkworth Road late in that century. This did not, however, mark the commencement of an era of shipbuilding by the Coquet, for it seems to have been the first and only ship built by the river until the late 1830s, when a Mr Douglas (and/or George Surtees) of Monkwearmouth in County Durham, began to build ships on Amble Braid. Then, in the decade 1851-61, Messrs Leighton & Sanderson built seven ships before closing down their operations.

A single ship is believed to have been built on the north side of the river in 1868, but it was not until the Harrisons began their boatyard that any permanence was given to boat building activity at Amble, mainly building fishing cobles and sailing boats, and making blocks and masts.

With the withdrawal of the 1884 Bill, the harbour commissioners had faced financial restraints over further improvements. They did, however, obtain a loan of £15,000 which enabled them to further deepen the harbour, and provide an additional staith room. Later, in 1890, the north pier was extended in concrete by 120ft (36.6m) using direct labour, thereby making the harbour easier for vessels to enter in rough weather.

The first shaft of what would become Togston colliery was commenced in 1890, but the pit does not appear to have produced its first coals until 1903. Meanwhile, Radcliffe Colliery had come up against a geological fault which threw the strata down to the south; it closed in 1892-3 as a consequence, but a new mine, to be called Newburgh Colliery, was sunk about 1 mile (1.6km) to the south-east, opening in 1896. In 1900, however, all the collieries in the immediate district of Amble came under a single proprietor, the 'Broomhill Collieries Ltd', and a new railway, running from Broomhill Colliery to the line between Radcliffe colliery and Amble, enabled this concern to operate independently of the NER. Coal outputs increased steadily and, sometimes as a response to requests from the colliery proprietors, piecemeal improvements to the harbour continued. Dredging remained an ongoing and essential activity, as always within a river harbour, and staith rooms were further extended. This work culminated in a 1905 slightly-angled extension of about 220ft (67m) to the south pier, aimed at limiting sand bar formation while at the same time allowing storm driven sand into the harbour from where it could be quite easily dredged out; this extension was facilitated by constructing a jetty from the quay across to the south pier, along which the extension construction materials could be carried; a useful spin-off of this jetty, according to McAndrews, was the creation of a 'fine perambulation'. The north pier was also repaired with huge concrete blocks where needed. Still, coal shipments only rose relatively slowly, reaching 758,000 tons in 1908, but falling back to 629,000 tons in 1913, with about three-quarters of total shipments being carried overseas. In total about £250,000 had now been spent on the harbour.

A new shipbuilding concern came to the harbour in c.1915, when the Amble Shipbuilding Company was established on the Braid. An associate company of this concern, the c.1918 Amble Ferro-concrete Co. Ltd, in which Palmers of Hebburn on Tyne had a interest, was one of 19 yards around the country to answer the admiralty's call to build small steam tugs and barges in ferro-concrete. The rationale behind this stemmed from the national steel shortages in the years towards the end of the First World War, and the need to build up shipping tonnages after wartime losses. The Amble yard seems to have employed 200-300 people including, unusually for a shipyard, a large proportion of women. Two out of the 12 tugs suggested by the Admiralty were built there, the *Cretebow* and the *Cretestem*, both launched in 1919, but both were to have relatively short lives, being dismantled in 1924 and 1925 respectively. However, of all the yards set up by the Admiralty under this crash programme, only the Amble yard continued to operate after the Admiralty dropped the idea in 1920. A few tugs were built for the Anglo-Mexican Oil Company, to be employed in Mexico, and oil storage tanks, derricks and pylons were also fabricated before the yard finally closed in 1926, another victim of the depression, leaving only Harrisons to continue their boat-building skills at Amble. Probably as a result of the war and the depression, the population of Amble actually fell from 4,851 in 1921 to 4,205 in 1931.

Fortunately, coal shipments from Amble gained a boost after the Co-operative Wholesale Society (CWS) bought the nearby Shilbottle royalties in 1916. Shilbottle's shallow coals had been mined at least from the thirteenth century, and a commentator noted in 1585 that there was 'a good and riche myne of coles verye profitable to the countrey thereabouts' at Shilbottle. Its coals continued to hold a very high reputation, but its distance from navigable water, some 3.5 miles (5.6km) from Alnmouth or 5 miles (8km) from Amble, had limited its coals to immediate landsale. In order to gain better access to a ready market, a horse-drawn waggonway, with iron rails, was constructed from the Shilbottle pits to Bondgate in Alnwick in 1809; although the colliery continued to be worked, the waggonway may have had a relatively short life, for it is not shown on mid-nineteenth-century maps. A tubway was subsequently built for a Shilbottle pit which lay about 1 mile (1.6km) north-east of the village, taking a more direct route than the earlier waggonway to a depot on the 1850 Alnwick Branch of the Newcastle to Berwick line, a few hundred yards south-east of Alnwick Station; a number of coal-using industries were developed around this depot, including a gas works, saw mill and an electricity generating station. But what Shilbottle really needed, to make significant profit from its fine coals, was rail connection with the sea, a fact that was plainly obvious to the CWS.

The CWS extensively reorganised Shilbottle Colliery; two new shafts were sunk to create the Grange Pit, a new village – 'Shilbottle Grange' – was built and a new railway line constructed to connect with the Newcastle to Berwick line, only 2 miles (3.2km) to the east. Although reversals were needed at the junction with the main line, and again at Chevington, nonetheless the Shilbottle coals could now be shipped from Amble. Capital expenditure on the whole undertaking at Shilbottle had reached £400,000 by 1926, but the new mine was already producing 850 tons of coal per day, as opposed to the 250 tons per day under the previous owners. Moreover, the CWS had even greater ambitions, for they bought the adjacent South Shilbottle Colliery in 1930, with freehold land and mineral rights over 5,640 acres (2284ha), and here they developed the Whittle Drift mine, again connecting it by rail to the main line, some 3 miles (4.8km) south of the Shilbottle junction, for shipment from Amble. This was quite a catch for the Warkworth Harbour Commissioners, for Shilbottle coals continued to

38 Coal staiths at Amble harbour, with commissioners' paddle tug (possibly *Ayr*) at the Broomhill Quay in centre foreground and steam-powered crane to the left. Beyond are the coal staiths at the Radcliffe Quay; photograph probably taken in the 1940s

enjoy an enviable reputation in the market, and a considerable portion of their output was now being shipped from Amble for use on the Swedish railways.

Although Newburgh colliery had closed in 1926, the Broomhill Collieries Ltd had opened Hauxley Colliery at about the same time and, located just a mile (1.6km) or so south of Amble, the addition of Hauxley coals made the harbour busier still; some coals were even finding their way to Amble from Ashington, Stobswood and as far away as Scremerston. So coal continued to dominate Amble's exports, but some timber was also exported, while grain and phosphates were brought in. The fishing industry, which had never been strong, falling to just two cobles at Amble and seven at nearby Hauxley Haven by 1905, had picked up slightly, such that by 1928 there were three motor boats and one sailing boat, plus a number of cobles catching lobsters, crabs and some salmon in the season; by 1936 there were 13 motor boats and 10 sailing boats, keeping 29 men in full employment and five in part-time work, plus the cobles.

Coal shipments from Amble peaked in the late 1920s and early 1930s at around 600,000 tons per annum, the harbour doing much trade with the Scottish east-coast ports, Scandinavia, Germany and London, but they slowly declined thereafter to around 300,000 tons per annum by the end of the thirties. Attempts were made to establish a local woodworking industry based on imported timber from the Baltic countries, but the outbreak of the Second World War effectively stifled that concern before it had made much progress.

39 Above Colliers at the Broomhill Quay coal staiths, Amble. Probably in the 1950s

40 Below Visten enters Amble harbour watched by people, seemingly in their Sunday best, from the South Jetty. Probably in the 1950s

With nationalisation of the coal industry in 1947, representation on the Harbour Commission took a new turn, and National Coal Board representatives ultimately formed the majority of the nine commissioners; the commissioners' clerk and office staff were also employed by the NCB. Thus, the harbour which had been created to serve the coal trade was now effectively run by and for the NCB, and consequently it could not survive the pit closures of the 1950s and '60s; Radcliffe Colliery had closed in 1955, and its quayside brickworks had gone by 1958; the Broomhill and Bondicarr mines closed in 1961, and Hauxley Colliery in 1966. There had also been factors at work which were beyond the control of both the harbour commissioners and the NCB. For example, the absence of an effective national fuel and transport policy militated against Amble when the Central Electricity Generating Board decided, in 1959, to convert the coal-fired power station at Poole in Dorset to oil firing, costing Amble some 1,500 tons of coal exports per week; the CEGB also decided to use 4,000-ton colliers to supply its coal-fired stations, far too large to use Amble harbour, so that Shilbottle and Broomhill coals would now be exported from Blyth. At the same time the NCB were unable to retain German orders for Shilbottle coal, up to 100,000 tons of which had been exported from Amble every year up to 1958. Finally, the ongoing conversion of Scottish trawlers to oil firing was steadily reducing bunker coal requirements at Aberdeen, previously a good market for Amble-shipped coals.

In fact, the harbour was by now quite outdated. The depths on the bar at the entrance varied constantly, and pilots were always recommended to ship's masters when practical. A large black ball was displayed at the inner end of the south breakwater by day to indicate whether there was a sufficient water depth over the bar; it was hauled down if the bar was dangerous. North-easterly gales caused difficulties at the entrance when nearly the whole space between the entrance to the harbour and Coquet Island could be filled with broken water. Nevertheless, some coals from Shilbottle, Whittle and the Widdrington opencast mine, plus small amounts from Ashington and Stobswood, continued to be shipped, mainly to Newton Abbot for power stations in south-west England; small amounts were also sent to Fraserburgh, Inverness, Aberdeen, Denmark, Sweden and Germany. But the coal trade declined by about 50 per cent in the period 1964 to 1967, only 250 ships using the harbour in the latter year and carrying out only 125,000 tons of coal. Alternative export cargoes were sought, barley and stone chippings for example, and although there were great hopes for these exports in the mid-1960s, and special conveyor-loading facilities for grain handling were installed in 1966, the harbour could only be economically viable by shipping 200,000 tons of coal, or its equivalent, per year. The relatively small amounts of barley and stone which were shipped for a few years in the 1960s (and this continued into the 1970s), could in no way make up for the steady draining away of the harbour's coal traffic. Neither the harbour commissioners nor the NCB were able to pull through this steadily worsening situation, and the NCB effectively pulled the plug on Amble by announcing, in 1968, that all coals presently shipped from Amble would be diverted to Blyth harbour. Amble's last cargo of coal was shipped in September 1969, the coal staiths being demolished and the rail tracks lifted in 1971. Moreover, after a century of successful if small-scale boat building, even J & J Harrison, after some good years in the 1960s, were now finding the commercial waters more than a little choppy. Employing about 20 people, but finding a declining demand for cobles, the company's land was probably more valuable than their business.

Although Amble still had its fishing fleet, with about four seine netters in the white fishing, and a dozen cobles for crustaceans, the town's prospects looked grim, and only the most optimistic could have envisaged a future for the harbour. However, even as the last coal was being shipped, the construction of a yachting marina was being considered as an alternative use for the harbour. Nearly 20 years were to pass before that idea became a reality when the Amble Braid Marina was officially opened in July 1987, with 250 alongside-deep-water pontoon berths; later that year the harbour commissioners increased their borrowing powers from £150, 000 to £500,000. Ironically, just two years later, J & J Harrison, with over 400 cobles, pilot cutters and sailing cutters behind them, were in the hands of the receiver. Fortunately the concern was bought by Marshall Branson Ltd,

41 An Amble coal staith during demolition, February 1971

42 Amble harbour without its coal trade, March 1985

better know for JCBs than coble building, being a Blaydon-on-Tyne plant hire firm. The workforce was soon expanded and RNLI contracts were obtained so that, together with English Harbour Yachts, its associate company next door, Amble retained a maritime industry. And it still does, for when the Marshall Branson concern was put into receivership late in 1994, the yard was taken over by the Amble Boat Company, now (2004) specialising in building all-welded aluminium-alloy vessels, up to 22m in length, including 'state of the art' all-weather lifeboats, as well as refitting work.

The Warkworth Harbour Commissioners are still in business, but now, like others elsewhere, serving the demands of leisure rather more than seaborne trades. However, a new fish dock was opened in 1988 for the three seine netters and 20 or so cobles then at work, and the fishing fleet still works out of Amble. It is undoubtedly true that the original promoters lost money in creating Amble harbour, hundreds of thousands of pounds which might have been better spent in constructing a mineral railway to link up with the Tyne. But then we should not have had Amble, nor its marina.

43 Amble Harbour Commissioners boundary post, March 1985

10

The Port of Blyth

In the rear of these hills, and on the river of the same name, stands the town of Blyth; not by any means a pretty place, though if a crowd of staiths and ships are a sign, it may be profitable ... The pier, built partly of stone and wood, extends into the sea for nearly a mile; and 'ought to go as far again' says one of the men, 'to be of any use'. (Walter White, 1859)

Blyth stands on the south bank of the mouth of the river Blyth, just over 14 miles (22.5km) south of Amble, much of the coastline between the two harbours being comprised of long sandy bays, notably the beautiful Druridge Bay immediately to the south of Amble. Like other ports immediately to the north and south of it, Blyth developed initially as a fishery with ancillary salt pans, but for a brief period of the twentieth century it shipped more coal than any other port in Europe. The river Blyth runs in an easterly direction to the sea for its last few miles, but it is forced east-south-east for about three-quarters of a mile (1.2km) by a ridge of rocks – the Coble Hole Rocks – just before entering the sea. These rocks, covered at high water but dry at low water, long marked an entrance, difficult to enter or leave in strong winds, to a sheltered anchorage beyond; a haven which served as a harbour at least from the fourteenth century and possibly from the twelfth century.

The early history of salt making at Blyth is only evident through a series of often disparate and usually brief references, and although it may result in an oversimplification, it is useful to consider the industry as comprising four groups of salt pans. Firstly a pan or pans on the south side of the river at 'Blyth-snook', established close to the mouth of the river by 1208, and being reserved by Gilbert Delaval, together with a fishery, in that year. Secondly, and also on the south side of the river at Cowpen Shore, a salt pan operative at least from 1153–65, when James de Bolam and his son Gilbert, granted it to the canons of Brinkburn. Thirdly, another group of pans on the south side which were in the hands of private persons. Fourthly, some pans and a fishery at Cambois on the north side of the river which Robert de Wincester granted to Newminster Abbey in 1138-40; there were seven pans here by 1534. This concentration of salt-making activity near the mouth of the river Blyth, together with the fact that coal mines at Cowpen were being leased at least by 1315, tends to support the notion that coal was being used to heat the lead pans producing salt at Blyth, at least by the early fourteenth century. Thin seams of coal which outcropped in the area may have been worked at the outcrop or from shallow pits, to provide the fuel for salt making, but it is just as likely that seashore coals were collected for this purpose. No doubt some salt would be used locally but some may have been exported.

The mouth of the Blyth was certainly in use as a natural haven by 1323, for the Bishop of Durham collected a total of 3s 4d for the anchorage of 10 ships there in that year, an amount which may only represent anchorage on the north side of the haven, for the north side of the river had come to be owned by the Bishop as part of Bedlingtonshire, a detached part of the county of Durham. The fisheries, coal mines and salt pans seem to have continued in use over the following centuries. For example, the Prior of Tynemouth leased a coal pit lying in the fields of Bebside and Cowpen for seven years to John Preston and Nicholas Mitford at 22s 0d per year in 1530; the same partners obtained another lease for seven years in 1535, at 26s 8d per year, while another pit plus two salt pans were leased to Richard Benson. There were at least 14 pans in use by 1533, seven of them, together with a coal mine, belonging to Newminster Abbey. Presumably the pans were now being constructed of wrought-iron plate since such were in use at nearby South Shields by 1489.

At the dissolution of the monasteries in 1539, the monastic properties, coal mines and salt pans, were appropriated to the Crown and then leased out to various individuals. Thus, the Cambois pans went to one Oswald Willesthrop, and a bill of lading from the period of his tenure indicates that some of his salt was carried to London on the *Thomas* of Newcastle; salt was also being sent to Yarmouth, Hull etc. The Cambois pans eventually came to Sir Ralph Delaval of Seaton Delaval, by which time both the pans and the coal mine were said to be decayed, and at the expiry of his lease in 1590, Sir Ralph removed the sole intact pan to Hartley and the old site belonging to the Bishop of Durham was abandoned. The Newminster Abbey pans were eventually leased, after 1547, to Sir Robert Delaval, who was thereby able to further extend his Hartley salt-making enterprise. A few harbour facilities had been created by 1589, for a lease of that year, when there were some 20 active salt pans around the harbour, referred to 'anchorage, beaconage, wharfage, [and] ballast quay'. But salt making at Blyth was to diminish somewhat thereafter as a result of the exclusion of Blyth merchants in the granting of monopolies on the selling of salt in parts of the country which had formerly been served by Blyth.

However, attempts were made to extend Blyth's coal trade towards the close of the sixteenth century, in particular after the Crown leased all the Cowpen and

Bebside mines, plus nine salt pans, to Peter Delaval for 21 years at £22 13s 8d from 1595. Delaval was a London merchant and a kinsman of the Northumberland family of that name, and this was neither the first nor last occasion that southern adventurers would seek to profit from north-eastern undertakings away from the immediate Tyne area where the monopolistic powers of the Newcastle Hostmen were generally absolute. Delaval developed new pits and salt pans at Blyth but the venture soon proved to be a commercial failure, and the remainder of his lease was assigned to Thomas Harbottle in 1602, he in turn handing it on to a group of Midlands' entrepreneurs which included Huntingdon Beaumont. This simple and common transaction was to have most uncommon, indeed ground-breaking effects.

Beaumont, described by William Gray in 1649 as 'a gentleman of great ingenuity and rare parts', was responsible for the first horse-drawn waggonway in Great Britain, evidenced by a lease of 1604 on coal mines near Nottingham which allowed him to carry coals from Strelley through Wollaton 'alonge the passage now laide with Railes and with suche or the like Carriages as are now in use for that purpose'. Beaumont and his partners took over Harbottle's lease for mines and salt pans in Cowpen and Bebside, and possibly also in Bedlington, in the following year, and although no details of this assignment have survived, it seems likely that permission would be simultaneously granted to build a waggonway and also that Beaumont began to build it very soon after the assignment came into force. William Gray also noted that Beaumont had:

> ... adventured into our mines, with his £30,000; who brought with him.... Waggons with one horse to carry down coales from the pits to the staiths to the River etc. Within few years, he consumed all his money, and rode home upon his light horse.

It is generally believed that the sum of £30,000 is a considerable exaggeration, but certain it is that Beaumont's venture failed. He was bought out by his partners in 1614, but they only continued in their north-east venture for two more years before withdrawing and leaving behind three boats 'and many and diverse Rayles, Utensells and implements'; Beaumont died in a debtor's jail in Nottingham in 1623. Coal shipments from Blyth in 1609 were just 644 tons, but reached 3,053 tons by 1616, a clear increase, and one perhaps stimulated by Beaumont's waggonway, but hardly a signal of the rail revolution that was to come, for the waggonway was the true harbinger of the railway system of the nineteenth century. Blyth's coal and salt trades stagnated following the collapse of Beaumont's adventure, for the shallow seams of coal which were then available yielded an inferior quality of coal, suitable for salt making but not for much else and consequently there was not much hope of expanding the coal exporting trade.

So Blyth's coal continued to remained subservient to its salt making, but the extent of these activities are difficult to determine for the seventeenth century. For example, although the Crown coal mines and four salt pans in Cowpen were leased to one David Errington in 1636 for 21 years, at £16 1s 3d per annum, Errington seems not to have fulfilled his tenancy, for he paid no rent, and the mines and pans were said to be lying waste 13 years later. Still, a colliery at Bedlington did remain active at a rent of £12 per year, while records for 1670 show that the pans and a colliery at East Sleekburn were worth £40 per year. Blyth was attached to the Port of Tyne in that year and remained so until 1848, when it was attached to the newly constituted Port of Shields.

Towards the end of the seventeenth century, there were moves to exploit the better inland coal seams just to the west of Blyth at Plessey, which had been worked as early as 1349, but whose distance from navigable water, some 3 or 4 miles (4.8 or 6.4km), had limited the market for its coals to landsale. Ralph Brandling, who bought land at Plessey in c.1690, opened its coals up to the coastal trade by laying a horse-drawn waggonway to Blyth before 1699. Then, Thomas Radcliffe of Dilston, near Hexham in Northumberland, acquired an interest in the Plessey and adjacent Shotton manors in 1700, and leased Plessey colliery to George Errington of Grays Inn; at about the same time he bought the Newsham property immediately south-west of Blyth; by 1713, control of these properties had, in effect, passed to Lord Widdrington, already the owner of collieries at Winlaton and Stella on Tyneside. Mining operations in the Blyth hinterland were still on a modest scale, however, consisting of three small pits, mainly supplying the salt pans, but also garnering a small export trade; some 300 tons of salt and 8,000 tons of coal were exported in 1715. Widdrington and Radcliffe paid for their Jacobite sympathies in the same year, their Plessey, Shotton and Newsham estates being forfeited to the Crown. Alderman Matthew White, a wealthy merchant of Newcastle, purchased these Crown properties for Richard Ridley of Heaton, his son-in-law, in 1722, and also bought the Blagdon estate, adjacent to Shotton. Successive generations of the Ridley family came to dominate the development of Blyth and its harbour, and to live at Blagdon Hall as they still do.

Some 58,000 tons of coal were being carried along the Plessey waggonway for shipment from Blyth by 1723; some of this coal was exported overseas, with 78 vessels, only one of which was Blyth-based, clearing the harbour with coals for foreign ports between August 1723 and August 1724; overseas exports were to dwindle thereafter following an increase in the export duty on coal. The White–Ridley concern continued to expand, mines at Bebside being willed to Matthew White in 1727, while a West Hartford royalty, near Plessey, was absorbed by Ridley in 1728. To better service his growing coal interests, Ridley now began a programme of harbour improvements aimed at providing better coal handling facilities at Blyth. The 'Bishop's Quay' had already been established on the north side of the river in c.1689, but the earliest facility on the south shore seems to have been Ridley's coaling quay of 1723. This was followed by a ballast quay in 1727, and in the following year Ridley engaged one John Hindmarsh to build 800 solid yards of quay; in successive years Hindmarsh constructed a Pilot's

Watch House (1729), a lighthouse and a quay extension (1730). Nearly 80,000 tons of coal was taken down the Plessey waggonway to Blyth for coastwise export in 1734, most of it destined for London and King's Lynn (115 and 127 ships respectively out of the total of 296 vessels which sailed coastwise in 1733), plus 2,700 tons for the foreign trade. In addition, Ridley now had 14 salt pans at work (including six brought north from Cullercoats in 1726), and was producing about 1,000 tons of salt per year. But a new venture was to bring a different trade to the river – the Bebside Slitting Mill.

The township of Bebside was located on the south side of the river Blyth, at the river's tidal limit some 3 river-miles (4.8km) from the sea; at first glance an unlikely setting for a slitting mill, that is a mill to produce wrought-iron rods from which to make, mainly, nails. The precise beginnings of the Bebside works are a little unclear. In 1736, Mary Johnson, the owner of Bebside, granted a lease to William Thomlinson, a merchant of Newcastle but originally from Cumberland, whose family had been concerned with a number of ironworking concerns in the North East. Thomlinson was granted rights to timber, clay and quarry stone, to erect buildings, and to have access to water power for a rod-slitting and nail making operation, but Johnson reserved to herself the coal and ironstone beneath her land, and the right to erect fire engines, mills, furnaces etc. It may be that she was intending to set up an ironworks on the site, but that did not happen and Thomlinson was to die in 1737, having only just commenced his Bebside works. Even so he would appear to have completed the construction of some slitting mills for nail rods and some water-powered forges, the whole being sold to an unknown buyer for £1,250 in 1739. Precisely what happened next is uncertain, but it seems likely that nail making continued on the Bebside site, eventually giving rise to the saying 'Hartley Pans for sailors, Bedlington for nailors'. But little more is known until March 1750, and again in February 1759, when the apparently successful enterprise was advertised for sale. The latter advertisement informed interested parties that:

> The Slitting-mill and Warehouses ... at Bebside near Blyth ... with Workhouses for about forty Nailors (now employed in an established trade) and all Manner of Work Tools and Utensils suitable to the same, with Dwelling-houses for the Workmen, and a large and commodious Dwelling-house fit for a Gentleman's Family, consisting of ten Fire rooms, (four of which are hung with genteel paper) with good Cellars, a Stable, a large Garden, and other Conveniences, and about 30 Acres of land ... the whole held by Lease, of which about 78 Years are unexpired, under the yearly rent of 28£.
>
> Also a Place called Watson's Key, near the aforesaid Works, with a Warehouse for landing and shipping Goods.... And also a Sloop called the NANCY, of the Burden of 35 tons, with her Tackle and Furniture....
>
> N.B. There is Proper Convenience for erecting a Forge or other Ironworks on the Premises. The Work is conveniently situate for Coals and Water, and within a Mile of the navigable Part of the River Blyth.

This is the earliest documentary evidence to indicate that the concern used the river Blyth as a navigable waterway by which to import wrought iron and export finished nails and rods, as well as a source of power, its location just above the river's tidal limit having presumably been carefully chosen with such considerations in mind. The same factors must also have led Malings & Co. of Sunderland, better known as potters, to develop land opposite Bebside Mill, but on the north (Bedlington) side of the river, for an ironworks, and here they erected a coke-fired blast furnace and achieved a 'Good Vend for Cast Ware', before 1766. The two works, facing each other across the river, were quite unrelated at this time, the Bedlington ironworks producing cast-iron ware from iron ores, the Bebside mill continuing to work up imported wrought iron. A horse-drawn waggonway, from West Bedlington to near the ironworks, and known to have been in existence before 1787, may have been built by the Malings to carry coal to the ironworks, but the enterprise proved to be commercially unsuccessful after a relatively short period, and its blast furnace was closed down before 1788, in which year the works was occupied by Hawks, Longridge & Co., the senior partners being brothers in law of Gateshead on Tyne.

William Hawks and Thomas Longridge had already acquired the Bebside slitting mill in 1782, when its sale notice indicated that it was capable of producing more than 500 tons of rod-iron and iron hoops per year, and that iron could be brought from London to Blyth as ballast 'on the most moderate terms'. Hawks and Longridge were already involved in ironworking in County Durham, and they now adapted both the slitting mill and the ironworks to slightly different functions, abandoning the blast furnace, but adding rolling mills. Their endeavours were eventually to bring more trade to the river Blyth.

Plessey coals had continued to dominate trade at Blyth harbour throughout these developments at Bedlington and Bebside, although considerable quantities of grain were also exported from the granaries of North Blyth and salt was still being made and exported. Moreover, the coal trade was attracting a few coal-burning industries to land adjacent to the mouth of the river, as an advertisement in a Newcastle newspaper indicated in 1744:

> At Blyth, a good sea-port [is] a new wind-mill, built with stone and well accustomed; a fire-stone quarry for glass-house furnaces; a draw-kiln for burning limestones; two large sheds for making pan tiles and stock-bricks, with a good seam of clay for that purpose; also at Link-house, one mile from Blyth, a large new malting, well supplied with water.

Most of the vessels working out of Blyth were still owned at places like King's Lynn, Whitby and Scarborough, even if some of them had been built on Tyneside or Wearside; indeed Wallace suggested that the *Olive Branch* was the only Blyth-owned ship in 1750. However, Edmund Hannay, a young shipwright from Leith in Scotland, set up a shipbuilding yard at Blyth in that year, apparently after having spent a while building small boats at Alnmouth; this signalled the beginning of a long history of shipbuilding at Blyth. Hannay also became a shipowner, and continued to build ships at Blyth until the end of the century; his son-in-law, Edward Watts, also became a shipbuilder at Blyth in his own right.

Trade on the river had clearly grown during the first half of the eighteenth century, but few port facilities had been provided other than Ridley's quays, the lighthouse and some beacons on the sandbanks to the southward of the entrance to the river. There were no coal-handling staiths as such, the Plessey coals simply being deposited on the quay before being loaded into the waiting colliers by barrow and plank. The river channel remained as nature had made it, and the reefs of rocks to the north-east continued to make its entrance very dangerous. The channel was also very prone to sanding up and it is likely that, at certain times of the year, coal loading would have to be completed at sea from keels. Further improvements to the harbour were now badly needed.

Matthew White's interests in the area had descended to his son Sir Matthew White, but they were devised by Sir Matthew, in 1755, to his cousin and brother-in-law, Matthew Ridley, son of Richard Ridley, who had married Sir Matthew's sister Elizabeth in 1742. Ridley clearly stood to gain most from further harbour improvements and yet it was not until 1765 that any significant change was made; the 'North Dyke', a long wall of loose stones designed to form a breakwater, was laid upon the Coble Hole rocks which formed the eastern side of the river channel as it entered the sea. Sir Matthew White's title and estates passed in their entirety to the Ridley family in 1763, and when Matthew Ridley died in 1778, the title and estates descended upon his son Sir Matthew White Ridley. He progressed further harbour improvements, causing the first coal-loading staiths to be built in 1788, as well as the high lighthouse, which still survives, although heightened, behind Bath Terrace. These developments, together with the shipyards, encouraged a growth in shipowning at Blyth, rising from only three vessels in 1761 to 15 in 1770, and 25 in 1789.

But the 1790s brought challenges to Ridley's monopoly on Blyth's coal trade. Firstly a small colliery opened near Bedlington, using a quay on the north side of the river; it soon failed and was bought up by Ridley. More importantly, a colliery was opened up at Cowpen on land which belonged to the Bowes family. The adventurers in this enterprise included John Clark who was said to have arrived at Blyth in 1760 as a poor boy but was now involved in rope-making, sailmaking and shipping; William Row, probably the shipbuilder and glass manufacturer of that name of St Peters, Newcastle; and Aubone and John Surtees, members of a family banking concern in Newcastle. This was a major undertaking, for they were aiming to win the deep, good quality coals which lay at 92 fathoms directly beneath Blyth. The successful sinking of this pit, the Cowpen A pit, between the years 1794 and 1797, marked the beginning of a new era, the exploitation of the deep coals of the Blyth district. A new but short waggonway was laid to the 'Flanker' at the mouth of the river, and the whole undertaking promised great success, even though issues of mine drainage and ventilation, and in breaking into the market, seemed problematical. Nor was all well at the harbour, much to the amusement of the agents for John Hussey Delaval's rival harbour at Seaton Sluice, just 3 miles (4.8km) down the coast, for the Cowpen concern had been seeking to undermine Sir Matthew's control over the estuary. As agent John Bryers informed Delaval in September 1798:

> Sir Matthew has been pulling down some erections that the Cowpen owners had made as sluices to keep their harbours clear of sand by stopping the water back until low tide and part built on Sir Matthew's premises. He has also threatened to make them remove the sand, gravel, stones etc. that they had carried into the river, to change its bed towards their New Quay. If this is done the expence will be great, their harbour from all appearance rendered nearly useless but most likely they will get it compromised.

Bryers continued to keep Delaval informed of Blyth's problems over the next few months, of the sanding up of the harbour, of ships using Seaton Sluice in preference to Blyth – 'We got 2 ships belonging to Blyth to sea yesterday', of low water depths in the entrance channel, and so on.

Blyth's shipyards may have been particularly busy during the Napoleonic wars, for several Blyth vessels were taken by the French and would presumably have to be replaced. The *William and Frances* was taken in 1797; John Clark's *Robert* was taken in 1803 and 11 years were to pass before her surviving crew were returned home; the *Elizabeth*, the *Ceres* and the *Hesperus* were all captured during 1807. The shipyards of Hannay and Watts had not survived into the nineteenth century, and other shipbuilders came and went in the decades before and after the beginning of that century, some of them seemingly building only a few vessels before going out of business. There were three active yards at Blyth in 1804, and two of these, Messrs Davison & Co. and H&W Wright, built naval vessels; the former concern employed 36 people of whom 20 were apprentices, while the latter employed 24 and 16 respectively. Blyth's first dry dock was constructed around 1811, being operated by a builder named Stoveld (or Messrs Linskill & Co., according to Wallace); there were also two rope makers and three or four sailmakers in the town.

The Cowpen colliery concern had sunk another shaft, the Cowpen B pit, by 1804, but the concern only produced 48,000 tons in 1812, a year in which 136,206 tons of coal were imported into London from Blyth. But the Plessey pits were approaching exhaustion, output having remained at about 60,000 tons per year throughout the eighteenth century, and the Cowpen owners, presumably aware of Plessey's likely closure, now made overtures towards Ridley. They suggested that if he now closed his Plessey pits, they would offer him an interest in the Cowpen collieries in return. More pressing preoccupations may, however, have lain behind this offer of mutual co-operation, for the Surtees bank had crashed in 1803 and Ridley was an important banker in his own right. The Plessey pits had been closed down by 1813 and Ridley was then a partner in the Cowpen concern.

Another partner in the Cowpen concern was a Mr Taylor Winship of Gateshead, and he seems to have taken on the active direction of its subsequent affairs. Winship and Ridley now turned their thoughts to possible harbour improvement and they asked John Rennie, the famous Scottish engineer/architect, to report on possible schemes of improvement. Rennie and his son John (later Sir John) visited Blyth in August 1813, the year in which he was also commissioned to prepare a report on possible improvements to the Tyne. Rennie spent one day viewing the harbour at Blyth, then left his son, just turned 19 years of age, to carry out the survey. Their final report was delayed due to pressure of other work, notably on the Royal dockyards, and in the meantime, anxious to obtain some immediate practical advice, Winship sought the views of Charles Mansen, a Master Mariner from King's Lynn who had frequently used the harbour. Seemingly the North Dyke upon the rocky reef of the Coble Hole Rocks had been breached, and Mansen suggested that:

> ... the ensuing summer must be directed to the chasm of the rocks, that is to the eastward of the channel, by filling that gap up. The advantages will be that your backwater will have a free course, and with an increased rapidity towards the outward extremity of the channel that will not fail to carry away any obstructions that a continuance of strong gales from the southward has too often a tendency to throw across the entrance of the harbour. As to the west side let Dame Nature have free play, it would be dangerous to counteract her on that part.... This Sir, is my opinion, grounded upon acquaintance with Blyth, as Master for the last thirteen years, but still they are only the suggestions of a simple individual.

Rennie was far from being a 'simple individual', but he would have approved of much of Mansen's analysis, as his report and plans of October 1814 indicate. Rennie first outlined the problems inherent in the harbour. The rocky reef made getting into and out of the harbour particularly dangerous in southerly winds; stones were carried over these rocks in high seas, altering the river channel as a consequence; the entrance channel only held a 10in (25.7cm) depth at low water, even though there was 6ft (1.8m) of water at the quay; the river, whose bottom was itself rocky in part, had an insufficient flow to enable it to scour the harbour. Rennie also noted that it had been suggested to him that a direct cut might be taken through the Coble Hole Rocks to the sea, but he was not convinced of the practicality of this idea; he was aware that such had been done at Seaton Sluice, but argued that the Cut there was much longer, and better able to be defended than a similar cut at Blyth could be. To remedy Blyth's defects, he proposed that a proper pier, some 1,370 yards long, should be built on top of the Coble Hole rocks, and made large enough to permit of vessel towing; this would cost £38,015. A new and straight river channel, some 200ft (61m) wide, should be cut parallel to the new pier but 150ft (46m) from it. Stone-built groins should be built out from the sand hills on the west side towards the new channel, for these would trap silt and sand so that river water at low tide would be entirely confined to the new channel, thereby assisting scour; this channel work would cost £9,064 making total costs of about £47,000. Rennie acknowledged, however, that his plan might not be the end of the matter, and noted that a wet dock could easily be formed should trade increase sufficiently to justify one.

In fact, Rennie's plan was not even the start of the matter, for nothing was done to implement his proposals, although some deepening of the river channel was carried out at a cost of £500, the North Dyke was repaired for £956 and a ballast crane, to the design of John Rastrick of Morpeth, was erected on the south quay in 1817. Nevertheless, trade continued to grow throughout the early years of the nineteenth century, in spite of the absence of significant harbour improvements, and the frequency of the southerly winds which often prevented loaded vessels from getting out of the harbour. Little was more annoying for a ship's master than to be loaded and unable to leave and, recognising this, the Cowpen colliery proprietors provided a diversion in 1819, albeit gastronomic rather than physical:

> On account of the wind remaining some time in the south, the laden vessels could not get to sea, and several continuing to come in almost daily caused such a grand display .... A dinner was liberally given by the owners of the Cowpen colliery at Mr. Bowes' to all the Captains in the harbour, and the afternoon was spent in the most agreeable manner.

Formal dinners, no matter how agreeable, were hardly likely to encourage captains to continue to use a harbour where exit and entry were so difficult, but the colliery owners also offered a more practical solution to the problem, one which should mollify the undoubtedly fractious captains, even though it was a temporary expedient and bore no relationship to Rennie's plan:

> The owners of the Cowpen colliery, in endeavouring to obviate the inconvenience of vessels not being able to get out of Blyth in a southerly wind resolved to make an experiment with a steam boat belonging Newcastle to tow ships to sea. The boat arrived in the harbour between 7 and 8 in the morning of the 18th June, 1819. In the forenoon the *Resolution* Captain T. Hogg, coal laden, was towed as far as the outer beacon, to the great satisfaction of a great number of spectators. A brig and a sloop, both laden were towed to sea in the same style. The steamer then returned to the quay, when a party of shipowners, etc., went on board, and spent the afternoon in great conviviality.

Tugboats, developed specifically on the Tyne to deal with becalmed or wind-disadvantaged sailing colliers, were an undoubted blessing, and soon the Cowpen company bought their own tug; they also built a new ballast quay on the north side of the river in 1820 and a new stone breakwater on the Coble Hole Rocks in 1822.

Sir Matthew White Ridley was sole owner of the Cowpen collieries by 1823. There had been heavy recent expenditures on eight new ships and a new pumping engine had been acquired. But trade was not buoyant in the aftermath of the Napoleonic War and competition from the Tyne-based coal owners remained strong; the Cowpen collieries were not yet profitable. Even so, new winnings were being made by other concerns, higher upriver in the Bedlington area, as at Netherton in 1819. This colliery offered no competition to Cowpen for it produced just 32 tons of coal in that year, carrying it by carts to keels on the river Blyth. Later, in 1829, the Netherton pits utilised a waggonway to a landsale depot in the inland market town of Morpeth. Other inland collieries were shipping from the Bedlington ironworks quay, using keel transhipment to Blyth, but the need for keels militated against their profitability and their outputs remained small. A new winning was made in 1823 at 'High Cowpen', just opposite the Bedlington ironworks, but it failed within two years.

Consequently, the Cowpen Collieries continued to dominate trade at Blyth harbour and, by 1828, their vend had risen to 80,000 tons. Ridley died in 1836, and was succeeded by his son, also Sir Matthew White Ridley who, in 1840-41, gave up his direct control of the Cowpen collieries by leasing them to Messrs Carr & Jobling. The latter concern also held the rival Hartley colliery, immediately to the south of Cowpen, and they effectively became tenants of Blyth harbour, enabling them, if they so wished, to stifle the potential of the upriver pits.

John Carr (1799-1860) was to become the more important of the two partners. His father, also John (1753-1829), had developed colliery interests while acting as bailiff to the Ford estate in north Northumberland, then owned by the Delaval family of Hartley and Seaton Delaval. He and Jobling had leased Hartley colliery near Seaton Sluice in 1809, then re-opened Walker-on-Tyne colliery in 1814 and later bought Felling-on-Tyne colliery from the Brandling family. Carr also had Seghill colliery by 1823, and used the 1823 Cramlington colliery waggonway to carry Seghill coals to staiths at Howden-on Tyne. The growing demand for steam coals was about to give new life to the colliery districts of south Northumberland and although both the Cramlington and Seghill collieries had been sunk at considerable expense in the hope of finding good household coals, their failure in this respect was soon to be matched by success in the steam coal trade. After his father's death John Carr inherited, extended and developed his colliery interests by taking in the Cowpen pit, and also the north Northumberland pits of Scremerston and Shoreswood. In 1839, impatient with the problems of being confined to using the Cramlington company's waggonway to the Tyne, he built his own line from Seghill to Howden-on-Tyne. Although Carr & Jobling had taken the Cowpen royalty in 1840-41, they did not exploit it until after 1849, when the Isabella pit was sunk. Probably in recognition of the limitations of Blyth harbour, Carr & Jobling now embarked on a more ambitious railway scheme, a line which would run between the Blyth and the Tyne. Such a line would enable them, if they wished, to ship all the coals of their Cowpen, Bedlington, Netherton, Bedlington Glebe and Hartley collieries, from staiths near the Low Lights, North Shields, bypassing Blyth and Seaton Sluice altogether. Carr & Jobling began to construct a part of this line in 1845 and by 1846-7 the line was opened from Cowpen to Seaton Sluice and on to a junction with the Seghill railway to the Tyne. This was the genesis of the Blyth & Tyne Railway and potentially the nemesis of the harbours of Blyth and Seaton Sluice, for even the unimproved Tyne offered much deeper water.

Jobling had left the partnership in 1847, but the concern was continued by a partnership which included at least five members of the Carr family. The new company was now shipping from the Blyth, the Tyne and from Seaton Sluice, but other coal owners were not so fortunate in the availability of outlets. Bedlington colliery had reached rich seams of coal in the 1830s, but its owners found it difficult to gain a good outlet on the Blyth. At first, they loaded keels at the ironworks quay, the coals to be transferred into waiting brigs near the river mouth, but by 1841 the Bedlington coal owners had built a railway to a staith at Sleekburn Gut, on the north side of the river Blyth opposite Cowpen; however, only the smallest of colliers could reach it. The Bedlington proprietors then conceived of a novel scheme to overcome this problem, as well as the unaccommodating attitudes of the Cowpen collieries in their dominance of Blyth harbour. They sought to gain access to the larger Tyne-served colliers, and the Tyne's deeper water, not by rail as Carr & Jobling had done, but by sea.

The SS *Bedlington*, built for the Bedlington colliery owners at T.D. Marshall's yard at South Shields, was a steam-powered, screw-propelled, water-ballasted container vessel, specially designed to carry loaded waggons of coal, 40 at a time, from the Blyth to the Tyne at Shields. It was launched in 1841 and had cost near £5,000. Its deck was a totally open hatchway and the hold beneath was fitted with three sets of rails to support coal waggons which could be lowered and raised by a derrick powered from the ship's main crankshaft. This novel vessel seems to have had constant maintenance problems when in service, and she suffered severe damage at Blyth in 1846 on becoming grounded while fully laden, just as she was leaving the staith. The Bedlington Coal Company did not feel it prudent to finance its repair for further use, perhaps influenced in their decision by the partial removal of coal export duties in 1845, for this concession, and the complete removal of duties in 1850, offered the potential for all collieries in the area to re-establish a foreign trade from Blyth. Moreover, the now fast-growing demand for steam coals, with which the area was well favoured, threw open more new markets for all the collieries of the district; the future now lay less in direct competition and blocking tactics between coal owners, and more in co-operation and amalgamation. The Cowpen concern, still effectively controlling Blyth harbour, seems to have been aware of the new opportunities, for they allowed the Bedlington company to construct a rail link to the Blyth & Tyne Railway at Newsham in 1850, thereby enabling Bedlington coals to be shipped from the Tyne but not from the Blyth, although the latter restriction was more of an indication of the inadequacy of Blyth's shipping facilities than a demonstration of ongoing competition; this line required a large timber viaduct over the river Blyth, designed by Robert Nicholson, which cost some £26,000. Now redundant, the *Bedlington* was patched up and offered for sale in 1851, being bought by a Scottish concern who rebuilt it as a ferry for the Firth of Forth. In 1854, however, it was requisitioned to sail to the Baltic, but was sunk by the Russians just before the official outbreak of the Crimean War.

It must have been apparent to all by the early 1850s, that Blyth harbour was failing to fulfil its potential, and that it could neither satisfy the needs of local ship and coal owners, nor the anticipated expansion of the local coal trade; some Netherton coals, for example, were now being shipped from the river Wear, while the Blyth & Tyne Railway carried much of the district's coal to the Tyne. About 1,200 ships were still entering the harbour each year, in addition to the 14 keels and four steamboats, presumably tugs, permanently based there, but saturation point had been reached in coal handling capacity. Yet, with the incorporation of the Blyth & Tyne Railway as a public railway in 1852, Blyth was now, at least in theory, an open port and at last, in an attempt to progress the situation, it was resolved to form a public dock company. A prospectus was drawn up for the Blyth Harbour Docks & Railway Company in 1853, to be established by an Act of Parliament. The company's appointed engineer was to be James Abernethy of London, a man who had previously carried out work at Aberdeen and Silloth harbours, and whose initial assessment of the situation at Blyth echoed the earlier one of Rennie. Abernethy noted that the river channel, some 4,500ft (1,373m) in length, was extremely tortuous and dry at Spring tides in many places; it was exposed to the direct action of north-easterly seas so that hardly a winter passed without vessels being stranded and wrecked on the beach on the southern side of the river; the estuary within the river mouth, which actually formed the harbour, was exposed to the run of the sea during onshore gales. The new company's prospectus went on to note that it was often necessary to load colliers from keels outside the harbour, and that much of the area's coal was being taken to the Tyne for shipment. It was argued, however, that the new company would redress this situation by creating a harbour at Blyth capable of taking vessels of 1,000 tons burthen, according to Abernethy's designs. His objectives were to provide protection to ships entering and departing the river; to confine and direct the outgoing current at low tide thereby increasing its scouring power; and to prolong the outgoing current seaward so that river-borne detritus would be carried out to sea. In all, this was rather similar to Rennie's plan of 30 years earlier, as Sir John Rennie was to point out to the Institution of Civil Engineers in 1862!

Abernethy's plans, based on his experiences at Aberdeen harbour, involved the building of breakwaters, the formation of wet docks and the deepening of the channel. There would be an outer half-tide basin of 7 acres (2.8ha) leading to an inner dock of 25.5 acres (10.3ha), and a graving dock accessible from the basin; the improved harbour would be able to ship 750,000 tons of coal per annum. In addition, new railway links would be made from the dock to the Blyth & Tyne Railway, to Hartley and to Cramlington. All this could be achieved, according to Abernethy, for £150,000, to be raised in £20 shares; the first Bill was rejected by Parliament after strong opposition from Lord Hastings, proprietor of the neighbouring but declining Hartley harbour at Seaton Sluice, but another Bill successfully gained the Royal Assent in 1854 and Sir Matthew White Ridley was installed as the company's first chairman.

Another Act was obtained in 1858 which gave the company jurisdiction as far upriver as Bedlington, a move which may have been spurred by a desire to assist the ailing Bedlington ironworks, whose decline had occurred quite suddenly after decades of considerable success and growth. The works had been able to profit from the growth in shipbuilding at Blyth during the second half of the eighteenth century, for the yards generated a considerable demand for nails, chains, anchors etc. The ironworks had come under the control of a London-based company, Gordon & Biddulph in 1809, and was placed, then or a little later, under the management of Michael Longridge, nephew of the previous co-owner. Longridge had close friendships with George and Robert Stephenson, and it is therefore hardly surprising that the Bedlington ironworks should become involved in the railway revolution. The ironworks made boiler plates, axles and wheels for George Stephenson's first locomotive in 1814, and a succession of orders for locomotive parts were to follow. By producing the first successful wrought-iron (malleable iron) rails, as patented in 1820 by the works' agent John Birkinshaw, the concern was able to capitalise on the spread of the national railway system. Although wrought-iron rails had been used earlier on the Tindale Fell waggonway in east Cumberland, their employment on a 2-mile line (3.2km) between a coal mine at Choppington and the ironworks in 1821, provided an important test bed for railway track engineering of the future. Bedlington rails were used for the Stockton & Darlington Railway of 1825 and the Liverpool & Manchester Railway of 1830; George Stephenson was company engineer to both of these railway concerns and their projection and progress were to have profound influence on the subsequent promotion of railways throughout the kingdom and elsewhere.

Indeed Michael Longridge was one of the original partners in Robert Stephenson & Co., the world's first locomotive building works, established in Forth Street, Newcastle, in 1823. For a while, in the absence of the Stephensons, Longridge acted as general manager at Forth Street, but he announced his intention to commence locomotive manufacture at Bedlington in 1836, a move which caused no little consternation at Forth Street where he was still acting as finance manager. Robert Stephenson, admitting that the Forth Street works were only performing 'tolerably well', considered handing the whole affair over to the Bedlington concern, but ultimately decided not to do so. Longridge, however, went ahead with his plan, and began building locomotives at Bedlington under 'Longridge & Co.' in 1837, while remaining a partner in the Forth Street

44 Part of the Bedlington ironworks in 1827

company until 1842. That the Stephensons and Longridge did not fall out over the matter is instanced by the fact that George continued to correspond with Longridge until the last months of his (George's) life.

The first locomotive from the new works, the *Michael Longridge*, was supplied to the Stanhope & Tyne Railroad, for which Robert Stephenson was the engineer; the first train to run from King's Cross was hauled by a Bedlington locomotive, as were the first railway services in Holland and Italy. It is probable, however, that these locomotives were shipped from the Tyne rather than the Blyth. To gain greater control over their supplies of raw materials, Longridge & Co. established Barrington colliery in 1840, and erected blast furnaces at Bedlington in 1849 and 1854, on or near the old Malings' site. Here they smelted a mixture of local and Cleveland coast ores, the latter presumably brought by sea to Blyth harbour for keel transhipment. By 1850, the year in which Longridge acquired sole ownership of the Bedlington works, it had reached, or possibly passed, the height of its importance. Having no rail connection to the region's main line system, and no easy access to deep water, the chances of continued prosperity must have looked shaky when compared with the better situations of rival concerns. Michael Longridge retired from the works in 1853 and it was offered for sale in that year. There were to be three more owners of the works, including Messrs Mounsey & Dixon; the latter partner, John Dixon, being a member of the famous Dixon family of Cockfield, one of whom, a Jeremiah, gave his name to the Mason-Dixon line in the USA, while John himself was to be responsible for bringing Cleopatra's needle from Alexandria to London and erecting it on the Thames embankment. The last owners of the Bedlington ironworks were the Bedlington Coal Company who finally closed it down in 1867. Better access to navigable water would undoubtedly have helped the works to survive profitably, and this may have been in the minds of the Blyth Dock Company's directors in going for their 1858 Act, for jurisdiction over the river up to Bedlington at least offered the possibility of a longer navigable river.

But it was not to be, for the Dock Company soon experienced financial difficulties. Work had begun on Abernethy's 1853 plan, but progress on the eastern breakwater was soon threatened; there were problems in obtaining suitable stone, and consequently the design was changed so that it might be constructed of creosoted timber with rubble infill. About 900 yards of the breakwater had been completed by 1857 and a timber training jetty appears to have been constructed. By 1862, the company had purchased and removed the old Bishop's quay and built a new one, they had carried out some dredging, and performed extensive works on the eastern breakwater and west jetty but, with only £48,000 of their authorised capital left, they had not even begun work on the basin and dock. Moreover, coal shipments remained stubbornly static at around 250,000 tons per year, mainly going to French and Baltic ports while, in contrast, the Blyth & Tyne Railway carried more than 1.5 million tons of coal for export from the Tyne in 1860. Amongst new colliery concerns now using the Blyth & Tyne Railway were the owners of the nearby Ashington collieries, later to be the major users of Blyth harbour, but sending their coals to the Tyne and the Wear rather than the Blyth in 1860.

Given the vast amounts of coal now being raised in a district for which the Blyth should have been the natural outlet, the harbour's potential could not have been more obvious to the dock company's directors, yet they seemed quite impotent. Although they obtained another Act in 1860, one which gave them additional powers including the privilege to operate ferryboats across the river, the company continued to suffer serious financial and operational embarrassments; all attempts to prevent the accumulation of sand at the harbour entrance were failing and copper-bottomed ships would no longer enter for fear of grounding. The directors had now spent almost their entire capital, but without significant improvements to the entrance channel the coal trade, and therefore the company's income, could only remain stagnant. It was time for a change of direction, and that meant a change of engineer.

The directors terminated Abernethy's appointment in 1862 and put Thomas Meik, engineer to the river Wear Commissioners and later to the commissioners for Warkworth harbour, in his place. Coal shipments slowly increased after Meik's appointment, but there was never sufficient capital to implement his many proposals. Complaints from shipowners continued to flood in, with requests for reductions in harbour dues because of the poor state of the shipping berths and eventually, in 1866/7, the directors were persuaded to purchase their own dredger, a wise move for the only immediate solution to their major problem, of insufficient water depth in the harbour, was dredging and yet more dredging. It was perhaps in anticipation of deeper water following this acquisition, that the Cowpen Coal Company, owned by Messrs Straker & Co. since the Carrs great losses consequent on the failure of the Northumberland & Durham District Bank in 1857, were led to purchase the *Weardale*, the first iron-built screw collier to work out of Blyth. The Cowpen Company were also busy with a new winning at Cambois, and that colliery's first coals were shipped from the north side in 1867.

The dredger soon began to pay its way, and it enabled the company to build some new staiths on the north side, but it was too little and almost too late, for the directors were running against the tide and blindly into trouble, failing especially to see that the days of the sailing collier were numbered. Ship ownership at Blyth had risen from 132 in 1854, to 201 in 1874, but there was then a fall in numbers as steam power took over from sail. Unless urgent action was taken soon, Blyth's trade was bound to fall, for even with the ongoing dredging, the larger steamships would not find sufficient water to load at Blyth. Meik realised the seriousness of the situation and, now based in Edinburgh, he reported to the directors in 1877:

> We beg to bring before you our opinion of the present state of trade and the general condition of the harbour. And our opinion stated briefly is that Blyth is now at a crisis in its history and unless a move is made forward it must inevitably go back. When an improvement takes place in the general trade of the Country, Blyth instead of sharing in it, will be left out in the cold while neighbouring Ports will profit by its loss. The trade of your Port has hitherto been largely dependant [sic] on the shipping owned in itself, and now that this is generally on the decrease there is an absolute necessity for encouraging a trade from elsewhere. Should you consider the subject worthy of your consideration at the present time, we should be prepared to go further into detail, meantime we think we have said enough.

This warning could not have been clearer, yet it went unheeded; what actually followed was inaction. Matthew White Ridley died in 1878 and was succeeded by his son, also Matthew White Ridley. He candidly informed his fellow directors that he knew little about the business, and that he was happy that they should decide whether it was, therefore, appropriate for him to succeed his late father as their chairman. It was an offer made with magnanimity and, it seems, proper honesty, but in their wisdom the directors promptly appointed him to the chair. The first action taken under Ridley's chairmanship appears to have been an attempt to restart a fishing industry at Blyth, but even this modest objective failed; the company appears to have been in inexorable decline. Meanwhile, the Blyth & Tyne Railway company had been extending its sphere of influence in south-east Northumberland, not just in coal-carrying but in passenger traffic as well. Eventually, however, in 1874, the company succumbed to the all-powerful NER and eventually the railway company became the real driving force behind harbour development at Blyth; but that still lay in the future.

Meik & Son knew that the prospects for Blyth harbour were deteriorating fast by June 1881; only 181,000 tons of coal had been shipped in that year, compared with 343,000 tons in 1873. However, an agreement had been made with the NER in the previous year, enabling the railway company to construct, at their own expense, a new deep-water quay with two coaling staiths on the south side of the river, but Meik was worried that the Dock Company would be unable to profit from collaboration with the NER unless further steps were taken to improve the harbour. In seeking to alert the directors to the problems, he pointed out that there was only 3 or 4ft (0.9 or 1.2m) of water at the bar, and that while ships of 1,000 tons could still get in and out of the harbour, vessels of 2,000 tons were now becoming the norm in the coal trade; the implication was that the larger vessels would not even attempt to cross the bar. Meik argued that matters and the director's attitudes must change if the NER was to be persuaded to continue its interest in Blyth. He warned the directors that:

> These increased facilities [the NER's] will however only make more apparent the chief drawback to Blyth as a port for regular and constant trade – we allude to the want of water on the bar and in the channel. The channel can easily be improved by dredging, but it is useless doing this until means are taken to obtain the same depth at the bar. As you are well aware, this can only be done by lengthening the East pier and building a new West Breakwater. These works will entail a considerable expenditure and it is the best method of meeting it that is the subject we now submit for your consideration. As a private Company you are not in the best position for raising money advantageously ... we wish you to consider whether in doing so you should not take steps for dissolving the Company and handing over the undertaking to a Public Harbour Trust or Commission, consisting of representatives of the different interests involved. The advantages of following such a course will be that you can follow the example of the Tyne, Wear, Tees, and other Harbour Trusts in borrowing money at a low rate of interest from the Public Works Loan Commissioners.

This time Meik's advice seems to have been accepted, and a Bill to establish the Blyth Harbour Commissioners received the Royal Assent in 1882, but almost the first act of the new commissioners, chaired of course by Matthew White Ridley, was to replace their engineer. They now turned, as several other harbour authorities in Northumberland were to turn, to J. Watt Sandeman of Newcastle, and with the NER urging further improvements, presumably supported by Matthew White Ridley who was also on the NER board, developments were now to be fast and furious. By 1884, the NER had constructed 1,100ft (336m) of staiths at Low Quay, a new dredger had been bought, the entrance channel had been improved and a ridge of rock in mid harbour removed. A new west breakwater, 2,470ft (753m) in length, was completed by 1885; the east breakwater had been extended 300ft (92m) in mass concrete by 1886 to minimise bar formation in the channel; in the following year a new channel, some 4,000ft (1220m) in length, and with a depth of 10ft (3m) at low water, was dredged about 210ft (64m) to the west of the old channel; in the same year the 1788 lighthouse was raised some 14ft (4.3m) to make it visible above the new staiths. The Ashington Coal Company was provided with easier rail access to the harbour in 1888, thereby obviating the previously circuitous route from its collieries to Blyth. At long last Blyth had a harbour worthy of the name, and good rail links direct to the collieries which sought to use it.

The town of Blyth had also been developing fast, and associated industries were expanding. Salt manufacture had ceased in 1875, but shipbuilding, ropemaking and sailmaking were all being actively pursued, and glass bottles had been made at Cowpen Quay since 1868. There were now two shipyards in the harbour area, a large dry dock capable of taking vessels up to 3,500 tons register and a floating dock for the repair of vessels up to 300 tons burthen. Wooden ships had been built at Blyth since Hannay's time, and the quality of the brigantines built by the Blyth yards was highly regarded, but wooden ships were giving way to vessels built of iron by the 1870s, and the last wooden ship was launched at Blyth in 1873-4. Blyth's first attempt at iron shipbuilding began c.1878, and although that venture soon failed, Hodgson & Soulsby, formerly wooden shipbuilders, had more success with the transition, launching two iron hoppers for the Russian government in 1880. Then the Blyth Iron Shipbuilding Co. was formed in 1883, aiming to take advantage of the promise of deep water following the establishment of the Blyth Harbour Commission. This company took over Hodgson & Soulsby's yard and added another dry dock in 1897; known later as the Cowpen Dry Docks and Shipbuilding Company, they eventually operated six shipbuilding berths at Blyth and in 1914 built Britain's first aircraft carrier, the HMS *Ark Royal*; it carried seaplanes which were lifted on and off the boat by steam-powered cranes. Blyth now had two lifeboat stations, one on either side of the river.

Blyth's municipal development was also obvious. A gas works had been established in 1852 and a waterworks just two years later. A new catholic church had been built in 1861 and a new parish church in 1885. The nonconformist societies were, of course, well represented – John Wesley had first visited Plessey in 1743. A Methodist New Connexion chapel of 1818 had been replaced by another in 1864; a Wesleyan Methodist chapel of 1815 was replaced in 1867, and a Presbyterian church in 1877; there were also Congregational, Primitive Methodist, United Free Methodist and Salvation societies by 1887. A Mechanics Institution had been established in 1847, but a new building was provided in

45 Blyth High Light, 1978

1881-2, with the Thomas Knight Memorial Hospital alongside. Not surprisingly, the town had its own brewery and various manufactories, whilst among its citizens it boasted a botanist, five consuls, numerous master mariners and pilots; the 'Coban, Cognac, Crane, Creole, Phoenix & Sancho Shipping Cos. Ltd' had a base there and John Fraser was publishing the *Blyth and Tyneside Comic Almanac.*

Coal shipments had reached 1 million tons by 1887; the harbour improvements, the continued support of the NER, the expansion of the Ashington coalfield and a pricing policy which made shipment from Blyth cheaper than from the Tyne, all contributed to this late-in-the-day success story. The commissioners, with their new-found vigour but still prompted by the NER, did not stand still, and improvements continued apace. Two additional coal staiths were constructed by the NER on the south side to the east of Low Quay in 1888 and in 1896, with new collieries being sunk to the north of the river, the harbour was enlarged and deepened and four additional coal staiths erected by the NER on the north side. The entrance channel was further widened and deepened in 1898, to give 16ft (4.9m) at low water, and a new 'South Harbour' with some 23 acres (9.3ha)

46 Loading a collier at the Blyth North Side Staiths, October 1972

47 The harbour ferry boat and part of the Blyth North Side Staiths, October 1972

of deep water, 30–38.5ft (9.15 to 11.7m) at high tide, was opened in 1899 to accommodate the growing number of ships seeking to use the harbour; this new harbour area was provided with wharves, cranes and railway connections to encourage general trade. The harbour area now totalled about 83 acres (33.6ha) of deep water and it was capable of holding over 100 large steamships, with vessels of up to 10,000 tons capacity capable of being accommodated. The change from the situation only 20 years earlier was astonishing, for the harbour area had only been about 25 acres (10.1ha) in extent in 1880, and could only accommodate about 40 small sailing vessels; most of harbour dried out at low water at that time, and even the channel to the sea would be frequently shoaled.

The timber and rubble section of the 1857 eastern breakwater was encased in concrete in 1907, extended by 900ft (275m) and provided with a timber superstructure and lighthouse in the following year. Nearly 3,000 ships used the harbour in 1909 and coal shipments from its ten staiths reached 4 million tons; the Bedlington Bomarsund pit had recently opened (1905), and Newbiggin colliery to the north (1911) was soon to add its output to Blyth's coal trade.

The Port of Blyth Fishing Co. was formed in 1912, with the intention of engaging in the herring and white fish industries, but the time was not propitious for such a venture, for with the outbreak of war in 1914, the company's vessels were requisitioned by the Government, along with their curing houses; the ice plant was dismantled and its machinery sold off as the site was developed as a submarine base; insufficient plant remained to justify the company in recommencing business when the war ended. There were also some organisational changes in 1912, as a result of agitation by coal owners who were seeking to reduce (the second) Viscount Ridley's power on the commission, by increasing their own representation. The coal owners argued that the number of commissioners should be increased from 13 to 20, and compromise was achieved through a new Act which allowed for 19 commissioners, but with an increased coal owner representation.

The new Act also authorised more new works, with a new timber jetty, the West Blyth Staiths, to be financed jointly by the commissioners and the NER; the west pier would also be replaced, and new dock offices would be built. Lastly, more dredging would be undertaken to give a depth of 24ft (7.3m) at low water throughout the harbour and at the bar, which would necessitate the removal of 500,000 cubic yards of rock. Blyth was now handling nearly half of Northumberland's coal shipments, and the commissioners had seen their revenues rise from £1,000 to £71,000 per annum. The new commissioners' offices were opened in 1913, but the outbreak of war curtailed progress on the other intended new works, and these were not completed until well after the war had ended,

48 Blyth harbour West Staith at centre, the power station to its left, and the tugs *Tynesider* and *Hillsider* at Bates Wharf on the extreme left. *M.R. Longbottom, 1969*

49 Blyth Power Station and the majestic West Staith, 1974

50 Loading a collier at Bates Wharf, Blyth, October 1972

the new West Staiths, for example, some 1,600ft (488m) long, opening in 1928. Coal exports continued to expand after the war as the Ashington Coal Company became the largest shipper of coal from the harbour, its four pits producing some 14,000 tons per day by 1929. The opening of the Ashington Coal Company's Lynemouth colliery c.1930, brought even more coal to the staiths on the north side of the harbour and the opening of the Cowpen Coal Company's Bates pit, just by the southern edge of a deep-water area of the upper harbour, led to the erection of two more south-side staiths in 1934. These developments led to total coal shipments in excess of 6 million tons in the years 1934-37.

At the nationalisation of both the coal and railway industries in 1947, the Cowpen collieries' staiths passed to the National Coal Board while the railway-owned staiths (the North, South and West) went to British Railways. Coal shipments continued to remain high, reaching an all-time record for the harbour in 1961, when 6,889,317 tons of coal were shipped; that figure made Blyth the largest coal shipping port in Europe. But this was Blyth's high-water mark and coal shipments were to decline thereafter, not just through pit closures. Blyth

51 Bates Wharf and the power station, Blyth, July 1975

'A' power station had opened in 1958, burning coal which would otherwise have been shipped from the harbour, and Blyth 'B' station opened in 1962. The South Staiths closed just two years later, when coal shipments had fallen to 5.2 million tons; a general cargo quay was created on the site formerly occupied by the staiths. Then Cowpen North Staith closed in 1968. The Blyth Dry Docks & Shipbuilding Co. finally shut its gates in 1966, and the dry docks stood empty for three years before the commissioners filled in part of the yard to provide warehouses and made over the two remaining docks to insulation specialists Gregsons, who closed down in March 1975 after 15 months in the hands of the Receiver.

This period coincided with the construction of the Alcan aluminium smelter at Lynemouth, just 5 miles (8km) or so to the north of Blyth which, when it commenced production in 1972, siphoned off more of the port's coal trade, for Lynemouth colliery's output now went direct to the smelter's power station. However, the importation of the bauxite needed by Alcan brought a new trade to the harbour, and the North Staith area was developed as a bauxite handling facility with a deep-water berth capable of accommodating 22,500-ton, 32ft (9.8m) draft vessels. But the tonnages involved in bringing bauxite in and shipping aluminium products out, and also considerable paper imports, in no way compensated for the losses in the coal trade. Even the switch to Blyth in 1969, of coals previously shipped from Amble, failed to stem the inevitable decline in coal shipments. Coal exports continued to dominate Blyth's trade, however, even in their decline, for although they had fallen to 1.8 million tons by 1974, the total export and import trade for that year was only 2.2 million tons. Coal shipments stayed at about that level until the miners' strike of 1984-5 and, as pit closures were accelerated thereafter, Blyth's coal trade was further imperilled, especially with the closure of Bates Pit in 1987. However, a new £2.6 million project was launched in 1991 to transport millions of tons of opencast coal by rail to an upgraded Bates' staith, for shipment to power stations on the Thames.

Curiously, after two false starts, Blyth's fishing industry became quite brisk in the 1960s, and it had a fleet of cobles and two seine netters in the 1970s, although the ups and downs of the fishing industry have affected Blyth as much as anywhere else. In addition, an old Blyth trade returned. Hughes Bolckow established a shipbreaking yard, the so-called 'Battleship Wharf', on the north side of the harbour in 1910, which included a shop for the sale of salvaged furniture, fittings

52 *Opposite above* Aerial view of Blyth harbour in 1969, looking towards the entrance channel. The sinuous North Side Staith partly defines the channel, the settlement of North Blyth lying between the staith and the sea. A collier is approaching the Cowpen South Staith (Bates Wharf) and opposite this wharf is the shipbreaking yard of Hughes Bolckow. *M.R. Longbottom*

53 *Opposite below* Aerial view of Blyth harbour in 1969, looking upriver. Dry docks at centre bottom, the North Side Staith and North Blyth to the right. The railway-owned West Staith projects into the harbour just to the right of Blyth Power Station. *M.R. Longbottom*

54 The Alcan bauxite terminal, Blyth, July 1974

and timber. Although it closed in 1970s, it was re-opened in 1990 by Andover Marine whose first orders were for the breaking up of Russian submarines – Blyth's advantage from the peace dividend. There have been many other proposed developments within the harbour area, typical of the 1990's, such as plans for a multi-million pound housing and leisure complex for the harbour side.

As the oldest surviving coal-fired plant in the country, Blyth's 1965 power station was decommissioned in April 2000 and its subsequent demolition was completed when its massive chimneys were demolished at noon 7 December 2003. But that was not the end of electricity generation by the harbour, for nine wind turbines were stationed on the 100-year-old east pier in 1992 and more recently, in December 2002, Blyth played host to the UK's first offshore wind farm, with two wind turbines erected just offshore from the harbour. At the time of writing, Blyth harbour is undergoing a £5 million investment programme, involving a major redevelopment of the old Battleship Wharf site, which will be dominated by a huge crane to enable the port to handle heavy metal products and allow rapid handling of bulk materials. This follows on from considerable investment in Ro-Ro provision and the construction, on an 11-acre (4.5ha) site formerly occupied by a shipyard, of a large centre for offshore technology, complete with a wet test facility and direct access to a secure, deep-water quay.

Three former dry-docks have been refurbished and marine features such as seabeds added, together with the largest commercial wave machine in the UK; not even John Rennie had thought of that. But the port also handles day-to-day cargoes, large quantities of bauxite for Lynemouth, but also forest products, grain and stone etc. – it is very much a jobbing port. And Blyth has not forgotten its past, for that has been celebrated through a rediscovered enthusiasm, now common throughout the North East, for public works of art, with a 50ft (15.3m) high artwork the 'Spirit of the Staiths' overlooking the harbour.

11

Seaton Sluice (Hartley) harbour

Sir John ... has cut through a solid and hard rock a new entrance to his harbour ... this great work he did at his own private expense, which no person has any share or concern in but himself ... These works ... afford Sir John the means of constantly supporting several hundred people who live upon his estate in honest industry, in which he and Lady Hussey Delaval take great delight. (Hutchinson, 1776)

Just over 2 miles (3.2km) of sandy beaches, low-lying dunes and links separate Blyth harbour from Hartley harbour at the mouth of the Seaton burn to the south; the sandy and shingley beaches to the immediate south of the mouth of the burn are fringed by cliffs of modest height. The Seaton Burn, finally flowing northwards, into the sea through the village of Seaton Sluice, was once the scene of very considerable industrial enterprise, such that the creation of Hartley harbour, or 'Seaton Sluice' as it became known, was one of the most interesting port developments on the Northumberland coast in the seventeenth and eighteenth centuries. It was the creation of the Delaval family of Seaton Delaval, initially to better serve their coal and salt industries, but later to accommodate a wider range of industrial enterprises. However, the mouth of the Seaton burn had long served as a natural haven for fishermen and others before any harbour improvement works were carried out.

The early history of Hartley's ownership is complex, but suffice it to say that Gilbert Delaval of Seaton Delaval had acquired a moiety in the adjacent Hartley lands by c.1219, probably consisting of about 100 acres (40ha), a coal mine and some cottages; the Middleton family held the other moiety from c.1242 and this included a windmill by 1283. The township would appear to have been quite prosperous by the end of the thirteenth century, with a fishery, for which the lord of the manor provided boats in return for payment in kind, a coal mine and some salt pans; one Adam the Miller 'paid' a pair of white gloves and a penny each Easter as rent for his salt pan at Hartley. The ancient name for the settlement at the mouth of the Seaton Burn is, indeed, 'Hartley Pans', but whether this appellation dates from the thirteenth century or a later period, has not been determined.

The manorial system remained in full sway in the early part of the sixteenth century; the maintenance of the fishing cobles was enforced by the manor court, limitations were put on catches, and the division of the haul between the coble masters and the lord of the manor was regulated; the playing of football was prohibited in 1500, and the sale of beer was restricted to licensed brewers. Lands in Hartley were held by four families, including the Delavals, by the middle of the sixteenth century, but also by the Crown from the time of the dissolution. Much of the township was, however, being leased to the Delavals, and Robert Delaval was able to effectively annex the manor of Hartley to that of his manor of Seaton Delaval by buying out all of the freeholders between 1574-77; Hartley remained with the Delavals from that time until early in the nineteenth century. Robert Delaval, as lord of the manor, seems to have begun a weakening of the manorial system at Hartley in 1576/7, when he first leased out his cobleshare, except that part needed for his own house provisions, and then leased out the fishing itself.

This change in the organisation of Hartley's fishing activities seems to have borne fruit, for there were some 18 resident fishermen at Hartley in 1626, and only Spittal, Holy Island and North Shields with Tynemouth, could boast larger numbers of fishermen on the Northumberland coast at that time. The salt industry was still in evidence – a natural corollary of a coastal location with shallow coal and a fishing fleet. Moreover, Sir John Delaval's salt was to gain a considerable reputation the sixteenth century, it being said to be:

> ... esteamed by sutche as buye the same to be better than any other white salt, and to be as good as baye-salt or as salt upon salt.

This may have encouraged others to make salt at the same place and five salt pan owners were based at Hartley by 1600, but the haven was unsuitable for coastal and foreign shipping and consequently salt for export had to be carried a few miles overland to Blyth for shipment. The high value per unit weight of salt, when compared with the low value of coal, for example, made such overland transport a perfectly viable economic proposition. However, it was not always a straightforward affair, for a trespass dispute arose in the early seventeenth century which involved the cutting of ditches across the way, the removal of shoreline beacons, and near hand-to-hand fighting, before recourse to the law prevailed.

Coal was the spur to Hartley's subsequent development. A number of productive seams either outcropped, or were to be found at shallow depth in its vicinity, and it is not therefore surprising that coal winning in the district dates back at least to 1291. However, with its own haven unsuited to coal shipping, and Blyth too far away to make the overland carriage of coal economical,

Hartley's coals remained restricted to purely local and mainly domestic markets. Clearly both the salt and coal trades would benefit if Hartley haven could be made accessible to seagoing vessels, yet it was not until *c*.1670 (some authorities claim 1660 which could be correct while others claim 1680 which can not be correct) that a serious attempt was made to improve the haven at the mouth of the Seaton burn. The burn, running north-east towards Hartley, turned due east within a few hundred yards of the shoreline but then, obstructed by a rocky headland, it was forced to enter the sea in a north-west direction. Herein lay the problem, for the mouth of the burn was very exposed, and its approach from the sea was oblique, making it difficult for ships to enter; moreover it offered little space in which to tie up. In an attempt to improve matters, Sir Ralph Delaval decided to have a pier constructed at the mouth of the burn on its east side, to protect the haven from the north-east. According to near-contemporary accounts the first attempted pier was constructed of squared stone, laid dry and without clamps. Perhaps not surprisingly, this pier did not survive its first real test, and neither did its successor, even though its stones were cemented with the best hard-lime cement. The third pier, which was certainly completed before 1676, utilised the same stones, but each was now dovetailed to its neighbour, both horizontally and vertically, with pegs of heart of oak. Now, even if the strongest waves lifted the stones, they would sink down again into their original places. Soon, however, a new problem arose, for the haven began to silt up, probably because the pier was slowing down the movement of river-borne silts which were formerly discharged into the sea as the tide ebbed, but were now being deposited, along with sand washed in at high tide, within the haven. Sir Francis North was probably the first visitor to record Sir Ralph's method of dealing with the problem, whereby he arranged for the harbour to be scoured by low tide releases of river and high-tide water which had been dammed behind a sluice at high tide. Having visited Seaton Delaval in 1676, North discussed the earlier problems with the piers, and the eventual solution, but noted that:

> … another inconvenience, was to be fought with and that was the sand silting up his harbour every tide, for that he had the opportunity of a rill of water which ran downe from the hill, and had excavated for itself a channell, this water issued at his port but had not force enough to clear the rock from the sand which the tide had left, therefore he built Sluice Gates cross the hill, which being shutt at flood made a collection of Backwater, and then at low Ebb he let all goe at once, and that scoured his rock, and made it as bare as a trencher: And for the Incouragement of this work and the workmen King Charles 2 Made Sir R D the collector of the Customes of his owne port, without being subject to the Custome hous officers at Newcastle.

The sluice, situated somewhere near the present road bridge across the burn, appears to have been semi-automatic, opening as the tide flowed, closing as it ebbed, and being then opened manually at low tide after horse ploughing of the

55 The old river-harbour at Seaton Sluice as it runs into the North Sea, its piers and quays derelict, with the old harbour entrance to the Cut at extreme bottom right, possibly in the 1930s

sand and silt below the sluice; and so the name 'Seaton Sluice' came about. This sluicing system came to be admired by many visitors to the area, not least by the great eighteenth-century engineer John Smeaton.

Previous to these improvements, Hartley had been annexed to the port of Newcastle in 1670, and placed under the control of the Custom House officers at Blyth, one of whom resided at Hartley, but as Francis North indicated, the £7,000 which Sir Ralph had spent on the harbour works which were needed to enable him to export salt, coal and grindstones from Hartley, had persuaded Charles II to make him collector and surveyor of his own port. No doubt encouraged by this development, Sir Ralph then seems to have built a second pier, presumably on the west side of the burn, having been offered a £1,500 grant towards its construction by King Charles; one third of this grant had been paid at the time of Charles' death in 1685, but the remainder was never forthcoming. The harbour was further protected, but from man rather than nature, by the provision of a battery to guard against possible French or Dutch sea attacks. This was useful on at least one occasion when, in 1667, a Dutch privateer gave chase to a small vessel carrying merchandise which headed for the safety of Seaton Sluice. Sir Ralph

56 The old river-harbour at Seaton Sluice looking upriver; the sluice gates were located near the modern road bridge; photograph probably taken in the 1970s

sent two boats out to escort her in, and at the same time fired warning shots over or perhaps through the privateer's bows.

Some 14 vessels used the harbour in 1685 and 56 cargoes, mainly of coal but some of salt, were shipped in that year. But the Delaval estates around Hartley were in a parlous state, a condition which Sir Ralph attempted to rectify by making advantageous marriage arrangements for his sons; even so he was widely praised as an entrepreneur at his death in 1691. Sir Ralph's personal estate went to pay off his creditors, while Seaton Delaval and Hartley passed to his widow and subsequently to his son, Sir John Delaval. The tidal harbour was still far from ideal, sometimes possessing insufficient water for the complete loading of collier brigs within its waters, recourse having to be made to completing their full cargo at sea direct from keels. This situation was described by Greenville Collins in 1698:

> Seaton Sluce ... is a tide haven, where small ships enter to load coals. There is in the peer at high water on a spring tyde ten foot; and at neap tydes, when the ships have not water enough out, they go into the road and there take in the rest of their loading, which is

brought out to them in keels. There is good anchoring in the peer in four, five, six and seven fathoms. It floweth here at full and change south-west by south. The water riseth at a spring tyde ten foot in the peer, and seven foot at a neap.

Sir John soon faced familiar problems with ongoing maintenance of the pier and he attempted to recoup his £500 outlay on repairs by seeking to recover the remainder of Charles II's earlier grant offer. In his argument Sir John noted the great benefits that had accrued from Sir Ralph's work: eight salt pans were now at work, the excise on salt alone averaging £5,000 per annum, and some 1,400 chaldrons (near 3,700 tons) of coal had been exported during the year 1704. Sir John's memorial was submitted to the commissioners for salt duty, but they claimed that the grant should not be given, for the contribution in duties from the Hartley pans to the exchequer could just as easily come from other places on the north-east coast where salt works were more numerous.

Sir John's financial problems were then compounded when he was presented with a claim from his brother-in-law, Sir Edward Blackett of Newby, Yorkshire, for £8,000 under the terms of a marriage settlement of 1684; Sir John's total indebtedness to Blackett by 1713 was in excess of £14,000, for a court order had required the payment of 6 per cent interest on the £8,000 from 1691. Unable to meet this claim without selling off some of his property, Sir John sought salvation from his wealthy relative, Admiral George Delaval of Dissington, Northumberland, who bought out Sir John's estates in 1718, but left him a life interest in Seaton Sluice and Hartley. Even after paying off Sir Edward, the Admiral still held sufficient capital to allow him to commission Vanbrugh to design Seaton Delaval Hall – commonly regarded as Vanbrugh's finest work. Admiral George gained little from the fruits of his enterprise, for he was thrown from his horse in 1723 and died therefrom. Under his will, made a few weeks before his death, the bulk of his estates passed to his nephew Francis Blake Delaval, who had earlier also inherited the Ford Estate in north Northumberland. When Sir John died in 1729, Francis also inherited Hartley and Seaton Sluice. All these properties were settled on his eldest son, Sir Francis Blake Delaval in 1748, and he succeeded in 1752. Ever a fashionable spendthrift and an infamous legend in his time, 'the gay Lothario', Sir Francis soon found himself in debt to the tune of £45,000, but a private Act of Parliament of 1756 enabled him to redeem his debts by the sale or mortgage of all or part of his estate. In the event, the manors of Ford, Horton and Hartley were vested in the trusteeship of his level-headed brother John Hussey Delaval, and it was under his careful guardianship and eventual ownership, that the subsequent significant developments at Seaton Sluice occurred.

The Delavals had known that the harbour needed further improvements for either Francis, but more likely John, had engaged John Smeaton to survey the situation and suggest improvements. Smeaton, who had been elected a Fellow of the Royal Society in 1753, had then studied canal and harbour installations in the Low Countries during 1754 before beginning work on his famous

Eddystone lighthouse in 1756. In that same year Smeaton visited the North East in connection with a proposed bridge at Hexham and either then, but certainly within two years, he also visited Seaton Sluice and examined the harbour, producing a plan for improvement in 1758. Smeaton was still at an early stage in his career as a civil and mechanical engineer and his proposal for Seaton Sluice was quite simple, involving the construction or reconstruction of a short pier on the east side of the river mouth and a much longer breakwater running west–east from the shore to provide an entrance channel from the east and give protection from the north-easterly winds. This proposal was not acted upon, but his visit to Seaton Sluice made quite an impact on Smeaton, for he was sufficiently impressed with the sluicing arrangements to recommend a similar system at Cullercoats and for his famous harbour plan for Ramsgate.

A copperas, or 'green vitriol' works had been begun at Hartley in 1756 and also a small plate-glass works employing imported German workers; the plate glass works was soon abandoned, but the copperas works, probably the first in the North East, was to operate for several decades. The method of copperas production was simple. Coal with embedded iron pyrites (known locally as 'brasses' and sometimes as 'fool's gold') was first crushed and then allowed to weather for three to five years on slightly inclined clay beds. The wind and rain gave rise to an acid solution of iron sulphate which was collected in wooden vats lined with pitch. Eventually the solution was evaporated to produce green crystals which, when roasted, gave oil of vitriol (sulphuric acid) and a residue which could be ground to give the colouring agent 'Venetian Red' or 'Jeweller's Rouge', a red iron oxide. The great beauty of the process for the prudent coal owner, was that it converted unsaleable coal to profitable products, using equally unsaleable coal as fuel in the crystallisation of the copperas liquors. Some of the brasses were shipped to Hartley from Delaval's Ford estate in north Northumberland via the port of Berwick in the 1750s and '60s, and some from Alnmouth, a small indication of much greater coastal movements between Northumberland's ports and harbours.

The decision not to proceed with Smeaton's harbour plan did not mark the end of the discussions concerning harbour improvements, for Seaton Sluice was now losing some of its trade to neighbouring ports; the harbour works of Sir Ralph in the seventeenth century were no longer sufficient to guarantee trade and further improvements were necessary if trade was to be maintained, let alone expanded. A short, horse-drawn waggonway had been laid from the pits to the harbour by 1758, and whilst this would have lessened the cost of carrying coal to the harbour, it could not, of itself, benefit those collier masters who were now reluctant to enter the harbour. The main problem, as described by Greenville Collins 60 years earlier, remained; the waters in the harbour were frequently so shallow that collier brigs might only be able to take on one third of their load within the harbour, the rest having to be brought out to them at sea in keels. There was a price to pay for this costly, cumbersome and time-consuming process, and it was paid by the Delavals who were obliged to accept a price for their coals which was only three-quarters of that which could be obtained on the Tyne, with its deeper water and faster turnaround times. It was at about this time that John Hussey Delaval bought a half-share in the Hartley Collieries from his brother Francis, and it was probably John who engaged William Brown of Throckley, the eminent north-eastern viewer and Newcomen engine builder, to act as viewer to his colliery concerns. Brown, however, despaired of ever being able to increase the vend (sale) of Hartley coals while the harbour remained unimproved. 'Please think of either mending your old Harbour or making a New one; if that is not done, Dispairing of an agmentation to your Vend' he wrote to John Hussey Delaval in April 1761. Delaval obviously acted quickly to improve matters and not just to maintain the coal, copperas and salt trades, for he was about to embark on a new venture, one which would simultaneously create a new industry for Hartley and improve the profitability of his coal mines, but also place extra burdens on his harbour.

That new industry was to be glass bottle manufacture which, like the salt pans and copperas works, would use otherwise unsaleable small coal from the Hartley collieries as fuel. Other north-eastern coal owners had similarly diversified but, as befitted an imaginative and flamboyant family, the Delavals were to create in their 'Royal Northumberland Bottle Works', the largest such enterprise in the country. The creation of a bottle works seems to have been John Hussey Delaval's idea, but the new enterprise was initially vested in his younger brother Thomas, who appears to have established and originally owned the works. Thomas Delaval has almost certainly been credited with much more than he is rightly due, but his character certainly caught the imagination of one writer, admittedly a friend, who described him as being 'busy as a bee flying from flower to flower, extracting coals from the bowels of the earth, and bottles out of damnation fiery furnaces'. An improved harbour would be an absolute necessity when the bottle works came about, not particularly for the easier export of finished products from the works and the easy import of some necessary raw materials as ballast on returning colliers, but because the additional shipping would interfere with the existing collier brigs; the salt, and copperas trades would also continue to need harbour space and facilities.

By the August of 1761, that is before the bottle works had opened, a plan for a new and improved harbour had been conceived, but its authorship is not yet known and may never be known, for it seems likely that the plan arose out of face-to-face discussions between John Hussey Delaval and his agents and viewer. Delaval's brother Thomas has usually been accorded the honour of creating the new harbour although, as we shall see, the story is not quite so straightforward. The plan was simple yet, for the mid-eighteenth century, quite bold. A 'Cut' would be made from the Seaton burn near its mouth, directly through the rocky headland in an easterly direction, and this Cut, with stop-log gates at each end, would serve as an alternative entrance channel to the old harbour, but also as a small wet dock. In addition, the seaward end of the Cut would be protected with piers.

Brown advertised in local newspapers for contractors to cut the new harbour 'part in Clay and part in Stone' and to build piers and walls, but as the person nominally in charge of the project, he felt ill-suited to the task; he was, after all, a mining engineer. As he informed Delaval:

> I dare not take the derection and contriveing the harbour not being a judge of these matters but hears there is one Robson of Sunderland who is a good judge. Pray would it be right to have him over and see the spot to consult him? Several [ships] masters are desirous to see it done and promises to trade here if the harbour was made safe and commodious.

'Robson of Sunderland' was undoubtedly Joseph Robson, engineer to the river Wear Commissioners from 1755 to his retirement in 1779, but Delaval obviously deemed it unnecessary to ask Robson to view the proposal, and Brown agreed to press on slowly with the works until Delaval could advise in person or send some other skilled engineer to Hartley. There was a temporary setback in November when a flood took away the sluice and part of the road bridge, and repairs to these must have delayed work on the Cut. Certainly, during the last two months of 1761, Brown repeatedly warned Delaval of the problems of the old harbour, of the need to press on with the new one, and of the desirability of independent and knowledgeable advice on the proposals:

> ... our bad harbour will frighten masters so that few will come to lead until induced by a new one and therefore thinks it wou'd be well if you would give directions to have some engineer to view it and give his sentiments. There are a few good hands at it just now and many more may be got if we were sensible we were doing right.

Clearly work on the Cut was proceeding, although it would appear that it was not until August of 1761 that its dimensions were finally established. A trench 42ft (12.8m) wide was to be cut through the surface soil and clay until the underlying stone was met, but the Cut through the stone would be made 30ft (9.2m) wide, except for a passing place halfway along the Cut which would be 60ft (18.3m) wide and 90ft (27.5m) long; the Cut would also be made 60ft (18.3m) wide 'next the Sea', and a strong pier would be built out into the sea from the north side. Brown occasionally wrote to Delaval concerning the construction work up to January 1763, when he reported on the opening up of a flagstone quarry in the Cut which, by the sale of flags, might 'ease you of a part of the expense of that great Undertaking'. However, there is no indication that Brown was directly involved in the works after December 1761, and it may be that Delaval's brother Thomas, reputedly an 'engineer' who had spent some time in Hamburg, had been overseeing the completion of the work. In fact, after a temporary family disagreement, Thomas took over the administration of the family's estates and John departed from Seaton Delaval around the time that the Cut was officially opened in March 1764, some two years after the opening of the bottle works.

The *Newcastle Chronicle* gave a short account of the event:

> ... the new Harbour at Hartley Pans was opened for the reception of ships: on which
> account a grand entertainment was given by Sir John Hussey Delaval to a great number of
> gentlemen, masters etc. Three oxen and several sheep, with a large quantity of strong beer,
> were given to the workmen etc. on the same occasion.

The report went on to note how the rock-cut channel was 900ft (275m) long;
30ft (9.2m) broad and 52ft (15.9m) deep, that it was capable of taking 12 to 14 sail
of vessels, each of 200 to 300 tons burthen and that it had been superintended
by Thomas Delaval; it is apparent that the passing place was not completed, but
the wider quarried section on the north side of the Cut may indicate that it was
commenced. Two light ships in full sail passed through the Cut on opening day,
and two days later the *Warkworth*, under Captain Curry, left fully laden with 13
keels of coal, the first cargo from the new harbour.

The Cut, driven through the 'Pan Close', created 'Rocky Island' and to give
access to the otherwise isolated buildings on this headland, a 'draw bridge' was
provided across the Cut where the present footbridge is located. Perhaps from
the beginning this drawbridge was a side-swing bridge, for the remains of such
are still to be seen; recently demolished, however, was the small octagonal-plan
booth which stood near the south end of the bridge and which was presumably
constructed for the bridge keeper. The two lock gates, one at each end of the
Cut, and known as 'booms', were simple stop-planks, lowered into vertical
grooves hewn into each side of the Cut; the same system remained in use at least
until 1858. At the south-eastern end of the Cut, beside the eastern stop-plank site,
a level piece of ground with a quadrant of walling to the south, marks the site
of a windlass used for raising and lowering the stop-planks, and possibly also for
winching vessels into the Cut; the gate lifting mechanism at the western end of
the Cut is not apparent.

The existing horse-drawn waggonway needed a slight re-routing to run
along the south side of the Cut, but the method of transferring coal from the
waggonway into the holds of the colliers can not be precisely stated, although
some form of coal spout was probably used from the beginning. The method of
transferral was certainly being debated in the 1780s when Joseph Oxley, a Delaval
agent, was intending to do away with 'the gears'. His proposal was to carry the
coals from the pits in the corves in which they came to bank. Six corves would
be drawn on a 'framed carriage' along the waggonway by one galloway, and
these would then be emptied onto a coal heap by the Cut. The coal would then
presumably be simply hand shovelled onto chutes leading down to the colliers.
The first edition Ordnance Survey map for the area, surveyed only a few years
before the harbour closed, does not appear to show any coal handling devices,
and certainly the Cut is insufficiently wide to accommodate the coal drops
which became a feature of the Tyne in the nineteenth century.

57 The old river-harbour at Seaton Sluice in the lower foreground, the Cut and the footbridge over it at extreme right, possibly in the 1930s. Almost all of the buildings on the 'Island' have now (2005) gone; see 59

58 The old river-harbour at Seaton Sluice to the left, the Cut and the footbridge over it centre right, 1974

It has been suggested that Sir Walter Scott, who certainly referred to Seaton Delaval Hall in *Marmion*, based his description of the small port of Ellangowan in *Guy Mannering*, on Seaton Sluice:

> ...They pulled around a point of rock, and found a very small harbour, partly formed by nature, partly by the indefatigable labour of the ancient inhabitants.... A ledge of rock had, by the assistance of the chisel and pickaxe, been formed into a sort of quay. The rock was of extremely hard consistence, and the task so difficult, that, according to the fisherman, a labourer who wrought at the work might in the evening have carried home in his bonnet all the shivers which he had struck from the mass in the course of the day.

The cost of the Cut, its piers and machinery was said to have been £10,000, yet even so, the project seems to have been skimped or inadequately designed and the absence of a passing place came to cause difficulties. It was soon realised that ships loaded to full capacity could only get away at full tide. Consequently, in October 1771, John Hussey Delaval, only just returned from his 'exile' after brother Thomas found himself in financial difficulties, and now in full and rightful control of affairs at Hartley, issued regulations governing the use of the Cut. Essentially, those vessels which could get into the Cut, load, and get out again on the one tide, were not to be obstructed in any way. Vessels entering the Cut which could only be part-loaded before the next tide would, therefore, have to be taken into the old harbour, so that any vessel which could load and get away would be able to do so; the part-loaded ship would then wait in the old harbour for the next high tide, complete its cargo and get away. No ships could enter the Cut without an agent's permission, and the agents would only grant a ship such permission, except for those wishing to proceed straight into the old harbour, unless it could proceed directly to sea without obstructing any other ship from sailing. The coal spout nearest the seaward end of the Cut was to be reserved for those colliers which had discharged their ballast and could sail out of the old harbour, round the rocky headland, to enter the seaward end of the Cut in order that they could load and proceed immediately on their voyage, even when the rest of the Cut was occupied by fully-loaded ships awaiting a better tide, or ships whose captains thought it imprudent to put to sea. It was also possible, if the Cut was otherwise empty of ships, for light vessels to enter the Cut from the old harbour, load and get away on the one tide. It was probably to make the Cut more user-friendly that it, and presumably its seaward entrance, were deepened in 1772, giving a sufficient depth of water for complete loading and departure of the colliers at most states of the tide; it now had a 4ft (1.2m) greater depth of water than the old harbour.

With William Brown as viewer, coal-mining operations took great strides forward at Hartley. Brown was pre-eminent in his time in the building of Newcomen pumping engines and a new deep winning was being made as the Cut was being driven, using just such an engine. In addition, Joseph Oxley, who

59 The Seaton Sluice Cut looking towards the old river-harbour, 1974

was Delaval's agent at Ford, was also occasionally active at Hartley, and he was the first person to modify a Newcomen engine to enable it to produce rotary motion, thereby allowing Hartley coals to be wound from depth without the use of horses; Oxley's very imperfect device was seen by the celebrated James Watt in 1768, but he was later to forget the name of its inventor. The Hartley pits employed 300 hands by 1770, and more than 48,000 tons of coal were shipped coastwise from Seaton Sluice in 1776. The following year saw 185 shiploads of Seaton Sluice coal delivered at London, a total of 30,686 chaldrons (about 80,000 tons). Sailings were carried out throughout the year, although only two vessels arrived in February; the loads carried varied from ship to ship, between *Dorothy's Increase* which carried 201 chaldrons, and the *New Norwich* which took only 75 chaldrons. In spite of the earlier problems with the Cut, it was now clearly paying its way, and Hartley coals were competing with Tyne coals on an equal footing. As one of the Delaval agents was to observe in 1781, the average annual vend of coal before the Cut had never exceeded 6,500 chaldrons, whereas it had been 18,000 chaldrons since the new harbour had opened; collier brigs could now sometimes do ten London voyages per year, because of faster turnround times, whereas formerly they could not do more than seven.

The Cut also meant that the salt, kelp and copperas-carrying sloops had freer use of the old harbour, salt being carried to Yarm, Stockton, York, Boston and Spalding, while copperas was regularly sent to Newcastle and London, and kelp to London soap boilers; in 1776, some 100 tons of copperas and 300 tons of salt were exported, in addition to the much larger exports of coal and glass bottles. Good indications of the extent of these trades, but also of some difficulties with them, can be found in agents' letters to Delaval. For example, in March 1781, Joseph Oxley informed Delaval that:

> Our salt has been so badly made this year that the customers at Yarm and Stockton have quite left taking any from your works, so that out of the small quantity of 450 tons made last year, or since April last, 380 tons was last Monday in the warehouse unsent away. I really am afraid Mr Cooper [the overseer of the salt pans] will fall asleep as he has too much indolance & indiffrance hanging about him. I am now loading a sloop for York of 50 tons of salt and 800 dozen bottles, and have a sloop agreed for to go with 30 tons of salt to Boston and 14 gross of bottles to the same place, also 15 tons of salt to Spalding & 27 gross [of bottles] there, & have promise of Lord Mulgrave sloop coming here to load small coals for Whitby and to take in 18 gross of bottles, have sold 80 tons of the discol'd salt to be shipt in a little time by Mr Row for Copenhagen with 20 tons of copperas and som bottles, have sold 40 tons of old Potts [old glass-melting pots] to Bristol …. [Punctuation added]

When the two bottle houses, which were in production before the Cut was opened, were augmented by a third in 1788, the works could truly claim to be the largest in the kingdom, a position it held until the 1800s. London was the main export destination for the bottles, as it was for the coal, and although both commodities might occasionally have been shipped in the hold of a collier brig, locally owned bottle sloops, each carrying between 3,000 and 4,500 dozen bottles, were the preferred means of transport. For decades the total vend exceeded 100,000 dozen bottles per year, and by the end of the eighteenth century it had reached 200,000 dozen. The impact of Hartley bottles on the London market was considerable, for Delaval established his own bottle warehouse in London, enabling him to cost-undercut his rivals by circumventing the established London bottle merchants.

These developments considerably increased activity in the old and new harbours. Vessels could use either entrance to the old river harbour, the Cut if it was free, or the river mouth, according to the weather, but the collier brigs always shipped from the Cut, while the smaller sloops shipped from the old harbour. Ballast and other raw materials which might be needed by the glassworks were discharged in the old harbour where at some stage a tunnelled narrow-gauge tubway was constructed to lead directly beneath the glass works. This tubway may not have served the bottle works at the latter's inception, but may date from between 1778 and 1788 when John Hussey Delaval, who had purchased the works from his brother on his return from exile in 1771, oversaw a

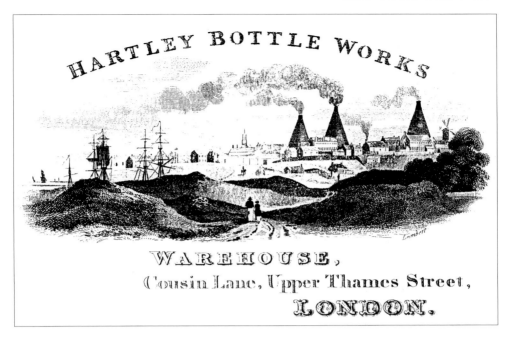

60 The Royal Northumberland Bottle Works, Seaton Sluice, with sailing vessels in the harbour to the left, probably *c.*1790

wholesale reconstruction of the works, including the replacement of the existing square glasshouses with improved round ones – glass cones. Certainly a network of underground tunnels, which still exist, were constructed to serve the works as it was extended to cover some 12 acres (4.9ha) by 1778. Coal from the Hartley pits was brought by waggonway to 'coal trunks' in the heart of the works, and lowered to the underground tubway for distribution to the glasshouse furnaces. Likewise imported raw materials such as clay, ashes, sand and lime were brought in through the quayside tunnel and distributed to wherever they were needed. Two more tunnels allowed slags and refuse to be dumped on the river bank to the west, and probably also served to supply combustion air to the glass furnaces. Finally, an underground 'bottles cariage way' linked the glasshouses to the main bottle warehouse, and also to the quayside tunnel and to the 'bottle crane' used to load the crated bottles into waiting sloops. It has sometimes been claimed that George Stephenson, the famous railway engineer, was in some way connected with the development of the tunnels and even that he designed the first narrow gauge railway to run on wrought iron rails here at Hartley. The evidence for such claims is weak, for most of the tunnels were in place by 1812 when Stephenson was just about to embark on his outstanding career. It is possible that Stephenson suggested the use of wrought-iron rails in the tunnels in the 1820s, following the patent taken out by John Birkinshaw of the Bedlington Ironworks in 1820, but even this remains in doubt.

61 A section of tunnel under the former Royal Northumberland Bottle Works, Seaton Sluice; the tunnel is some 5ft 6in (1.68m) high and 5ft (1.52m) wide. *Ian Standing, March 1979*

The tunnels were well constructed, mainly in brick, but reinforced in certain sections with sandstone masonry, having arched roofs over vertical side-walls while the floors were of ash clinker dumped over the natural boulder clay; the tunnels had probably been constructed using the cut and cover technique. The tunnel sections vary between 4ft 4in (1.3m) and 16ft 5in (5m) wide, and are between 6-7ft (1.8-2.1m) high. Some of them had served as air-raid shelters during the Second World War even though, in places, there was only 6in of ground cover above the crowns of the arches; internal walls were constructed to conceal lavatories and when these were inspected but not used by the author in 1978, their drainage systems appeared to be in good working order.

Other related industries had also been developed. A limekiln of unknown date was built against the cliff line just to the south of the Cut. A small shipyard had been established by 1766, and leased out to Anthony Topham, the first ship launched being the 63-ton bottle sloop *Seaton Sluice*; on at least one occasion it was used to carry groceries from Hartlepool to Delaval's London residence and, as will be seen, it had the odd scrape during its life. Although initially successful, with vessels of up to 236 tons being launched, subsequent tenants only held the shipyard for short periods of time before its final closure before 1812. Later there was an engine works at Seaton Sluice. But these were quite minor ventures when compared with the coal and bottle trades.

It was not only adverse weather conditions which affected these trades, for from the late 1770s through to the end of the Napoleonic wars, the shipping and the inhabitants of Seaton Sluice and neighbouring ports were occasionally threatened by 'friend' and foe alike. In March 1778, Stephen Watson, an agent at Hartley, warned Delaval that the naval impress might put a stop to the coal trade as 'all the sailors that have escaped [the press] are fled and flying to the mountains'. Early in the June of the following year there were reports of attacks on colliers by two French privateers and two cutters, which fired briskly on the colliers with their 124 guns but did little damage and were frightened off when two British ships appeared nearby. Towards the end of that month Watson's earlier prediction proved correct:

> ... last night the press broke out and took all three year servants which is a sufficient embargo on shipping – and I doubt will have a bad effect so as to intimidate all boys in the future.

A few days later he informed Delaval that he was experiencing difficulties in obtaining sailors, for all had been pressed into the navy and all trade had stopped as a consequence; Watson had to give up his agency soon afterwards 'due to Militia engagements'. A press in June 1779 saw one ship leave Seaton Sluice manned only by its captain and mate, assisted by 'a crippled sailor, 2 very old men, and 4 or 5 little boys'. And so it went on. The bottle sloop *Seaton Sluice* was taken by a Dutch privateer off Scarborough in February 1782, while on its return voyage to Hartley loaded with ashes for the bottle works. In what appears to have been an entirely formalised arrangement, the Dutch let the vessel continue, on condition that Delaval paid a ransom of 200 guineas, taking the ship's mate to imprisonment in Holland as security for the ransom; the mate was well treated in prison, but he was quite unused to such confinement. Seemingly the same vessel was captured by the French in February 1783, while on route to London, but was eventually rescued by a British frigate. More colliers were taken by the French as the Napoleonic wars heated up, as in the case of the *Honoured* which was taken off Whitley Bay in 1801, and ended up in France; the *Chancellor* was lucky to be rescued by a frigate in the same year. It is not surprising that, during this war period, a new block house and battery were constructed on a ballast mound which overlooked the harbour.

In spite of such excursions and alarms, the last 40 years of the eighteenth century saw Seaton Sluice reach the peak of its importance, when up to £24,000 might be collected in port revenues per annum. Such success did not enamour Delaval to the Tyne-based 'gentlemen of the coal trade', especially when he saw no reason to be bound by their rules, but his obstinacy in this context came to fracture his otherwise fruitful relationship with William Brown, for Brown came to have his own direct interests in the Tyne trade. When, in 1778, Delaval ignored the 'limitation of the vend' imposed by the 'Coal owners of the Tyne', insisting on setting his own level of vend, and also offered higher than average binding monies to pitmen to gain their services for one year, Brown found himself so compromised that he resigned from Delaval's employ:

> They [the Coal Owners of the Tyne] think the Quantity that you name (Viz) 23,000 Chalders [per annum] too great particularly as every Owner in both the Rivers of Tyne and Wear is under the Necessity to abate of their Stipulated Quantities in order to make way for New Collieries that are now in & coming into the Trade. They also think the Mode of giving such high Binding Money Viz 3 or 4 Guineas a Man to Pitmen a very bad precedent that may tend very much to the prejudice of the trade in General in future ... my Partner Mr Bell ... blames me very much for Endeavouring to serve a Gentleman that is Essentially hurting him as well as myself and indeed I find myself so Circumstanced that I can no longer serve you in the Capacity I have done for some time past.

It seems that Delaval did not appoint another viewer for several years, but relied on his customary agents (there were about 14 of them) to oversee colliery developments, just as they organised other estate affairs. There had been considerable investment at Hartley in the 10 years since 1771, but the agricultural depression of the 1780s, exacerbated by the American War of Independence, brought retrenchment; the period of bold development was now over and consolidation was now the main requirement. Still, as the glassworks were being developed, houses were built for the glassworkers as well as ancillary workers such as smiths, brickmakers, millhands, joiners and coopers. By 1790, the village of Seaton Sluice, now quite distinct from Hartley, had a market square, school, maltings, brewery, public house and 43 cottage houses in the predictably named John Street, Hussey Street and Delaval Street.

Delaval was to have financial worries in the decades either side of 1800. The 1790s, which saw the outbreak of the French Revolutionary war and the Napoleonic War, combined with some harvest failures in Britain and inflation from 1793 – a novel feature in the eighteenth century – brought problems for many. Delaval also had problems with his collieries; coal sales had been steady in the 1780s, but were falling towards the end of that decade as new winnings and slack sales affected supply and demand, causing Delaval to borrow money. But he had to keep the collieries going or else the bottle works, perhaps now proving a better revenue generator than the coal mines, would fail; unfortunately for Delaval the price of glass remained steady when almost all other commodity prices rose. Delaval was now in his 80s, and he sold off one of his houses in the south, perhaps to offset his declining income. Then, in a rather odd arrangement, he seems to have agreed to lease the harbour in 1796, together with seven public houses and all the agents' and pitmen's cottages, to his son-in-law, George Carpenter, 2nd Earl of Tyrconnel, for 21 years at £80 per annum plus £1 per annum for every cottage; Delaval himself would be allowed free use of the harbour for the 'Exportation and Importation of any Goods ... whatsoever'. This arrangement, if it actually came to fruition, may have been designed to remove one area of financial risk, or possibly to advance the husband of his favourite daughter, Sarah Hussey Delaval, in business affairs, either to ensure a succession, for Delaval's only son had died in 1775 aged 19 years, or simply to enable Tyrconnel to maintain his wife in her accustomed degree of opulence.

In fact, estate and harbour affairs seem to have continued pretty much as before. There were occasional attacks on Hartley ships by privateers, the pitmen sometimes went on strike and shipping continued to be at the mercy of the weather. Occasionally a sailing vessel would be entrusted to carry a special cargo, as in 1798 when Delaval wanted a pianoforte moving from Seaton Delaval to his London residence. One of his agents, John Bryers was deputed to organise the move, and although his first thought was that that a bottle sloop would have insufficient space in its cabin, 'the cabins so small & full of the hands lodging there', and that a collier would probably have to do the job, he soon reported that 'The *Polly* [bottle sloop] sailed last tide, on board the Piano Forte packed in a case as you ordered, & two paintings that Lord Tyrconnel ordered to be sent to you by the first vessel'.

At his death, in 1808, John Hussey Delaval's estate was split between his widow, who inherited the glassworks, copperas works and brewery, while the colliery and salt pans passed to his younger and only surviving brother Edward. The manufacture and export of white salt had ceased in 1798, after an Act prohibited the manufacture of white salt and alkali salt in the same place; thereafter, only alkali-salt was made at the pans for use in the glassworks. Edward, the academic member of a multi-talented family, continued to reside in London and showed little interest in the affairs at Hartley, except presumably to collect the rents, for he seems to have leased out the mines to John Carr, Delaval's agent at Ford, and James Jobling, a Newcastle colliery viewer, in 1809. When Edward died in 1814, lately married but childless, he was the last of the male Delavals, for neither he nor his seven brothers had left surviving male heirs. The glassworks passed to Susannah, Marchioness of Waterford, daughter of Sarah Hussey Delaval, and the works continued to thrive for a number of years under tenants, while the coal mines passed with the Seaton Delaval, Hartley and Horton Estates, to Sir Jacob

Astley, son of John Hussey's sister Rhoda; salt and copperas making seem to have ceased in the 1820s.

Precisely who was in control of the harbour immediately after John Hussey Delaval's death (the Earl of Tyrconnel had died in 1805) is unclear. It is probable, however, that it was leased to Carr & Jobling along with the collieries in 1809; the same partnership also took a lease on the glassworks in 1820, and since the Carr family ran both concerns until their respective closures, it seems likely that they gained control of the harbour by lease. Coal and glass bottles certainly continued to be exported from the harbour although this was to become increasingly difficult. A gale followed by an extraordinary high tide, in February 1825, caused considerable damage at several north-eastern ports. At Hartley, according to the ubiquitous 'oldest inhabitant', the tide had been 'the highest ever remembered' and had threatened to destroy the harbour; in the event, one of the piers, probably at the seaward end of the Cut, was breached but repaired before the next tide, while the whole of the east side of a pier in the old harbour was destroyed and the entrance of the harbour thereby blocked up; none of the vessels lying in the harbour had suffered any damage.

Mackenzie's *View of the County of Northumberland* had been published in the same year as the storm damage, and he described the twin settlements of Hartley and Seaton as fairly prosperous. Hartley, with its five public houses and a Methodist meeting house, was mainly inhabited by fishermen and coal miners. Seaton Sluice had four public houses, three butchers, a 'common brewery' belonging to Messrs Blackett & Co. who supplied all the publicans of the township, and a Presbyterian meeting house. A few 'respectable' ship owners, as well as glassworkers and seamen, resided there, and all together some 1,800 people lived in the two places. In the late 1830s, when Thomas Hair made a watercolour of Hartley Colliery, in preparation for his *Sketches of the Coal Mines in Northumberland and Durham*, he had been advised that the haven was a natural and artificial curiosity which was 'Worth gaun a mile to see'; regrettably he did not sketch the harbour, but he did note that 111 colliers had used the harbour in 1836, carrying away 35,660 tons of coal.

But the harbour and its associated settlements were now stagnating. When Joseph Lamb & Partners commenced new coal winnings at Seaton Delaval in 1838, with six shafts being simultaneously sunk within the compass of 600 yards, the first coals to be shipped, in 1842, were sent to the Tyne rather than to Seaton Sluice. And when the *Melton Constable Hotel* (named after the family home of the Astleys) was built overlooking the old harbour in 1839, it was observed that more than half a century had elapsed since any new buildings had been erected or any improvements made in Seaton Sluice and Hartley. However, a foretaste of things to come was the commencement, in 1843, of a twice-weekly passenger service on the *Venus* between the New Quay at North Shields and Seaton Sluice, the fare including the cost of tea and a plate of fruit in Seaton Delaval Gardens. With the development of the Northumberland steam coal districts and their huge outputs of coal, the little harbour of Seaton Sluice became increasingly inadequate, and colliery lessees who had used it for decades were now keen to leave it. As one such lessee, probably Carr, put it in the 1840s:

> We ship our Hartley coals at Seaton Sluice. Sometimes for ten weeks together a ship cannot
> get to sea from that port and it is of the utmost importance to the well being of the colliery
> that we should get a better place of shipment.

In fact, the harbour of Seaton Sluice was well located, geographically, to serve the expanding steam coal districts of Northumberland, but the result of agitation such as Carr's was to catalyse port developments on the Blyth and the Tyne, rather than at the outmoded, incommodious and now unsuitable Seaton Sluice; what had been appropriate for the 1760s was now no longer so. Carr & Jobling, who had also leased the Cowpen collieries at Blyth from 1836, now sought to carry at least some of their coals to the Tyne for shipment and by the construction of a branch to the line which was to become the Blyth & Tyne railway, they could, by 1846, take their Hartley coals to the Tyne. It may have been this railway link to Seaton Sluice which led W.K. Horsley & Co. to establish their ironworks and engine factory at Seaton Sluice at about this time. While active the works produced steam engines for local colliery concerns including, for example, a 200hp pumping engine for Burradon Colliery.

Some coal continued to be shipped from Seaton Sluice, however, for Carr & Jobling still had the glassworks and they therefore continued to need a rail connection between their pits and the harbour. Their main colliery, the Hartley 'Hester' pit, had been opened out in 1846, its coals being brought down the waggonway to the glassworks and to the coal-shipping places at the Cut. John Jobling sold out his interests in Carr & Jobling in 1847 and the concern was reconstituted as Messrs Carr Brothers & Co., but the commercial crisis of 1857, which resulted in the collapse of the Northumberland & District Bank, forced Carr Brothers & Co. to sell their colliery concerns at public auction in the following year; Burradon went to Joshua Bower of Hunslet, Leeds, where he already had collieries and glassworks in addition to being the major lessee of turnpike tollhouses in the country; Seghill was taken by Joseph Laycock; and Cowpen was purchased by Messrs J. Straker. Hartley Colliery was, however, withdrawn from the auction after special arrangements were made with Lord Hastings to enable the Carrs to continue there. It was to be but a short respite, for the dreadful calamity of the 'broken beam' at the Hester pit in 1862, resulted in the deaths of 204 men and boys and in the closure of the colliery; this finally brought coal shipments from Seaton Sluice to an end, the ironworks closing soon after. The bottle works, however, continued until their closure in 1872, when the sailing ship *Unity of Boston* cleared the harbour in July with a cargo of bottles destined for the Channel Islands. It was the last trading vessel ever to use harbour which, in 1887, was described as sanded up, useless and 'entirely abandoned'; thereafter it would only be used by a few fishing cobles. The depressed state of the area after the closure of its various industrial enterprises is indicated by the population figures for Hartley Township. Standing at 1,639 in 1801, the population had risen to 1,911 by 1841, but fell to 1,112 in 1891, before rising again to 1,716 in 1901 after a resumption of colliery operations in seams abandoned after the closure of the Hester Pit.

The abandoned glassworks remained until their demolition in 1897, to make way for new housing as the community, no longer dependent on its own industries for a living, now grew steadily. The large brewhouse also ceased working and rather unusually, if not uniquely, the brewery premises were converted to provide both an Anglican and a Nonconformist church under the same roof; the brewery bell which once summoned workers to its door now beckoned a more temperate flock of worshippers.

A plan was devised to provide a passenger rail service for Seaton Sluice early in the twentieth century, although its station was to carry the more refined name 'Collywell Bay'. A contract was let to build the branch line from the electrified Tyneside Loop line in 1912, and it had almost been completed when work had to stop with the outbreak of the First World War. The rails were removed early

62 The octagon building at Seaton Sluice, 1974

in the war period, and then temporary track was put in for a rail-mounted naval gun. It was not until 1924 that the London & North Eastern Railway, the successor to the NER, re-examined the scheme, but it was finally abandoned in 1931, although some embankments and bridge abutments remain in place.

Gradually, almost all of Seaton Sluice's eighteenth-century buildings were either purposely demolished or simply fell into decay during the twentieth century. The remains of the windmill, near the site of the Mill Pit just to the south of the glassworks, vanished under a modern housing estate about 40 years ago, the pantiled buildings on Rocky Island have collapsed in the past 30 years or so and the small octagonal booth by the footbridge over the Cut has also gone. Only the tunnels beneath the glassworks site, and the 'Octagon' building survive from Seaton Sluice's heyday; the latter building, which variously served as port office, custom house, colliery office and reading room, was converted to domestic accommodation some 20 years ago. The old harbour and its 'new' Cut remain, the former now home to a small informal marina and partially restored, but only the sites remain of the sluice beneath the road bridge, and the salt pans on the level ground to the east of the bridge on the south side of the harbour. Seaton Sluice remains a fascinating place for anyone interested in our maritime history and much more could still be learned by a painstaking archaeological survey of the harbour area. It is certainly worth 'gaun [at least] a mile to see'.

12

Cullercoats harbour

Cullercoats, a place otherwise of no great distinction, but worthy remembrance in this respect, that it is a very commodious little port, of artificial construction, or as the people stile it, an harbour made by hand. (Hutchinson (1776), quoting Snagg)

Cullercoats lies just 4 miles (6.4km) south-east of Seaton Sluice, St Mary's island with its 1897/8 lighthouse and the sands of Whitley Bay, lying in between the two former harbours. The attractive village of Cullercoats and its small harbour belie an industrial past. Unlike the other ports and harbours of Northumberland, the settlement of Cullercoats has had a relatively short history, and its harbour an even shorter one. The development of the harbour and its accompanying village derived from its local geology and geography, in particular its proximity to the 'Ninety Fathom Dyke', an east–west geological fault with an average throw of 540ft (165m), which is exhibited at the surface immediately to the south of Cullercoats Bay. A succession of coal seams outcrop north of Cullercoats, almost parallel to the coastline, while the effect of the fault to the south is to bring the same coal seams to the surface again, as well as pockets of the magnesian limestone more commonly found in County Durham. Coal was being worked as early as 1315, for it is known that some workings in the area were destroyed in a Scottish invasion of that year. In c.1600, the area which became Cullercoats consisted simply of 2 acres (0.8ha) of land called 'Culvercoats' (i.e. Dovecotes), a part of the demesne fields of Tynemouth and 'Arnold's Close' alias 'Mardon Close'. These lands seem to have been conveyed to Thomas Dove of Whitley in 1621; his forbears had been tenants of Tynemouth windmill and Mardon watermill in 1539, and his descendants were to exert considerable influence over the future development of Cullercoats. Dove leased a parcel of ground to a miller, Richard Simpson, in 1644, Simpson being allowed to build a house on the land, presumably for Mardon Mill, but he was also granted the right to fish with one boat, the latter to be built, repaired and managed by Dove and himself.

Seventeen years later two of Dove's sons, John and William, were temporarily imprisoned in Tynemouth castle for attending a Quaker meeting, and he created a Nonconformist burial place in Arnold's Close in the following year. When Thomas Dove died in c.1666 and was succeeded by his son John, Cullercoats was now becoming a small hamlet, detached from its parent town of Tynemouth, and indeed was about to take a further important stride forward.

Although Cullercoats stood just over 1 mile (1.6km) north of the mouth of the Tyne, its small-scale coal mining activities could nonetheless benefit by having shipping facilities even closer to hand. Consequently, when Lady Elizabeth Percy, heiress of the eleventh Earl of Northumberland, leased out her collieries at Whitley, previously tenanted by John Dove, to John Rogers and his partners John Carr and Henry Hudson in 1676, she also agreed that the lessees and herself would, at their joint expense, construct a 'pier', probably meaning a small harbour, at Cullercoats to encourage the shipment of coal. The pier seems to have been completed in the following year at a cost of £3,013 and, according to Maberly Phillips writing in 1892, the foundations of two wooden piers could still be seen. To assist the carriage of coal to the new pier, John Dove leased to John Carr, for 99 years from July 1677 at £5 per annum, a 2 acre (0.8ha) piece of ground near the pier and a strip of ground 15 yards broad 'as the same is now dowled, Marked & set forth for a waggonway or ways', to lead from the pier towards the upper dam of Mardon Mill and the Whitley collieries. Although the most easily won coals were within 1.5 miles (2.4km) distance from Cullercoats, and carriage by coal wains might have been economically feasible, a horse-drawn waggonway from the pits to the harbour would clearly be an advantage to the undertaking in minimising overland carriage costs. If this waggonway was indeed built at that time, it would have been the second such in Northumberland, pre-dated only by the Bedlington Way of the first decade of the seventeenth century. In the same month Lady Elizabeth petitioned the Lord Treasurer to make her new port a member creek of the Port of Newcastle, on the basis that she had:

> ... lately formed a colliery in her lands in Tinmothshire, which lyes so far distant from Tinmoth to carry her coals hither for exportation, that she hath a convenient place upon her owne estate called Caller Coates ... fitt to erect a key to export her owne coales and the coales of the neighbouring collieryes [and] as Seaton Delavall and Blyth Nook have been made member creekes to the port of Newcastle, she may obtein the like favor to make Caller Coates a member of the same, being much nearer for the use aforesaid.

This petition was granted in September 1677, making Cullercoats a member of the Port of Tyne, and like Seaton Sluice it was placed under the charge of a deputy custom officer at Blyth, for which service Lady Elizabeth would pay £10 per annum. Although the port of Cullercoats was described simply as a 'pier' at this time, we have seen elsewhere that this word was sometimes used to imply a small harbour. It was undoubtedly small, but even so it may possibly have been easier to access than, say, Seaton Sluice, although a bank of exposed rocks on either side of its entrance could present problems; the way was beaconed at least from the second half of the seventeenth century. The harbour was and remains tidal, so that vessels would always have to enter at high water and would lie dry at low water. Such arrangements were far from uncommon, and the collier brig was expressly designed with such working conditions in mind, whether for loading in the north or unloading in the south.

Dove and others leased lead mines in Arnold's Close to Carr for 31 years in the following month – a curious reference, for there are no known veins of lead in that area – and in November they leased out land near the pier on which a saltworks with two pans could be built, to Thomas Fearon of South Shields for 98 years, provided only that he bought whatever coal was needed by the saltworks from the Whitley mines at the going price on the Tyne. This project clearly went ahead, and Fearon was able to ship 118 tons of salt in 1679 and 179 tons in 1683. Thus, in the space of only two years, Cullercoats had embarked upon new ventures, its traders having direct access to the lucrative London and east-coast markets for salt and coal, but the still-small settlement was not about to become an industrial colony like its neighbour Seaton Sluice.

Some 14,000 tons of coal were shipped coastwise in 224 cargoes in 1678/79, an average of 64 tons per cargo, and prospects must have seemed good. John Dove died in the following year, but his son Thomas continued to build upon his father's enterprise and a number of plots were set aside for houses in the years immediately following. Thomas built a manor house for himself in 1681/82 and also leased a plot of land for house-building purposes near his mansion to a master mariner of North Shields. Coal shipments were growing and had reached 22,000 tons coastwise plus 2000 tons foreign by 1684/85, outputs over and above whatever coal tonnages were sold by landsale and consumed by the salt pans, and the limekilns at Mardon – a degree of success which 'excited the jealousy of the hostmen of Newcastle'. It may also be that some lime was being exported, for Henry Hudson, presumably a partner in the original 1676 colliery lease, had leased limestone quarries in the field called Maudlin Pitts at Mardon.

The continuing success of the harbour resulted in the further growth of the community around it, a process encouraged by Dove who, in 1690, conveyed several parcels of land in Arnold's Close and some houses, to the agent of the Whitley Colliery. These plots and houses, located on the point overlooking the sea at the north side of the bay, were to be held in trust for 15 people, including several 'yeomen', a blacksmith, a carpenter and two master mariners – a combination of skills, talent and wealth which would be useful to a growing and would-be self-reliant community. Such had been the rapid development of Cullercoats that it was decreed in 1690 that:

> ... whereas the towne of Cullercoates is growne numerous and populous, and but about a mile distance from Tynemouth, and many houses new built there, it is ordered that it be made a distinct constabulary of itself.

Thus, Cullercoats became a township in its own right, separate and distinct from Tynemouth. The coal and salt industries continued to be active into the early eighteenth century, although coal outputs seem to have stagnated with the export figures little changed since the 1680s, being 15,800 tons in 1705. However, salt exports had reached 1,789 tons, and in consuming about 8 tons of coal in the production of 1 ton of salt, the coal mines were clearly kept busy. A waggonway had certainly been constructed by 1704, for in that year a Newcastle carpenter was engaged to keep it and its 39 waggons in good repair for three years; this contract stipulated that the way could be ballasted with clinker from the salt pans, yet another example of an interrelationship between the coal and salt industries. There were now 19 salt pans around the harbour, 17 of which were in the hands of the colliery lessees, producing 2,180 tons of salt and generating a clear profit of £538 in 1708. Moreover, it was estimated that the revenues from the harbour and salt works would soon yield some £1,700 per annum.

But this was not to be, for although Cullercoats was now seeing its finest hour as a port, it was soon to undergo irreversible setbacks, before being finally eclipsed by the Tyne, the first being a violent storm which swept away the outworks of the pier in October 1710; it was estimated that rebuilding costs would amount to £1,200. It is uncertain whether or not any rebuilding work was carried out, but some 2,049 tons of salt were cleared in 1714, and 18,500 tons of coal shipped in 138 cargoes, an average of 135 tons per cargo. The continued increase in the size of colliers, evident since 1679 and surely set to continue, could only militate against Cullercoats' future as a coal shipping harbour; that particular fate was pre-empted by another misfortune at Cullercoats as the Whitley and Monkseaton collieries, the harbour's sole suppliers of coal, were about to suffer problems of their own. As the more easily accessible coal was being worked out, severe drainage difficulties were being encountered in the deeper workings to the dip. A new attempt was made to win this coal in 1722, and the acquisition of a Newcomen atmospheric pumping engine, which might have been able to deal with the water problem, was considered, but the lessees failed to come to satisfactory terms with the colliery's owners and the concern was abandoned for the next 90 years. (When Whitley colliery was finally re-opened in 1810, it was connected by a waggonway direct to the Tyne at North Shields.) The salt trade, deprived of its easy access to cheap pan coal, was inevitably disadvantaged by the loss of the nearby collieries, but some 756 tons of salt were exported coastwise in 1724, falling to 688 tons in the following year. Salt production at Cullercoats ceased completely in 1726, when six of the salt pans were transferred to Blyth and the rest were abandoned.

Cullercoats' days as a port were now over, but it continued to be an important fishing station, being described in 1749 as 'the best fish-market in the north of England [where] boats may land and go to sea when they cannot from any other place for several miles north and south'. In addition, the ownership of trading boats, and even a small export trade in lime, may have been retained, for the *Triton* of Cullercoats, laden with ballast, was lost on route from Hamburg in 1755. But Cullercoats was clearly taking on another aspect, one far remote from collieries and salt pans, for as Mrs Astley (Rhoda Delaval) wrote in *c.*1751:

> Tinmouth and Cullercoates are much in fashion; not a room empty. My Lady Ravensworth and my Lady Clavering were a month at Cullercoates bathing.

Even so, there were to be two more attempts to resuscitate Cullercoats as a coal and salt exporting harbour. Firstly, in 1759, the year after his survey at Seaton Sluice, John Smeaton produced a 'general plan for restoring the Harbour of Cullercoats' for the Duke of Northumberland. Smeaton had been so impressed by the sluicing arrangements at Seaton Sluice, that his plan for a new Cullercoats harbour incorporated the same principle. A north pier would be built, in part on the foundations of the old one, but re-formed to give twin pier heads in a Y formation, and a new south pier would be constructed in a northerly direction towards the north pier from the cliffs on the south side of the bay, to provide a narrow entrance channel; a coal quay and a ballast quay would be protected by these piers. Smeaton identified two areas within the harbour, one to serve as an inner harbour and the other where fine, sloping sands would enable ships to lie at anchor. He also noted a small brook which discharged into the sea, but which could be diverted to discharge directly into the harbour via a sluice; a reservoir could be formed behind the sluice 'which in dry seasons may be discharged at low water for cleaning of the harbour'. As at Seaton Sluice, Smeaton's plan for Cullercoats was to be thwarted and no reconstruction work was carried out, probably because the Duke could not envisage any significant returns on the investment which a new harbour would involve, especially as there were no working coal mines in the immediate neighbourhood.

The second expression of hope for a new harbour was, in reality, nothing more than that. A co-heiress of John Dove had married the Revd Curwen Huddleston of Clifton, the incumbent of Whitehaven, Cumbria, in 1742, and he thereby came into the ownership of former Dove properties at Cullercoats. He offered to sell this property to the Duke of Northumberland in 1770 and, surely only as a piece of 'soft sell', he argued that new coal mines could be opened, waggonways built and the port reinstated from its then ruinous state. The Duke displayed some interest in purchasing Huddleston's estate, and further correspondence ensued, but the harbour was not resurrected.

Little of incidence seems to have occurred over the next few decades, but it can be assumed that Cullercoats became increasingly more popular as a watering hole, perhaps especially after the occasion, in December 1805, when a cask of gin was driven ashore and consumed on the spot by any who chanced to hear of it and get near it. It was said that numbers of people were lying drunk on the sands, and that others rolled about around the cask for the greater part of the day; alas one youth literally drank himself to death. The small seaside resort of Cullercoats was augmented by salt-water baths in 1807 and by 1813 John Hodgson could describe the settlement as:

> ... a small bathing-town, inhabited chiefly by fishermen. Here are warm and cold baths, a ballast hill, the ruins of an old pier, of a waggon-way for coals, and behind the village a neglected Quaker burial-ground.

There was, as always, often a personal price to be paid for taking to the waters, and as reported in the local press in 1829, many lives had been lost while bathing at Cullercoats 'as the current which sets out is so very powerful, that it is almost impossible to stem it'.

Nearby industrial developments passed Cullercoats harbour by. The Marden limestone quarries remained at work, and coal mining was resumed in 1810 when Cullercoats Main was opened by the quarry lessees, William Clark of Benton and Thomas Taylor of Earsdon. To the north the ironstone deposits beneath the links at Whitley Bay were being worked by the Lemington Iron Company, but these, like the coal and lime, were taken by waggonway to the Tyne. The population of Cullercoats now numbered about 460, rising only to 542 by 1831, when 145 families lived in 89 houses, but it was soon to grow more steadily as more affluent people deemed the village to be a desirable place to live. As Parson & White's *Directory* for 1827 indicated, the village had four public houses at that time, plus a Methodist chapel, and several fine houses 'well provided for the accommodation of visitors during the bathing season'. As at Alnmouth, the intermingling of new villas and old mansions amongst the old fisherfolk's dwellings, all overlooking the semi-derelict harbour, was considered to provide a picturesque as well as a healthy environment, a situation well promoted by the several artists, such as Winslow Homer in the early 1880s, who found inspiration there. No matter how hard their labour or how poor their living, the 'Cullercoats fishwives' were also generally seen as picturesque, becoming famed for their 'symmetry and beauty'. The Findens, however, writing in 1838, saw the more prosaic, indeed arduous side to their labours:

> The duties performed by the wives and daughters of the Cullercoats fishermen are very laborious. They search for the bait – sometimes digging sand-worms in the muddy sand at the mouth of the Coble-dean, at the head of North Shields; gathering muscles on the Scalp, near Clifford's Fort; or gathering limpets and dog crabs among the rocks near Tynemouth; – and they also assist in baiting the hooks. They carry the fish which are caught to North Shields, in large wicker baskets called creels, and they also sit in the market there to sell them. When fish are scarce, they not infrequently carry a load on their shoulders, weighing between three and four stone, to Newcastle, which is about ten miles distant from Cullercoats, in the hope of meeting with a better market.

The Findens might have added that, as in all fishing communities, there was also a constant fear of disaster, a fear made real in 1848 when a coble with seven fishermen on board was stuck by a heavy sea as it was proceeding from Cullercoats; all men were drowned, some within sight and sound of relatives and friends.

But Cullercoats continued to strengthen its position as a desirable place in which to live. Even Robert Arkwright, son of Sir Richard Arkwright of Cromford, bought a house in Cullercoats in 1846, mainly for the benefit of his wife, who was a daughter of a member of the famous Kemble family of actors. Towards the end of his life, Mrs Arkwright's 'constant and affectionate friend' the Duke of Devonshire, also took a residence in Cullercoats. The Richardsons, a notable Tyneside family of Quakers, were to have a considerable impact on Cullercoats, particularly in facilitating better amenities for the fishermen and their families. George Richardson, after decades of preaching throughout all the countries of the British Isles, spent many of his later leisure hours among the fishing community at Cullercoats, and also assisted in the provision of schools and an efficient water supply. Even in his advanced years – he died aged 90 in 1862 – he would put to sea in a coble to present bibles to French sailors in their ships in the offing.

The pier, which may never have been properly restored after the storm of 1710, was finally rebuilt in 1848 to serve the interests of the fishing community. But white fishing gradually left Cullercoats, as it did most of Northumberland's smaller ports, especially after large sailing boats from Scarborough and Hartlepool began to fish the waters off the coast between Cullercoats and Newbiggin from c.1860 onwards. The steam trawlers of North Shields later further aggravated the situation for the inshore fisheries, and many of the Cullercoats' fishermen had to settle for summertime stake-net salmon fishing only, some finding additional seasonal work as labourers on the Tyne.

In common with other ports and harbours in Northumberland, Cullercoats established a lifeboat station, the first boat being donated by the Duke of Northumberland and later, in 1879, a look-out house was provided for the Volunteer Life Brigade. But the harbour was again dealt a severe blow, when part of a north breakwater, which was apparently under construction at the time, gave way in an extremely high tide in 1885, even though the massive facing stones had been firmly cemented together; the twin breakwaters were subsequently completed, sometime before 1893.

Concomitant with the steady decline in the importance of the Cullercoats fishing fleet from the late nineteenth century onwards, was the further development of Cullercoats as a small seaside resort, with Edwardian houses following on from the Victorian, and the rapid increase in house building towards the end of the nineteenth century saw Cullercoats even more firmly established as dormitory town and popular bathing place. But it was also put on the scientific map when the Northumberland Sea Fisheries Committee, formed in 1890, established their Marine Laboratory there in 1897; although it was destroyed by fire in 1904, the laboratory was rebuilt four years later and now serves as Newcastle University's 'Dove Marine Laboratory'.

63 Aerial view of Cullercoats harbour, with the Dove Marine Laboratory at centre below the cliff, built on the site of earlier Baths; the lifeboat house and the much altered north pier are to its right. Standing above the inner end of the pier is the Watch House. *M.R. Longbottom, 1969*

Cullercoats' population numbered about 1,800 by 1905, when 35 cobles still worked out of the harbour, a few in white fishing, but the decline in fishing continued through the twentieth century as Tyneside and Scottish fleets increasingly trawled the Cullercoats' herring and white fish grounds. The fishwives, who had formerly helped their menfolk to land, sort and prepare the fish on the beach, before selling them wherever there was a willing purchaser, gradually made recourse to the fish market at North Shields to supplement the lobsters, crabs and winkles which were still being brought ashore at Cullercoats. The railway network enabled the fishwives to travel throughout south Northumberland and north Durham, taking their barrows and creels with them – a familiar sight as late as the 1960s. All that has now gone. Only half a dozen cobles worked out of Cullercoats by 1974 and, as working boats, they have now all but disappeared. Moreover, most, if not all, of the fisherfolk's cottages have gone in recent years, yet, sandwiched between historic Tynemouth and the upstart Whitley Bay, Cullercoats retains its individual flavour.

64 Ground-level view of Cullercoats harbour, with the Dove Marine Laboratory, the lifeboat house and the Watch House. Fishing cobles drawn up on the beach. *M R Longbottom, 1969*

65 Fishermen's houses in Cullercoats, probably in the 1920s

Postscript

Glossary

Bibliography

Index

Postscript

We cannot be unaware that many once flourishing ports have now lost their former significance; many are undergoing great changes while others have completely ceased to trade, their facilities, once important, being now entirely surplus to any presently conceivable requirement other than leisure pursuits. And this is as true of a great port like Liverpool as it is of a minor harbour like Seaton Sluice in Northumberland. Of course, the growth and subsequent decay of our historic ports reflects changes elsewhere, in the economics of sea transport for example, in Britain's economic and industrial wellbeing, in 'globalisation'. But often, the changes which have brought about growth or decay at our local ports and harbours have been local, the rise of fish and chips as a sustaining meal in Britain after 1870 for example bringing growth, or the decline of the coal industry in north-east England in the twentieth century bringing retrenchment. One thing is for certain, and that is that the often gifted harbour engineers and promoters could never have foreseen the forms of development now gracing Northumberland's harbours, the wind farms, the 'marina villages', the high-tech applications of offshore technology and so on. The changes at our harbours over the past couple of centuries have never been predictable, and surely the same will be true of the next century or so.

Glossary

ASHLAR
Well-dressed and squared sandstone masonry.

BAR
A shifting sandbank forming and lying just beyond a river-harbour mouth, so reducing the depth of the entrance channel.

BARQUE
A barque originally implied a three-masted ship, with two square-rigged masts, and one fore and aft rigged mast. By the mid-eighteenth century it often just meant a broad-sterned boat with no ornamental figure on stern or prow.

BAY / BAYE–SALT
Salt produced by solar evaporation in 'salterns', either from sea water, brine lakes or brine springs.

BOAT
A 'boat', as distinct from a 'ship', usually implied one of the smaller classes of vessel, such as a keel, wherry, coble, fishing boat etc.

BOOM
'Boom' has several meanings; for example, a boom can be a floating barrier of timber across a river or harbour mouth. At Seaton Sluice, in the eighteenth century, the 'booms' seem to have been the sloplogs which formed the gates at each end of the Cut.

BREAKWATER
A linear structure projecting into the sea, built to provide protection to shipping and harbour facilities.

BRIG

A two-masted square-rigged vessel, with fore and aft spankers.

BRIGANTINE

A vessel whose aft rigging was like that of a schooner, and whose forward rigging was like that of a brig; it was sometimes called an 'hermaphrodite'.

CHALDRON/CHALDER

The Chaldron/Chalder was a volumetric unit of measure used in the coal shipping trade, but it was a measure whose absolute value varied in time and place and, although a volumetric measure, its approximate equivalent weight in coal was well understood. Thus, the 'Newcastle Chaldron' appears to have been equivalent to 43 cwt in 1616, to 52.5 cwt in 1678 and 53 cwt after 1695; the 'London Chaldron' was generally one half that of the Newcastle Chaldron. Historical units of measurement are a veritable minefield.

CLIPPER

A clipper was a ship with forward-raking bows and aft-raking masts, designed for speed and endurance.

COBLE

An open fishing boat, unique to north-east England and used for coastal fishing. A clinker-built boat about 30ft long, 6-8ft in the beam and flat-bottomed at the stern, built around a central 'ram-plank' but with a 'bilge keel' on either side of the ram-plank towards the stern to facilitate beaching above high-water mark.

COLE/SEA-COLE

'Cole' is simply 'coal', but sea-cole/sea coal can mean coal found along the foreshore, having been eroded from seams outcropping in cliff sides, or even on the sea bed, but the term has also sometimes meant coal which was exported by sea, as opposed to 'landsale coal' which was not.

COPPERAS

Copperas, which has nothing at all to do with copper, was obtained from the iron pyrites found in some coals, making the latter unattractive as a fuel to potential purchasers. It was made by weathering the pyrites in 'brassy' coals for up to five years, during which time a weak acid solution, a ferrous sulphate liquor, was run off and collected in wooden tubs lined with pitch. When such liquors were deemed sufficiently strong, they were evaporated in lead cisterns to give crystals of 'green' copperas. Strongly heated copperas gave 'green vitriol' (sulphuric acid) and a red iron-oxide residue which could be used as a paint pigment ('Venetian Red') or as a polishing agent ('Jewellers' Rouge') or as a dye in itself. Copperas was also used as a mordant to fix dyestuffs, as an ingredient in the manufacture of Prussian Blue and as an agent for the darkening of vegetable dyes and tea leaves etc.

CORF/CORVE

The corf was a wickerwork basket used in coal mining until well into the twentieth century for the carriage of coal underground, and up the mine shaft. A corf might hold about 6-8 cwt of coal each, and a hewers wage might be based on the number of corfs filled underground.

CRAYER

A small trading vessel.

CUTTER

A cutter was, strictly, a boat which belonged to a man-of-war, capable of being sailed or rowed; it was rigged rather like a sloop, but had a running bowsprit (the spar jutting out in front of the ship's prow to which forestays were fastened).

DEMERSAL FISH

Usually called 'white fish', they normally feed off smaller fish, worms, crustaceans etc. at the bottom of the sea, hence they were caught with baited hooks. Such fish include ling cod, haddock, halibut, whiting, hake, and the flat fish (skate, sole and plaice).

DUKE OF RICHMOND'S SHILLING

A Crown Duty on coal from Newcastle dating from 1368 had been allowed to lapse, but was re-imposed by in 1600 to meet the supposed debts incurred through the lapsed Crown Duty. Thus Elizabeth I now imposed a levy of one shilling on every Newcastle chaldron of coal from the Tyne sold to the free people of England. This duty came to be known as the 'Richmond Shilling' after 1677 when Charles II assigned it to the Duke of Richmond. The Richmond Shilling was sold to the government in 1799, for an annuity of £19,000 to the Richmond family, and soon the government was showing huge profits from its purchase. It was a duty which was peculiar to the Tyne trade and was not repealed until 1831.

FREESTONE

Another word for 'sandstone', implying that it can be freely split along bedding planes.

GROYNE

A low, timber frame or wall, projecting into a river or the sea, to check the drift of sands and silts.

GUANO

Generically, this can mean any kind of bird dung, but imported guano, to be used as an agricultural manure, was the dung of seabirds and was, in particular, brought in from Peru, Chile and some African coastal countries; it became a significant import into Britain from the 1840s. An 'artificial' guano was sometimes made from fish.

HARBOUR

A natural, enhanced or artificially created sheltered location for shipping, somewhat larger than a haven.

HAVEN

A natural and usually small sheltered area of sea water forming a suitable and safe location for boats and ships.

JETTY

A structure built to project out into sea or river water to facilitate the berthing, loading or unloading of vessels, but not designed to provide protection.

KEEL

Keels (and keelmen) were peculiar to the rivers Blyth, Tyne and Wear and to Seaton Sluice. They represented a key feature of the coal trade and a distinctive feature of river life up to the last quarter of the nineteenth century. The functions of the keel were twofold. Firstly, and mainly, to collect coal from upriver locations which were inaccessible to seagoing colliers, and to deliver that coal to the waiting colliers. Secondly, in certain cases, keels enabled partially-loaded colliers to complete their loading at sea, often beyond the bar. The keel was a strong carvel-built (the external wooden planking was not overlapped) craft, some 40-42ft long and with a 19ft beam amidships. It had a pointed stern, which made it easier to build and to handle, a flat bottom and a very shallow draught, of about 4.5ft when loaded. Its hold was only about 18in deep, but the sides of the hold were bulkheaded, and planks above the hold (i.e. above deck level) allowed its cargo (coal) to be piled high for easier unloading. The keel could be propelled by a 22ft long oar and steered, and partly sculled, by a 25ft 'swape' at the stern. Some, perhaps all, keels were also fitted with simple single-mast sails, but the prime mover for the keel while in the river seems to have been the tide.

KETCH

A 'ketch' was a two-masted vessel with a tall main mast and a small mizzen.

LIGHTERS

Historically, a lighter was a sloop used for carrying stores in HM Navy, but later the term was generally used to describe any small vessel used for the supply of ships within a harbour.

MIZZEN MAST

Here meaning the aft mast of a three-masted ship.

PELAGIC FISH

Fish which spawn on the seabed, but then live in the surface waters and feed on plankton, hence they can only be caught with nets. They tend to occur in shoals especially the herring, pilchard, mackerel and sprat.

PIER

The word 'pier' normally implies a linear structure projecting into the sea whose superstructure is capable of being used for some commercial purpose, for example providing access by road vehicles, the construction of ice plant, etc. However, there is some evidence that, in Northumberland at least, the word sometimes implied an artificial harbour.

PINK

A small, flat-bottomed trading vessel used in the coastal trades, distinguished by its narrow stern.

PORT
Technically, a port was a harbour with terminal facilities and other services for shipping, but legalistically it was a harbour which had been formally designated as a Port of Custom.

PRESS/NAVAL IMPRESS
The forced conscription of merchant seamen into naval service.

PRIVATEER
Any ship, brig, schooner etc., fitted out and crewed by private persons and usually licensed as such by the home state, for the purpose of cruising against foes with the intent to capture their ships and/or contents.

QUAY
Usually a wharf with mechanical handling devices such as capstans and cranes, but sometimes simply a harbour wall posessing mooring rings and ladders.

SALT UPON SALT
White salt could be dissolved in sea water and then boiled in salt pans to give salt upon salt. It was a Dutch speciality used for the preservation of herring.

SCHOONER
A vessel with two raking masts and rigged with fore and aft sails.

SETTS
Cobblestones made from whinstone.

SHIP
Historically, the word 'ship', as distinct from 'boat', implied one of the larger class of sailing vessel, those having a bowsprit and three or more square-rigged masts. More commonly nowadays, any seagoing vessel of considerable size merits the description 'ship'.

SLOOP
A sloop was a small merchant vessel, with a single-masted rig, carrying a single gaff sail.

SMACK
A small fishing boat, rigged rather like a sloop.

SNOW
A two-masted vessel, square-rigged on both and with a tri-sail mast.

SPANKER
A fore and aft sail set on the aft side of the mizzen mast.

STRANGER BOAT
Any boat using a port or harbour which was not registered there.

STRIKING MAST
Masts which could be lowered to enable a small sailing vessel's passage under low bridges.

TOMMY SHOP
Usually a company store from which employees could obtain goods in lieu of wages.

VEND
A term used particularly in the north-east coal trade to mean the quantity of coal sold, or to be sold, by a coal owner.

WHARF
A structure, which might also act as a retaining wall, situated alongside water for the berthing and unloading or loading of vessels.

WHERRY
The (Tyne) wherry was a clinker-built (overlapping external planking) river boat, and was a fairly late development. Of larger capacity than a keel, it was designed for steam towage and the carriage of a variety of river cargoes.

WHINSTONE
In north-east England this means the dark, compact, hard igneous rock, associated with the Great Whin Sill of Northumberland and Durham; it is not a 'freestone', being of igneous origin, and is therefore difficult to shape.

WHITE SALT
Strictly salt produced by solar concentration of sea water, then by fuelled evaporation in 'salt pans', but often simply implied salt produced in salt pans.

Bibliography

Archer, D., *Tyne and Tide: A Celebration of the River Tyne* (Daryan Press, 2003)

A Tourist, *The Border Tour ...* (Edinburgh, 1826) [By the Rev. Warner?]

Bates, C.J., *History of Northumberland* (1895) p 151

Brown, N., 'The Diary of Nicholas Brown', in 'North Country Diaries', *Surtees Soc.*, 118 (1910) 230-323, p 238

Bulmer, T.F. (ed.), *History, Topography, and Directory of Northumberland (Tyneside, Wansbeck, and Berwick Divisions) ...* (Newcastle upon Tyne, 1887)

Cartwright, R.A. & D.B., *Islands: The Holy Island of Lindisfarne and the Farne Islands* (David & Charles, 1976)

Craster, E., 'Beadnell in the Eighteenth Century', *Archaeologia Aeliana*, 34 (1956) 161-173

Defoe, Daniel, *A Tour Through the Whole Island of Great Britain* (1723-5)

Earnshaw, T.S., *Hartley and Seaton Sluice* (Seaton Sluice, 1957)

Emsley, K., 'A Circuit Judge in Northumberland', *Tyne & Tweed*, 31 (Spring 1978) 13-18

Finden, William & Edward, *Ports and Harbours* (1838; reprinted by E.P. Publishing Ltd, 1974)

Fordyce, W., *A History of Coal, Coke, Coalfields and Iron Manufacture in Northern England* (1860, reprinted by Frank Graham, 1973)

Fuller, John, *The History of Berwick upon Tweed* (Edinburgh, 1799; reprinted by Frank Graham, 1973)

Galloway, R.L., *Annals of Coal Mining and the Coal Trade*, 2 vols (1898, reprinted by David & Charles, 1971)

Gray, William, *Chorographia, or a Survey of Newcastle upon Tyne: 1649* (reprinted by Frank Graham, 1970)

Hair, T.H., *Sketches of the Coal Mines in Northumberland and Durham* (1839, reprinted by Frank Graham, 1969)

Hodgson, John, *History of Northumberland*, 2 (Newcastle upon Tyne, 1827; reprinted by Frank Graham, 1973) 167. *History of Northumberland*, 4 (1840)

Hutchinson, W., *A View of Northumberland ...[in 1778]*, 2v (Newcastle upon Tyne, 1778)

Jervois, E., *The Ancient Bridges of the North of England* (The Architectural Press, 1931)

Lamont-Brown, R., *The Life and Times of Berwick upon Tweed* (John Donald, 1988)

Mackenzie, E., *An Historical, Topographical, and Descriptive view of the County of Northumberland*, 2 vols (1st edn Newcastle, 1811; 2nd edn., Newcastle, 1825)

Martin, E., *Bedlington Iron and Engine Works, 1736-1867* (Frank Graham, Newcastle, 1974)

McAndrews, T.L., *Amble and District* (Amble, 1912)

McInness, R.G., *History of Amble* (Amble, 1880)

Monthly Chronicle of North-Country Lore and Legend (Newcastle upon Tyne, 1887-91)

Morrison, P.G. & Rylance, T., *Amble* (Amble, 1988)

Newcastle Chronicle

Newcastle Courant

North Sea Pilot Part III (1948)

Northumberland County History, various volumes

Parson & White's *Directory of Northumberland* (1827/28)

Perry, Richard, A., *Naturalist on Lindisfarne* (London, 1946)

Phillips, M., 'Forgotten Quaker Burial Grounds', *Archaeologia Aeliana* New Series 16 (1892-93)

Pococke, Bishop R., 'The Northern Journeys of Bishop Richard Pococke [1760]', in 'North Country Diaries', *Surtees Society*, 124 (1914) 199-251

Sykes J., *Local Records,* 2 vols. (Newcastle upon Tyne, 1833); a continuation 3rd. vol. by T Fordyce (Newcastle upon Tyne, 1867)

Tomlinson, W.W., *The North Eastern Railway* (reprinted by David & Charles, 1967)

—., *Comprehensive Guide to the County of Northumberland* (1889)

—., *Historical Notes on Cullercoats, Whitley and Monkseaton* (Walter Scott, 1893; reprinted by Frank Graham, 1980)

Victoria County History of Durham, v2 (1907)

Wallace, John, *The History of Blyth* (Blyth, 1869)

Wallis, John, *The Natural History and Antiquities of Northumberland; and of so much of the County of Durham, as lies between the Rivers Tyne and Tweed, commonly called, North-Bishoprick* (London, 1769)

White, W., *Northumberland and the Border* (London, 1859)

Wilkinson, D. & Morrison, P.G., *A Study of Amble* (Amble, 1985)

Wright, A., *The North Sunderland Railway* (Oakwood Press, 1967)

RECORD OFFICE SOURCES:

Crewe Trustee Papers, NRO 452 for Seahouses

NRO ZHE 26/3; NRO ZCR3 B19 for Beadnell

NRO 683/6/71 for Holy Island

NRO Delaval papers for Hartley

Index

If you are interested in purchasing other books published by Tempus,
or in case you have difficulty finding any Tempus books in your local bookshop,
you can also place orders directly through our website

www.tempus-publishing.com